Advance Praise for *A Very Short Time*

Keith Sykes has written a beautiful memoir. We get to meet his family, read about his wild adventures as a young man—hitching rides and going where the music brought him. I know my late husband, John, loved Keith through and through. They were alike in so many ways—quiet men, kinda shy, each a successful songwriter, but who could raise hell with the best of them. They shared so many good times with the odd misadventure thrown in for good measure!

As they grew older, and both settled into domesticity, their friendship deepened and the songs started coming.

Some of the most beautiful songs John recorded and performed were cowritten with Keith Sykes. "You Got Gold," "No Ordinary Blue," and "Long Monday" are among my favorites.

Keith has been married to his sweetheart, Jerene, for longer than I can count. We four had some wonderful, fun, and memorable times together.

Among the many gifts John left me, one of the most treasured is my enduring and loving friendship with Keith and Jerene.

I hope you read this amazing life story—you'll love it!

—Fiona Prine

A VERY SHORT TIME

A VERY SHORT TIME

KEITH SYKES

A Very Short Time - Keith Sykes

Copyright © 2024 by Keith Sykes. All Rights Reserved.

Cover photo photo by Dave Gahr
Back cover photo by Steve Roberts
Book design by Andrea Reider

I am all for copyright. Copyright gives writers the opportunity to create and offer their finished works to the public. When you purchase this work you reinforce the idea that the work is real and valuable. Thank you for complying with copyright laws by not reproducing this book by any means now known or devised in the future, and by not distributing any part of it without permission. By doing so you stand with me and all writers.

ISBN 979-8-9908104-0-2 (HB)
ISBN 979-8-9908104-1-9 (PB)
ISBN 979-8-9908104-2-6 (ebook)

Library of Congress Control Number: 2024913946

KSME Books, 1035 Big Bell Loop, Eads, TN 38028

This book is a work of non-fiction. As the author/publisher I make no guarantees as to the accuracy of the information contained in this book. I have told it as I remember it as best I can.

KSME Books

keithsykes.com

To Jerene

We've had fifty years of crazy good love, and
Without you this book would never have been written

to Gail and Ronnie

my life is better because you love me

to Dane and Jill

my life is full with you in it

CONTENTS

Foreword		xiii
1	It All Started in a Small Womb In Kentucky	1
2	Long Distance Information Give Me Memphis, Tennessee	6
3	The Guitar	9
4	Off Like a Prom Dress	13
5	Draft Sign-up Time	25
6	Look Out Pretty Babe, I'm on the Road Again	28
7	Holiday Inns	37
8	The Rhodes Show	39
9	Buffalo	42
10	The Coffee House Circuit	45
11	Jerry Jeff Walker	48
12	Fly To Memphis, Hitch to North Carolina	49
13	Life in New York	52
14	San Francisco and Larry Brooks	56
15	Michael Brovsky	58
16	Ronstadt	60
17	231 Thompson St #12 and Gary White	63
18	*Keith Sykes*, the First Album	65
19	Townes Van Zandt	67
20	Kris Kristofferson	69

21	Don Nix and Muscle Shoals	71
22	*1,2,3*	73
23	Loudon Wainwright III	76
24	Summer Soldiers	78
25	It Takes A (Greenwich) Village	82
26	Alex Chilton	84
27	Off to the Left Coast	86
28	Travel, Play, Repeat	95
29	Guy And Susanna	97
30	John Prine	98
31	Key West and Jimmy Buffett	99
32	Recording With a Band In New York	104
33	Austin and Mary Lou	106
34	Key West, Nashville, Memphis	113
35	The Highsteppers	122
36	Jerene	124
37	Things Get Rolling	126
38	Chris Bell	128
39	Keith and Jerene	130
40	Things Take Off	132
41	*The Way That I Feel*	144
42	Bob Kelly	148
43	Buffett Does "Coast"	149
44	Steve Goodman	152
45	And the Hits Just Keep on Coming	153
46	The Year of the Child	154
47	Coral Reefers	156
48	Montserrat	159
49	*I'm Not Strange, I'm Just Like You*	167
50	Back to My Real Job	172
51	Life in a Whirlwind	176
52	*SNL*	181

CONTENTS

53	And Then It Happened	183
54	*It Don't Hurt to Flirt*	184
55	This Was the Beginning of the End of My Early Life	187
56	*Play x Play*	189
57	*Fun Rockin'*	191
58	Publishing, Producing, and Writing	195
59	"Love, Love, Love"	197
60	John Kilzer	198
61	Hipbone	201
62	Pitching and Writing	203
63	Peter Asher	205
64	Terry Manning, Publisher	207
65	Buffett's Little Martin	208
66	"You Got Gold"	209
67	Co-Writing	214
68	Naomi Judd	215
69	*It's About Time*	217
70	Todd Snider	221
71	The Bienstocks	225
72	The Woodshed	227
73	Robilio	229
74	Teenie	230
75	Songwriters on Beale	231
76	Ben—Willie—Darrell	235
77	Cliff Harris	238
78	Kelcy Warren	240
79	*Advanced Medication for the Blues*	241
80	Ambergris Caye	245
81	MIDEM	256
82	Amsterdam	258
83	New Orleans	260
84	The Millennium New Year	262

85	Keith Sykes, Artist	266
86	*Don't Count Us Out*	267
87	I've Never Seen Anything Like It	273
88	LJT	276
89	"All I Know"	278
90	Kelcy	280
91	Cruisin'	281
92	*All I Know*, the Album	283
93	*Retrospective Vol 1*	290
94	Hot Springs	291
95	*Let It Roll*	293
96	The New Reality	298
97	Jed and Kelley	300
98	The Delta Fair	301
99	*Country Morning Music*, the Album	303
100	Start and Finish	304
101	Port A and *20 Most*	305
102	*Bucksnort Blues*	307
103	Jamaica	311
104	Phillip Stafford	312
105	*Songs From a Little Beach Town*	313
106	Note on Beale	320
107	President and Chief Manager, Ardent Studios	321
108	*Tree of Forgiveness*	325
109	The Pandam	327
110	Jerry Jeff	329
111	Keith Sykes Songwriter Weekend	331
112	Leo Goff and the Dolby Atmos Room	333
113	Jerry Jeff's Send-Off	335
114	Let the Show Begin	337
115	Leo Goff lll	339
116	Winds of Change	341

CONTENTS

117	A Night at the Halloran	342
118	You Got Gold, The Event	343
119	KSSW 2022	345
120	Last Phone Call With Betty Fry	347
121	The New Year and Port A	348
122	Bye, Ardent	349
123	The Beat Goes On	350
124	Star at the Halloran	351
125	Todd 2023	352
126	Thank You, Jimmy Buffett, One More Time	354
127	You Got Gold, The Event 2	356
128	KSSW 2023	357
129	Why I'm Here, Thank You, and Goodbye	358

Acknowledgments	361
Thank You	363
About the Author	367

FOREWORD

Paul McCartney said you shouldn't drop names.
    I know, he didn't say it to me, but even if he did there's no way I can tell this story unless I drop names. I'm gonna be dropping 'em like crazy the whole time I'm writing this because these people are as much a part of my story as I am. As a matter of fact, without some of these names I wouldn't be doing this.

    I could have easily gone down another path. Such is fate and luck and life. It's a series of things that happen. Some of them you make happen, and some happen in spite of what you do.

    We all have a story and this is mine.

1

IT ALL STARTED IN A SMALL WOMB IN KENTUCKY

Dammit, man! I wish I'd written that line, but I didn't. I heard someone say it on NPR. It's the first line of a book I did not read, but who could forget something that good? So thank you writer of that great line. If you will—should you happen upon this book—please get in touch with me and tell me the name of your book so I can get a copy. I'll read it!

I know, you could easily have your attorney make contact and tell me what a no good plagiarist I am and to cease and desist from the human race, and if I don't you will sue my balls off and I'll be another ball-less subhuman cretin with a faint itch that I cannot scratch because the object of my itching is no longer connected to my body!

Well, at least I started in Kentucky. We moved away when I was just shy of my ninth birthday so my memories from there are a bit faded.

All my Sykes relatives were there, and many still are. My aunt, Joan Sykes Capo, is the one I've stayed in contact with the most and the only one of her siblings still living. Her brother, my dad, Elroy Sykes, had five brothers and sisters of whom he was one of the middle children.

My mother, Neva Rutland Sykes, had two sisters and one brother. She was the oldest.

A VERY SHORT TIME

She was one year older than my dad. They were from Stewart County, Tennessee, and went to school in Dover. When the TVA dammed the Tennessee River all the families who lived along the river had to take what they were paying for their land and go elsewhere. My grandfather Sykes went just outside Murray, Ky, and bought a 48-acre farm and lived there until he died in 1965.

My sister, Marieva Gail Sykes Blair, was born in 1945 on an Army base in Milan, TN. My parents moved around a bit after my father was discharged from the Army, then settled in Murray. I was born there on October 24th, 1948, my mom's 24th birthday.

When I think about my roots, my mind goes to when my wife, Jerene Rowe Sykes, and I went to Ireland to celebrate the millennium New Year with John and Fiona Prine. I called my mother to tell her we were going to Ireland, and she immediately began telling me about my grandmother Sykes, whose father's name was Austin Quinn.

Austin came to America from Ireland, and my mom said he didn't know exactly how old he was when he arrived, but thought he was about 8 or 9. I suppose I can figure out what year this would be but what I'm getting at is I had long thought we were all from England. After all, her name being Rutland, which is the smallest county in England, and Sykes, which is known for the Sykes of Sledmere House with its 30,000-acre estate in Yorkshire.

Now, I'm absolutely, positively certain I am not in any way connected to the Sykes of Sledmere. It's just I thought we were English. But I was delighted to know about my Irish blood ties.

Everywhere I went and everything I saw in Ireland was a treat. If you ever get the chance to go there, by all means make that trip.

It turns out, according to ancestry.com, I'm 68% English and 22% Irish, with a 10% mix of Polynesian and European drizzled with a pomegranate and orange zest demi-glace.

I suppose some uncle got lucky in Hawaii way back in time.

IT ALL STARTED IN A SMALL WOMB IN KENTUCKY

Kentucky is rich in history. It was the 15th state to join the Union and has been known to race a few horses and play a bit of basketball.

Music has been played there as well. OK, a hell of a lot of music has been played there, including, but not limited to, old-time fiddle music, blues, rock 'n' roll, jazz, country, and you guessed it, bluegrass music.

I don't remember a lot about my school days there, but I do remember a TV show that came on after I got home from school each day. TV in Murray in those days was a one-or two-channel affair in strictly black and white.

As an adult I found out the shows I thought were hosted by Jimmy Dean had to be reruns of the original nighttime shows that he, or some other country star, hosted. Nevertheless, I believe that's where my lifelong love of country music began.

The radio in Murray, I believe, was pretty much like it was nationwide. We heard Patti Page followed by Chuck Berry, followed by Dean Martin, followed by Lonnie Donegan, followed by Nat King Cole, and on and on. It was a wonderful mash-up of music. We didn't need to have everything walled off from everything else. I didn't know who was black or white or any other color. I just knew if I liked a song, I liked that song. I didn't know if you liked Elvis it wasn't OK to like Frank Sinatra. Elvis sang some songs I liked more than others. All the singers did. They played "Tennessee Waltz" so much sometimes I thought it was the only song they played.

I do remember music being something very special in my life, but I was a long way from connecting with it in the way I eventually did. But even then, still in Murray, music was speaking to me. The songs that really got me took me away from everything else, and I became a member of the time and space they occupied. I could not only see the pyramids along the Nile, I was somehow transported there. I was there, and I didn't really have an idea about the realities of pyramids or rivers because I didn't look at it like that. I just knew I was there, and it didn't take any time to get there or cost any money to go. No passport required. I didn't even have to shut my eyes. I could look at the shadows of the telephone lines as Mom or Dad drove along, me with my hand out the window with the wind rushing by, pushing my hand up and down as I tried to keep it on the same path as the shadows, listening to the radio sing songs.

My father was a bad alcoholic — the kind you didn't want to be around after he started drinking. At least that's the impression it left on me. He couldn't have a beer or two with a friend, then come home to the family. One beer would lead him to the next, and the next, and the next, and the next, until that would lead to whiskey, then to moonshine, then after about six weeks would lead him to the hospital with alcohol poisoning with no friends, no money, and nowhere to go.

He was the best guy in the world when he was sober, but when he was drinking he was the worst man in the world. I gave my love to him fully, as only a young son can, to have him then become this terrible person who hurt me with the crazy things he would say and do. He would get better, and in no time I would forget all about the crazy man and love him unconditionally once again. This would go on through my entire adolescence, into my teens and early 20s, until a two-or three-day period when I was living in New York City and the crying drunk phone calls finally pushed me over the line. I still loved the man I loved, but I couldn't give anymore. I did the best I could to not think about having a father and simply tried to get on with the rest of my life.

He was married eight times. I knew three of his wives. There was my mother, of course, and she was his first. Then there was Juanita, who I think was number three, who I got to know and loved dearly, and Rosie, who I believe was number five, who I also knew and dearly loved.

My mother dealt with him the best she could, but divorce was inevitable. She took my sister and me to stay with her mother, Merle Trevathan, at her house in Paris, TN, which is about 20 miles south of Murray. We spent the summer of 1957 there.

Mom went to Memphis during that time to attend a business college to learn secretarial work. She was unhappy with this kind of thing but learned shorthand and typing like secretaries do, hoping to find work that paid enough to raise an 11-year-old girl and an 8-year-old boy. She finally found work at John Gaston Hospital where she learned to be a medical histologist. From there she went to Baptist Hospital, then later to the VA Hospital. In 1977 she retired from the VA and worked in Riyadh, Saudi Arabia, until she retired five years later.

On the weekends when she could, my mother would drive from Memphis to Paris, and I remember those being such joyous occasions for my sister and me.

My grandmother, who I called Grandmama, was a gem of a woman who had gone through living with an alcoholic husband herself. She grew strawberries, and people would come from all around to pick their own pint or quart. Pints were a dime.

Her husband, my step-grandfather, who everyone including my sister and I called Frank, built house trailers in a workshop behind their house and always had two to four for sale on the front part of the property on Highway 641 next to the strawberry patch.

On one of my mom's trips to visit us, she asked me if I wanted her to bring me something from Memphis the next time she came back. I asked for a copy of Elvis Presley's "Peace in the Valley." The next time she came back she brought it to me, and I was so proud of it. Turns out it was an EP, which had four songs rather than the standard two that a regular 45 had. Who knows how many times I played that record? I have no idea. I also have no idea where it is, which is sad because I'd love to have it back. Oh, well. If I had all the records I ever owned over the years it would be a great collection.

2
LONG DISTANCE INFORMATION GIVE ME MEMPHIS, TENNESSEE

My sister and I went to Memphis with our mother and moved into a duplex on Crump Avenue near Treadwell School. Right away I started the 4th grade and my sister began the 7th grade.

I've talked about this with my sister, and we both think I would have fared better in school if I had been held back a year. I was still 5 when I started 1st grade. In those days it was up to the parents to make that decision, and with the turmoil going on in our lives we both figure Mom had all she could cope with without the thought of me taking another year to start school. Mom would have most likely preferred leaving Murray sooner but held off as long as she could given the chaos of my father's behavior going on all around her. The crap single mothers have to put up with.

Nothing seemed easy to me in school. I was new, didn't know anyone, and didn't know how to make friends. One of the teachers saw me alone every day during recess and introduced me to a fellow who was in the same grade as me, so I could know someone. I still remember him to this day, which is rare for me because I meet people all the time and cannot for the life of me remember their names.

LONG DISTANCE INFORMATION GIVE ME MEMPHIS, TENNESSEE

But after all this time I can tell you this fellow's name was Jack Dodd. He smiled when we met, and he let me hang out with him, which did me a world of good. I didn't know it at the time, but Jack was smarter than most of the other kids in school, though he never gave me any indication of that. He never let on to be anything other than the really nice person that he was. Jack was friendly and made me feel like a part of the situation, and that helped settle me.

One of the two biggest records at that time was "Whole Lotta Shakin' Going On" by Jerry Lee Lewis. I remember the DJ saying it was recorded in Memphis. I didn't know anything about recording, but that record sure was exciting to listen to. And since they made it in Memphis, all the better. The other one was "Great Balls of Fire" and it hit me like, well, great balls of fire. It sold a million copies within a few weeks and talk of Sam Phillips and Sun Records was ever present, even in my elementary school.

Elvis was huge, and I thought he was so grown up at 21 and sounded better than anyone — completely unchallenged number 1 in every category. I was still living in Murray when "Love Me Tender," the song and the movie, came out, and to me, all the singers who followed him were imitating him in one way or the other.

"Blue Suede Shoes" by Carl Perkins was huge, and when Elvis did it that was the first time I'd heard a song by two different artist and I could compare the two. I thought Elvis' voice was better, but Carl Perkins was still great.

I never looked at who wrote the songs back then. I thought songs were just always there, and singers sang them and that was that.

Once, my Aunt Reva, my mother's sister, who I thought was the most beautiful woman in the world with her coal black hair and high cheek bones, and Grandmama, who looked like the very definition of a grandmother, came down to visit and to see where we lived. Mom took us all to see Graceland. My sister and I hadn't even been to Graceland, so this was a big deal for us.

A VERY SHORT TIME

Elvis was in the Army at this time, so there weren't many people gathering by the gates of Graceland since he wasn't there. Elvis' Uncle Vester, who was the gatekeeper and would be for many years, came out from behind the gatehouse to greet us. To my utter astonishment he let us drive up to the front of the house so we could take a picture or pick up a leaf if we wanted. We were all so excited about this simple act of amity, and I still think about it.

Gail still has the leaf she picked up and placed between two pieces of wax paper.

After almost three years of living in a duplex, Mom was able to buy a house at 799 Freeman St. It was still in the Treadwell school district but actually quite a bit closer to the school so the walk didn't take as long. The house was a whopping 895 square feet, even smaller before my step-grandfather Frank came down from Paris and enclosed the side porch so I could have my own room. But it seemed spacious compared to the duplex.

Before long I met some neighborhood kids, and if you add those to the kids from my former neighborhood, I knew quite a few folks I could call friends. Some of them I still stay in touch with, especially Larry Raspberry, who would one day become my best man, and Phillip Rauls, who would become a record promotion man for Stax Records, Atlantic Records, and Capitol Records. Also, there was Larry Wall, who would join Raspberry to form The Gentrys, a band who's first single, "Keep On Dancin,'" went to number 4 on Billboard's Top 100 Singles chart while they were still in high school!

3
THE GUITAR

It was while living in this neighborhood that I learned to play guitar. It was the fall of 1965, I was a senior at Treadwell, and my friend James Winberry had a Goya nylon string classical guitar. I believe it was a gift, or belonged to one of his siblings, I don't remember.

James and I had similar tastes in music. We were best friends all through high school and did everything together. His room was upstairs in one of the few two-story houses in the neighborhood, and we could listen to records and talk and do whatever high school kids do in relative privacy.

At that time we thought pot was what you made coffee in, but we did manage to do a little bit of drinking from time to time, courtesy of the fact someone had given me a fake ID. Though I looked even younger than I was, we scouted out the liquor stores that would sell us orange or cherry vodka, and we would have a high time on the occasional Friday night.

James' parents often included me in special events. They invited me along to see Peter, Paul and Mary at Ellis Auditorium in '63 and '64. Those were the first, second, and only concerts I'd ever been to, and they still stand out as being among the best I've ever experienced.

James let me take his guitar to my house one weekend when my sister was home from college. She had taken lessons on clarinet and piano, and she had a little spinet in her room. So she was the musical one in our house.

At the University of Tennessee-Martin, someone had taught her a few guitar chords. So, using James' little Goya, she showed me G, E minor, C, and D.

I can remember slowly getting my left-hand fingers placed on the strings at what I thought were the right spots and then running my thumb down the strings with my right hand. The sound that emanated was something like a bicycle tire running over a one-inch diameter rope. Although, occasionally, I would hear one of the open strings faintly ring, if only for an instant, and think to myself, 'OK, getting there.'

Then I'd carefully set my left-hand fingertips to the position of the next chord and then ask Gail if it was right, to which she would reply, as if not even looking at my fingers, "No." I'd say, "Show me again." She would. And we would repeat the entire sequence. This went on until Gail was about to spontaneously combust and fled the house with one of her comely college girlfriends.

After a few days I could play a very bad rendition of "You Cheated" by the Shields. As I look back, I can hear that the chords Gail had taught me were mostly right, but rather than the C, or 4 chord in this instance, it should have been the 2 minor, or A minor. But at that time she could have told me anything, and I would have taken it as gospel. This reminds me of an old joke. What do you get when you toss a piano down a mineshaft? A flat minor. Sorry. I can't help it.

After a few days James called and asked me if I was ever going to bring his guitar back. I did. But by then I was fully infected with the fever. It was happening a lot in those days, a full-fledged musical epidemic brought on by folk music happening in a huge way, and the Beatles overtaking America from '64 on. And now I had it, too.

Around the end of 1964, when I was in 10th grade, I began to write song lyrics in study hall. Rather than study, I would read Ian Fleming, or Tennessee Williams plays that I could check out in the library, or just stop everything and write—or try to write—song lyrics. I have no idea what I did with those lyrics, because even then I could tell there wasn't much going on. I do remember thinking they were pretty bad imitations of Hank Williams songs. Today, I can't, and don't, compare my stuff to Hank Williams. Just the thought of that sounds wrong. What I mean is, no one can compare to Hank Williams. In any case, my musings were only vapors of lyrics.

After I learned those first four chords all I thought about was learning how to play guitar. Just a few weeks later Christmas came, and I got an adult present. That is, one of my gifts was a $20 bill.

The very next day I went to Beale Street and found Nathan Novick's Pawn Shop. Nathan looked like my idea of a gypsy. He had dark eyes and wore a suit, albeit a bit untidy, and had black, slicked-back hair. I think he wore a ring. But what I'll never forget was he would spit on the well-worn wooden floor, in any of the rooms in the shop.

Stuff was piled everywhere, and guitars were hung on the walls in a couple of rooms. I most likely walked in wearing my dark green Hush Puppies, corduroy or Levi's pants, and an Oxford cloth shirt. Altogether it just screamed—of course I'm just surmising here—"Here comes my next 20 dollars" to Nathan.

He asked me what I was looking for, and I said a guitar. He asked me how much I wanted to spend. As I could see, he had a lot of guitars, and of course he wanted me to have just the right one. All I knew about guitars was I wanted to play one. But I did have a crucial bit of information. I knew some guitars, especially the lower-priced ones, the action, or the amount of space between the strings and fretboard, could keep you from enjoying playing, let alone get proficient.

I said I'd like to try one in the not-too-expensive price range to see how it played. I followed him to another room where the guitars were not as fancy as the ones you could see from the street, and he handed me one and then spat on the floor. I played it, and to my surprise the strings felt pretty good. About like James' Goya. And these were steel strings. I didn't even know if it was completely in tune, but it was just about what I was looking for. I handed it back and asked to see another. He obliged me, and we did this another time or two before I was ready to get serious. I went back to first one and asked, "How much?"—and this is the classic part—he said "How much have you got? I said—and this is so me—"$20." He said—and I'm not making this up—"Well, that one just happens to be $20."

At the cash register Nathan told me I could get a case for this much … and of course I'll need another set of strings for that much … and the tax is so and so … until I finally said, "I really do have $20, and that's all I have." He spit on the floor and I walked out with that little guitar. No case. No extra set of Black Diamond strings. Just a guitar that was made wherever they made cheap guitars at that time.

I played that thing until I learned how to make barre chords. At that point Mom must have said something to Elroy, because he came down to Memphis with a red sunburst Gibson B-25, case and all. Those little guitars were not gifted with a very resonant sound, but the action was great, and just having something that was a real guitar was such a treat.

Not long after that I graduated from Treadwell. I was finally free to be me!

4
OFF LIKE A PROM DRESS

The day after I graduated high school, I knew I never wanted to spend another day in any school, anytime, anywhere. I was accepted by Middle Tennessee State University—it may have still been a college at that point—but I was a mediocre student at best, and it just wasn't what I wanted. I did do well with things I enjoyed, such as mechanical drawing, architectural drafting, American literature, and American history. Outside of that I was just sitting there doing just enough to get by.

That day my mom drove me to the edge of Memphis, which at that time in our neck of the woods was where Summer Avenue and the newly opened Interstate 40 intersected.

I didn't say too much along the way. Neither did she. She drove up close to the on-ramp which was going east toward Nashville. Just as I was ready to close the back door after getting my suitcase and guitar, she leaned over the seat and said, "Keith, don't forget to have fun." I have to say that was the last thing I expected to hear from the woman who had spent the last 17 years trying to get me to behave. I was thinking she would say almost anything but that. Still, it really was a comfort to know that's what she had in mind after all those years.

Maybe it was because she had so little personal time for anything, much less fun, that she didn't want me to forget the things in life that can bring you joy, whatever they might be. To me, at that point, just getting out in the world would be, if not fun, at least liberating. And I needed that.

I hitchhiked to Murray that day to spend a little time with Elroy. He was self-employed in the antique business, and I needed somewhere to start. Murray was as good a place as any.

I had been hitchhiking the last couple of summers, so this was nothing new to me. In those days people hitched rides all the time. Those days are gone. It only takes a few serial killers to take the fun out of everything for everyone. The fun, and freedom. Such is life.

I stayed in Murray long enough to get a couple of jobs and I saved $60. At that point I was ready to go.

My first destination was Washington, DC. I got rides with all kinds of people. My feeling is they saw a kid on the edge of the highway who looked like he didn't have any other options and decided to give him a ride. And they would be right about the no other options part. Some people were going a few blocks. Some people were going hundreds of miles.

That summer I figured out a lot more about being a hitchhiker than I did just hitching up to Murray or down to Florida for a few weeks. First off, the suitcase thing is for amateurs. A lot of hitching is carrying your stuff to a place that people might actually stop to pick you up. Like after the intersection, not before it. Like on the outside of town in the direction you're going, not the other way around. I walked through a lot of small towns and a suitcase gets heavy fast. They didn't have wheels in those days. I had to carry the guitar no matter what, because this was before the days of the gig bags. But a suitcase is easily replaced by a backpack, and I would do that the very next year.

Long-haul truckers were always cool because they were usually traveling at least to the next town. I was picked up by everything from station wagons already crowded with families and their belongings to the lone person in a sedan who was going my way.

When I got to DC I found the YMCA and met a fellow from West Virginia who, like me, was fresh out of high school and had come to see some sights. As we got to know each other that week we found we both loved folk music. When I meet someone and we talk music I usually feel comfortable around them right away. We exchanged numbers and addresses, and I felt like I had met a new friend.

I walked over a bridge to get to Arlington National Cemetery. I walked to the part of the Smithsonian that has airplanes. I walked to the White House and took the tour! I think they let us see a few rooms downstairs and that was about it.

After a week in DC I set out for New York City. This was the big one for me. This is where all the folk music that I knew about was happening. I had only been playing for a few months, but I wanted to see where Bob Dylan and all the rest made their stand. I looked a good three years younger than I was, had not written a single song—at least with words and music—but I wanted to take a look around the most famous city in the U.S.

So I held out my thumb on the edge of this gigantic expressway and was hoping for the best when the longest black Cadillac in the history of Cadillacs pulled up just in front of me and waited for me to get in. As I settled in after stowing my guitar and suitcase in the back seat I couldn't believe my luck—or this car. I had never been in a Cadillac that was actually moving down the road. I take that back. My friend Jimmy Ray's dad had a '59 Caddy with those cool fins and taillights, and I rode with them to Mississippi once.

The man driving this Cadillac wore a black suit with material that looked very soft and pliable. He was handsome and spoke in a voice that I couldn't trace to a region. He spoke like people do on TV. He made me feel welcome in this car that was more like a first-class hotel room cruising about 70 mph on a road that had so many lanes it seemed like it should have its own zip code. The thing I couldn't help but notice was the "Wonderbar" radio. I asked him what it did. He pressed the bar and the radio went looking for the next station. I'm sure my smile was as wide as the mouth of the Amazon, but I was trying not to show it. It had black leather seats and, in another first for me, we were riding in the comfort of air conditioning. I was sure this guy was Howard Hughes. Or someone who was "somebody."

When he asked where I was going I replied, "New York." He said he was too and again asked me where I was going. I said New York City. In a very polite way he asked again where I was going specifically. He said he could drop me off just about anywhere I'd like. That's when I realized I didn't know where I was going, other than to New York City. He said if I could think of someplace in the meantime to tell him because he knew the city well and didn't mind if he went a little out of his way because he wasn't in any particular hurry.

As we got closer to the city and I could see the skyline, I was flooded with thoughts of how big it was. I still didn't have a clue about where I was going, so I kept to my "I'm going to New York City" line. When we came out of the Holland Tunnel and suddenly Manhattan was upon me, my eyes must have looked like saucers. My ride said since I was going to New York City he would drop me at the corner of 42nd Street and Broadway. That should be New York City enough for anyone. He didn't say it, but he surely must have been thinking New York City enough for a dumb-ass, green-as-a-gourd hick like me.

I thanked him sincerely for the ride, got out and grabbed my stuff and looked around. "Damn. This place is big!" Now here is the part that's played over and over in my mind countless times since then. I didn't know north from south, or east from west. I asked the first person who looked like they knew their way around which way to Greenwich Village. That one wasn't sure, but the next two people I asked came up with roughly the same directions, so I began my trip. On foot, of course.

They said walk two blocks that way, go right on 5th Avenue, then Greenwich Village is about 40 blocks away. I thought to myself, '40 blocks or so sounds far, but I can make it.'

After three of those Manhattan blocks it dawned on me what kind of trip I was looking at. One of these blocks is about as long as it is from Murray to Paris. It's not that far, of course, but damn! I don't remember how long it took me to walk to the Village, but it was not just a few minutes. It was maybe closer to an hour. Along the way it finally dawned on me that I should have told Mr. Cadillac I wanted to go to Greenwich Village.

When I got there and started looking for a place to stay, I found out that a lot of people like me—meaning lost, with little money, and a complete unknown—stay at the Earle Hotel. I think it cost $6.00 a night. It may have been as much as $7.00. I don't have the receipt, but I think I had enough money to stay for five nights and then I'd have to move on.

Subway tokens were 10 cents, or maybe 15 cents. I made my way around a bit, talked to people occasionally and saw a few things. I played a little chess in Washington Square Park.

Here's what happened: I would sit down. Some unassuming person would walk over and ask if I'd like to play. I would say yes. In approximately 45 to 90 seconds, the unassuming person would say "Check," and I would make another move after which the unassuming person would say, "Checkmate. Do you want to play another?" To which I would reply in the affirmative and the process would continue for two more times, max, and then I would decline any further trouncing.

After my outings I'd go back to my room, pick up the guitar for a few minutes, then stop to think about the possibility of writing something that was supposed to be a song. Nothing came forth. I was as blank as a pure white sheet of typing paper. If you've ever looked at a sheet of paper in that way it can begin to look as big and unwelcoming as a New York City block. Or Greenland in winter. Just a vast, cold, treeless, nothingness.

When I checked out of the Earle Hotel I got some help with directions at the front desk. I remember the clerk saying something like "take the tube" or "the tunnel," or a bus from Pennsylvania Station to New Jersey and hope for the best from there. I finally broke down and asked, "What is the tube?"

"The subway."

"The subway?"

"Yes, the tube."

Oh.

After I made it to New Jersey I decided I wanted to try to go to Alaska. I hitchhiked back to Memphis to get the last bit of money I had at Mom's.

I was there for a couple of days and ran into Charlie Durham, a buddy from school who told me he was going to Nassau in the Bahamas to gamble, and if I wanted to meet him in Miami he would cover my plane ticket to the Bahamas, and I could share the room where he was staying. I told him about my Alaska idea, and he said if I changed my mind the offer was still good.

I hitched to Denver, and my last ride told me about a place I could stay for the night. It was mighty rough, but I stayed as quiet as I could and took a shower in a tub that looked like it was last cleaned sometime just after the invention of the wheel.

I made it out of there, and after a few local rides, a good-sized flatbed truck hauling some heavy equipment picked me up. The driver looked to be in his early 20s, and the fellow with him was about my age, 17.

As we took off the guys asked where I was headed and I told them Alaska. The driver said they were going to El Paso.

'El Paso,' I thought. 'Now this is interesting.'

OFF LIKE A PROM DRESS

When I was about 4 or 5 years old, my family went on a trip to El Paso to meet up with some of Mom and Dad's friends they knew from serving in the Army. I don't remember much about that trip, but I do have some memories that have stayed with me all this time.

One of them is our car had a device that automatically dimmed the headlights, and Dad was never happy with that thing. It seems if he wanted the bright lights on they would go off, and when he wanted them off they turned on.

I also remember seeing White Sands, New Mexico, and the Petrified Forest. Strange the things that stay with you.

These truckers said I should ride with them. It would be a lot more fun than Alaska, and when we get there and drop off the load we could go to Juarez for a night. All this sounded right up my alley, and I didn't waste time mulling over the particulars. We were in Golden, Colorado, and having a nonstop ride that far was enough info for me.

Man, oh man, what a time that was. Somewhere, I have a picture of us in the Juarez bar. It has their names written on the back, and I'm gonna find that thing one day. Maybe even before I finish this book.

We made our way down to El Paso, delivered the freight, and got a room somewhere. After we had a chance to wash up we walked over the bridge to Juarez and went to a bar that seemed very friendly and carefree. The bartenders didn't care how old you were. If you wanted a drink, that was old enough for them.

Our fearless leader, the 20-something, left the table for a few minutes and came back to tell us if we wanted some pussy all it would take is $5, or about 50 million pesos. The exchange rate in those days was very lopsided, but not that lopsided. I just remember thinking you could get a lot of pesos for a dollar. I couldn't think of any reason not to do it, so I said "I'm in."

I paid my $5 and was sent to a small room that looked like any number of roadside motels of that era. Pretty much a bed, a sink, some sort of chest of drawers, a nightstand and a small bathroom.

A VERY SHORT TIME

At 17, I didn't have a frame of reference for this kind of thing. As I think back on it, the price of the "girl" I had prepaid for should have been a red light—pun intended—right there. But before the activities would begin, a small lady who looked to be in her 70s came in, and in broken English said, "Inspection." To which I replied, "Inspection?" "Yes, 5 pesos," she said. I grumbled about the money because no one had mentioned this before but I begrudgingly gave it to her. She said, "let me see the dick!" "You mean you want to see my dick?" I replied. "Si, si" she said. So, according to the rules of the house as I understood them, I had to pull out my dick so she could take a look. So I did. And there it was in all its naked wonder. By this time it had shriveled to a measly inch or so and what this old lady wanted to do with it was way beyond me. She took it in both hands. Or, I should say, a thumb and finger from each hand. She looked up and said it was OK and left like a languid turtle.

In anticipation of my rendezvous, I kept going over what I would do with my hour with a girl I didn't know, had never seen, and who did this sort of thing for a living. I didn't have to wait too long. The "girl" looked about 40, a little heavy—let's just say she was not my type, physically. She was, however, very interested in getting the ball—pun intended, again—rolling. Within three minutes we were stripped, in bed, in and out, and done.

I was still in bed when she was ready to move on. "What about my hour?" I asked. In broken English she informed me that this is what is known as an hour in Juarez. Oh. Well. I guess $5 didn't go as far as I thought it would.

We rolled out of El Paso while the sky was still black, and we each described in some detail our experience in Juarez.

For me, in a way, I'm glad I did it. Being right out of high school where the women in my life were my Mom, sister, and girlfriends from school, I can't say it's something I'm proud of. But on the other hand I guess it's one of those things in life that tells better than it actually was. Sex is enough to figure out on its own, and I found out that night that this kind of sex was not for me and not the way I'd approach it thereafter. It's just something I did at a point in my life. No less, no more.

My new friends and I—I did regard them as friends—finished our time together when we reached San Antonio. They were home, and I was on the road again and a long way from Alaska, so I called Charlie Durham. He said the trip to Nassau was on and I was still welcome to meet him in Miami.

It took a few days of hitchhiking, but I made it to Miami and met Charlie to take my second trip out of the country. Of course, neither of these trips involved a passport, but I was an international traveler.

It was also my first time to travel by air. I remember the plane was very crowded and the engines were loud. The props were in full swing when the pilots released the brakes, and the entire thing and all of us in it were moving down the runway and then we were off. As I usually do the first time I do something, I just went along with it. Charlie was just as scared as I was, but he never let on. People are just a little different when they are scared.

In about half an hour we touched down at the airport in Nassau and were greeted with banana daiquiris being given out by a fellow dressed in a suit that wasn't a military or pilot's uniform, but close enough that I knew it was a uniform. And since the guy in the uniform was handing me a daiquiri, it must be OK to drink it. Pow! My first daiquiri, and it was lovely. I thought to myself, 'I like Nassau.'

Charlie had a room that was small, but big enough that if we tried to be out of each other's way some of the time everything would be fine all the time. He came to gamble, and that's about all he talked about and all he did. I didn't have much of an agenda, but I was very glad I was there.

I went on a glass-bottom boat ride that I really enjoyed. The water there is so beautiful, like nothing I'd ever seen. The boat took us to see fish small and large, and coral, and more. Just the fact this water was clear as pool water was enough to wow me. And the colors! Everything paled compared to them.

I sat on a seawall one afternoon reading a book of poems that had Ben Jonson's "To Cecelia" in it. I had a large Coke that I set beside me. I was reading the poem and trying to memorize it when I noticed a small arm in my peripheral vision to my right slowly reaching for my Coke. I quickly turned, but I was too late. A boy who looked about 10 was running across the sand with my Coke in his hand, heading to the shelter of wherever he went after pulling such a heist. I was peeved at first, but then it made me laugh. I guess Cokes don't come easy for a street kid in Nassau. Or do they?

The lobby of the hotel was a nice place to play my guitar. Whenever Charlie needed some space, I went there and just played things I was learning and things I knew reasonably well.

When I was in Murray I would go to an all-night service station and Danny Roland, who would go on to play with Townes Van Zandt for many years, would drop by sometimes. I would sit and listen to him play as long as he would do it. I'd watch his fingers while he made the guitar sing and try to pick up as much as I could. I would work on some of the things he did to keep trying to get better.

A young man about my age came in one afternoon. Turns out he could play guitar, too. I'd be trying some finger picking thing and he told me I should learn chords. I didn't care much about learning chords back then. I never do well trying to learn something I don't care about. But as the years have gone by I've learned I do like chords and wish I knew more of them. And if I could see that fellow today, I'd ask him to show me one or two.

In a few days I was back in Florida with three cents to my name, trying to hitchhike across "alligator alley," and let me tell you, I was getting nowhere, fast.

Alligator alley was a two-lane affair in those days with very little traffic. And the traffic I did see must not have seen me. I was passed by way more than I was picked up. But I did make it across, and I was hungry and tired by the time I did.

There is a strange thing I noticed about being hungry. The first couple of days I noticed it all the time. But by the third day it was somehow not as noticeable. I think I just forgot to think about it. And then someone would feed me.

Just after getting past alligator alley, we turned into a large, oyster shell parking lot with a hamburger place in the middle of it. My ride bought me a small Coke, small burger and small fries. I felt like I couldn't finish it all. But somehow I did, and was so happy.

I hitched up the west coast of Florida, and in Valdosta, Georgia, a VW bus with several hippies in it picked me and took me all the way to Richmond, Virginia. I'm guessing there were two guys and three girls. It could have been just the opposite. I do remember one of the girls gave me six cents as they dropped me off, so I almost had a dime. I kept thinking how lucky can one guy get? I made my way to Highway 64 and hitched up to Charleston, WV, to see my friend I had met in DC just a couple of months before.

By the generosity of some of my rides I had maybe 50 to 75 cents by the time I got there. I called my friend, and he picked me up in his family's station wagon. I spent a couple of nights with them, and this is when I first heard Tom Paxton and Hedy West records. My friend was a folk music fan and had some really cool records. He invited some of his friends over, and we all listened to and talked about those records.

It was October, and I had to get back to Memphis to sign up for the draft. My friend took me to the edge of town, and I was off again.

I slept in cars parked at gas stations on the outskirts of towns. I slept on the ground. A fine meal was a five-cent pack of crackers, a can of either potted meat or Vienna sausages, and a Coke or a small carton of milk. When it rained, I stayed under a bridge or the canopy of a gas station. I washed up at those gas stations, too. Many times the people I had a ride with asked me to stay in their homes. I owe them a debt of gratitude. There were coin-op laundries when I needed that. Believe it or not, I can't remember anyone ever being mean to me. So, I really am a lucky fellow.

5
DRAFT SIGN-UP TIME

Once back in Memphis I did my part and signed up for the draft. I was completely broke when I got there, but Mom never minded me coming home to start over again. At least she didn't say anything to me about it if she did.

Since its inception, Memphis has been a major distribution center. Sears had a huge building in the Crosstown section of town. The department store was on the first few floors, and the rest of the building was floor after floor crammed with everything that was listed in the three to five-inch thick Sears catalog that was ubiquitous at that time.

Every October, Sears would start hiring people to power them though the Christmas season. I was hired at minimum wage to do some heavy lifting. I was little, but no one seemed to care. As long as I could pick up a box, I was good to go.

I rented a small apartment that was over Mr. and Mrs. Coker's grocery store in my old neighborhood. I worked all day at Sears and played my guitar every other waking moment.

After the Christmas season, I was just about to take off again when an old friend, Charlie Lopez, asked me if I'd like to work at a title company.

Well, I had been going to Melody Music store to drool over the Martin and Gibson guitars that were hanging on the walls. If I was lucky, I would hear a really good player. That was the treat. To listen and watch and learn. You never knew who might be there.

Memphis was a hotbed of great musicians, and the studios were recording hit after hit. Once when I was there Charlie Freeman came in. Charlie played sessions at Stax and when he played he sounded like his fingers were angels. And of course when I told him I thought he was great, he just said "Oh man, this is nothing. I'm not that great." Well, I thought to myself, 'that ain't what Chips Moman says. Or Jim Dickinson. Or Elvis Presley. Or on and on, counting every music person who's living in Memphis.'

Inspired by an insatiable lust for a new guitar, I answered Charlie Lopez by asking, "What's a title company?" He told me you sit in a room full of people drawing property lines on big Mylar maps. They give you the lot description and you find the address on one of the maps and draw the lot lines in by following the description. I always loved drafting, and this was in the same wheelhouse, so I took that job.

The lot description went like this: Beginning at an iron stake 50 feet from the center line of Canada-Seed Tick Road and continuing for 862 feet to … whatever the description says. And you just read the description and draw it in on the map. I could do the crap out of those things. The main benefit of that job was I would be able to buy a better guitar.

I talked to my mom and told her about all this and asked if I could move back home. She said I could. I asked if she would co-sign for me to buy a guitar on time. She was a little more cautious about that. I promised I wouldn't let her down, and the guitar I wanted was one of the best guitars made. It's even guaranteed for life! She said yes and we went to Melody Music, where Joe Golden sold me my 1966 Martin D-28. I still have it, and it's still under warranty.

DRAFT SIGN-UP TIME

I worked for the title company until mid-April, and thanks to my mom I paid off my Martin. It's still my most prized guitar. I had to trade my Gibson B-25 to get the Martin, and I have no idea what happened to the pawn shop special, but I have some very nice guitars, and I love them all. They each do what they do a little differently from each other. And yes, in the event of my passing please tell Jerene not to sell my guitars for what I told her I paid for them.

6

LOOK OUT PRETTY BABE, I'M ON THE ROAD AGAIN

When I left Memphis this time I hitched straight south to New Orleans. I had friends from school there, brother and sister Dub and Dawn Overhue, so I used the phone book or got a number from someone, but however it happened I got in touch with them. They had a friend who had an apartment and a car—an Oldsmobile Toronado to be exact—something a hitchhiker tends to remember, and I stayed there for a bit.

After that I stayed with two other "street people" in the French Quarter on the second floor over a bar that was being built. I don't even remember the name of the street it was on. There was zero anything on the second floor of this building, so after the carpenters had left the-soon-to-be bar, we grabbed a broom and swept the dust from the floor enough to lie down and get a little sleep. I used my backpack for a pillow, and that's all I had for a bed.

I used the showers you could rent at that time at the French Market. And there used to be these breakfast joints where you could get 2 eggs, toast, and maybe a strip of bacon, perhaps some grits, and coffee for a total of about $1. Or it could have been 50 cents. That cheap meal could last me all day. I was eating to live, not living to eat, so eating only came to mind when I felt hungry. Of course, I weighed about 115 pounds. Maybe I should have tried to be a jockey.

One thing about those showers. The humidity in New Orleans is not like your ordinary, run-of-the-mill humidity you may have in your neck of the woods. I lived in Memphis for eight years and believed I knew all there was to know about humidity. Turns out I knew nothing. I would take a shower, and by the time I dried off I was completely wet again. It makes it hard to put your clothes on when you're wet. But at least I was clean and wet.

I heard all manner of the music that creates the ambient sounds of the Quarter, coming from all directions. I took in Babes Stovall singing on the street. I heard those street corner preachers with their rattling syllables of "this place is hell, and you better redeem yourself unto the Lord or risk certain eternal damnation." You couldn't miss the loud, screeching streetcar brakes, and I loved the clip-clop of carriage horses passing by, all decked out with flowers and hats and colorful beads.

It's a shame I can't remember the names of everyone I've met along the way. If I could I'd tell you the names of the two guys I stayed with above the in-progress bar. It's with those two guys I first smoked marijuana.

One of the guys was black and the other was white. And none of us ever thought a thing about it anyway. No one ever brought it up. I was just glad to be there doing what I was doing, being who I was, with who I was with.

One night the taller guy brought in what I thought was the skinniest cigarette possible. It's a wonder anything was inside it. It couldn't have been much. But when I was offered a puff, I took one. I inhaled as deeply as I could. The joint went around, and when it got back to me it was pretty much toast. I tried, and maybe I got a little smoke, mighty little. We talked a few minutes, and lo and behold, I felt a fraction of a high coming on. After we talked a bit more, I said to myself, "I like pot."

And thus began the rest of my life.

A VERY SHORT TIME

I hitched from New Orleans to Johnson City, Tennessee, to visit Bruce and Virginia Taylor and their kids Susan and Allen. Bruce had been an Army buddy of my Dad's since they met in El Paso. It seemed Allen and I had always known each other, and his sister and my sister were about the same age and we all enjoyed each other's company. So when I came knocking on their door they took me in like I was part of their family. They had an easy way of being together, and I was comfortable with them. They were a loving family, and I felt it, too.

Allen had a green Gretsch Anniversary guitar and I had my new Martin D-28, and we played what we knew just about every day. He was better than me, so I could learn something every time we sat down. He also had some cool records, and we liked the same artists. It didn't matter what genre it was. If we heard a new song on the radio, we both liked it. Or didn't like it. We were brothers to one another. I feel it still.

Bruce found me a job at an all-night filling station on another side of town. There wasn't a lot of business at the station when it began to get late. After 11 p.m. it was pretty much dead. I thought it was an excellent time to do some reading, and I brought a book every night. I read a few mysteries and was working on *Catcher in The Rye* when I got the news that the boss had other ideas about how I spend my time at the station.

I received a duty list. 'OK,' I thought to myself. 'I better get cracking.'

The list consisted of jobs like cleaning the restrooms using the prescribed methods the boss would personally demonstrate. Hosing off the lot was near the top of the list. It was one the biggest lots in all of Johnson City, and hosing it went a lot slower than you might think. Mopping the office floor. Emptying the ashtrays. It went on to cover emergency procedures, important phone numbers and probably a bunch of other stuff. I don't know. I could only do so much. If by some strange circumstance I completed all the duties listed above, the ones listed below could just stay there at the bottom of the list. Sort of a purgatory for unattainable quests that only the few, the brave, the proud, the good, could manage to accomplish.

Johnson City is where I recorded for the first time. I was trying to write music and lyrics and had a few rudimentary songs that sounded kind of like a Hank Williams type of song. Nowhere near as good as Hank. Maybe the same zip code but lacking any originality.

Allen had a friend, Larry Clawson—everyone called him Bubby—who played pretty good lead guitar. Allen played pretty good electric rhythm, and I played acoustic. Together we recorded two songs. One for the front of the 45 and one for the back. I guarantee you can't find a copy of that record.

Bruce went over and above trying to make it a success, but to no avail. We played live one time in Johnson City. I was scared beyond measure, but Larry and Allan played pretty well and I sang and played. I have no idea what I sounded like.

Looking back, the studio had the egg carton things that hold maybe three dozen eggs each that covered the walls. It had a control room where the recorder was and a studio where the musicians played, and that was it. The entire thing was in a garage. Bruce had records pressed, and there you go—we had a record. It had my name on it. It just shows to go ya, you never can tell.

I had saved about $60 by the time Virginia's nephew, Mose Tipton, Jr., was leaving for Portland, Oregon. If I wanted, I could go with him. I could help drive and navigate.

That sounded like a plan to me, so I packed my things and said my farewells. In a way, I never really left that beautiful home, because that family meant so much to me at a very pivotal time in my life.

The trip to the northwest was a wondrous journey. Buddy—that's what everyone called Mose—and I made good traveling companions. The scenery was amazing. Until you see outside of your own world, you can't fully appreciate how great it is.

I stayed with Buddy's family in Portland—all cool people who made me feel welcome.

When I left, I headed south. I'd been to Mexico the year before but never to California. So, California here I come.

1967 was a wild year for the hippie movement. The media was always reporting on love, peace, and all things psychedelic. I thought hippies were cool, but I was still a folkie and liked it that way. So when I got to California and had the chance to hitch over to San Francisco or head back east, I chose the latter.

I had the experience of being in New York to compare it to, and I knew I wasn't ready to delve into San Francisco. I wanted to go the Newport Folk Festival, so east it was.

I got a ride in a baby blue VW convertible and made it to Reno. Just outside of Reno the driver asked me where I'd been, and I said New Orleans. He asked how the grass was there, and being the old grass smoking pro I was, I said it was good. He asked if I'd like some for the road. I said yes. He pulled off the road and rolled two joints—this time the joints were nice, full joints. Then he asked if I like to do some right then, and I said no.

I hadn't developed any pot etiquette, and looking back it was an assholey thing to do, but I didn't know. I was just overwhelmed thinking I now had some actual marijuana of my own and I could do with it as I pleased.

Outside of Reno I got a ride in a red-and-cream, '56 Chevy Bel Air. I wish I could remember the driver's name. He was black, outgoing, and confident, and 10 years or so older than me. He asked me where I was going, and when I told him he said I could ride all the way to Salt Lake City, and I loved the sound of that.

We had hours ahead of us, and we talked about everything traveling through that desert. When we were so far out that I couldn't see anything but desert—no town, no signs, no telephone lines, nothing but maybe an oncoming car once in a while—I asked him if he'd ever smoked pot. He said he had. I told him I had some and if he wanted to we could fire it up. He was game, and the game was on.

We needed a pee break anyway, so when we stopped I opened my guitar case and got one of the joints from its hiding place inside an old kazoo. We fired it up and had a few pulls. I said he could keep what we didn't smoke, and he did. Not long after, the radio was actually getting a station and "Creeque Alley" by the Mamas and the Papas came on, and I didn't recognize it at first. I'd heard it all over the radio, but this time was different. When the vocal came on it dawned on me what it was. Kinda wild, in a cool way, but I couldn't find the "one." Musicians will know what I'm talking about. Non musicians, please ask a musician friend to show you. Let them play you a song and show where the one is.

My ride asked me if I knew what a "fright high" was, and I said I didn't. In hindsight I think he may have been talking about being paranoid. If you're not used to pot it can make you magnify your feelings. So, if you get overcome by good feeling it makes that larger. Like uncontrollable laughing. Conversely, if you get lost on a bad thought it gets magnified, making you feel paranoid. If you focus on something else and remind yourself you're high, you'll usually be fine. It wasn't long before we were talking about something else, and what happened 30 seconds ago stayed 30 seconds ago.

We made to Salt Lake City, and my new friend let me stay in his room that night.

Inside city limits you tend to get very short rides, and after a few I finally made it to the edge of town on a road headed to Colorado.

Just outside of Grand Junction I got a ride with a woman who said her kids who were into music. My guitar was a dead giveaway about my interests. She asked if I wanted to stay at her house and meet her son and some of his friends. So I spent the night in Grand Junction hanging out with them. That night I heard "If I Were a Carpenter" by Bobby Darin for the first time. It's funny how I remember these things.

The next day I was on the east side of Montrose when I got a ticket for hitchhiking. I asked the cop how I was supposed to get out of Colorado if I couldn't hitchhike? He told me—and I am not making this up—I can stand on the opposite side of the highway. If a car stops and asks if I want a ride, then that would be legal. I replied with something along the lines of, "You mean I stand on the west bound side of the road even though I'm going east, and if a car in the eastbound lane stops and asks if want a ride, that's my only option?" He really did say yes.

Well, as soon as he left the vicinity, I was back on the eastbound side with my thumb out every time a car came by. I still have that ticket. Once every blue moon I get it out and take a look at it.

It wasn't too long until I got every hitchhiker's dream ride. Every young male hitchhiker anyway. It only happened to me this once, and I'm so glad it did.

Two young women stopped and gave me a ride. They were roommates and friends. They were from Oklahoma City and said I was welcome to ride all the way there with them. They were a few years older than me, really pretty, had a good sense of humor, and seemed so carefree with an aura that led me to think they could do anything and get away with it. I have to say at that moment I wished I was a little older and tons less shy, but I was none of that and still completely happy with my circumstance. Again, I just wish I knew their names. It would be fun to ring them up once in a while and reminisce about that trip.

They had beer. They had cigarettes. They had attitude! I was 18 and had very close to nothing, but what a trip it was.

When night came there was a storm, and the rain was heavy. Out in front of us some cars had stopped, so we slowed to a stop. I was about to open the passenger side door when a car came up from behind and didn't slow down. In the next second it had left the road and went down an embankment, finally coming to a stop well ahead of us down in that ditch. It must have been going 60. The girl who was driving was already out of our car when this went down. She was trying to figure out if it was a wreck or car trouble or what. She came back and said there was nothing we could do, so we slowly went around the cars in front of us and kept traveling.

Maybe we pulled over to catch a nap at some point and maybe we didn't, but early in the morning we made it to one of the girls' home in OKC. I spent the night on a couch or floor or bed—I don't remember—but later that day I was on my way again with Newport, Rhode Island, on my mind.

Newport was a mythical place to me. All the great folk artists played there, and there were big crowds who came every year.

I got a cot at a hostel that had showers. I could leave my backpack and guitar there and walk around the festival grounds during the day and go to the concerts at night. The daytime events were called workshops, and I heard people playing in small gatherings sprinkled all around.

Judy Collins was hosting a contemporary folk song workshop, and I talked with her a bit. She was so damn pretty I could barely put a sentence together. There was one guy who had a song I fell for immediately. It was called "Just a Little Brown Boy." The fellow was a black guy who had a great voice and great playing style and the lyric went, "He's just a little brown boy five months old, and before he can read he will know the score." I think Judy Collins liked it, too.

Another workshop featured Arlo Guthrie. A lot of people were talking about this guy because he was the son of one of the greatest names in folk music. It would not be long before everyone would stop talking about that and start talking about him.

A VERY SHORT TIME

Of all the workshops I went to, the largest crowd was about 20 people. This workshop was on Saturday afternoon, and it looked like about a thousand people were there. Arlo was introduced and came up to the microphone wearing a dark shirt, suspenders, a fedora and a necktie. He may have said something before he began to play, I can't remember. But when he played his Martin guitar in that familiar Travis picking style I loved so much and started singing what is now the famous "You can get anything you want at Alice's Restaurant" all my attention was drawn into that song.

Five minutes came and went. 10 minutes came and went. It was 20 minutes before the song was over, and when it was over I was forever an Arlohead. Even though there was no such thing as an Arlohead, I was one. Hell, the only thing that was a head at that time besides that thing that sits on your shoulders was a pothead. It didn't matter. I was sold, lock, stock and barrel.

If nothing else happened at the 1967 Newport Folk Festival, Arlo Guthrie did.

7
HOLIDAY INNS

I was getting better on the guitar. I thought I could sing. I still don't know why. I was perfectly normal in other aspects, but why I thought I could sing is still a mystery to me. It doesn't matter. What I was doing was getting better at writing songs.

I stopped in Johnson City and got work cutting and stacking in the tobacco fields. The Taylors were as kind as ever, and I stayed with them once again. Before long I had a bit of money so I hit the road. By the time I got to Memphis, Arlo Guthrie's album was out so I bought a copy and learned "Alice's Restaurant" in its entirety.

There were some bars that had live music, and I got a few gigs. I met some music people from time to time and wound up getting an audition for Holiday Inns. I was so nervous, but outwardly it must have not shown as much as I feared.

The auditions were held at Phillips Studio on Madison Avenue. The engineer—who I found out years later was Sam Phillips nephew, Judd Phillips—asked me what songs I was going to play. I said "Alice's Restaurant." "Is that it, he asked?" "Yes," I replied. "That's it."

I was thinking he'd never heard of "Alice's Restaurant," and I was only too happy to surprise him with it. Sure enough, when it was finally over he came running out of the control room with a grin from ear to ear, holding his thumb and forefinger about an inch apart and said, "You have this much tape left on the reel."

A VERY SHORT TIME

I got the job!

My first professional gig—it was professional to me—was February 1968, at the downtown Holiday Inn in Charleston, South Carolina. Holiday Inns paid for my round-trip airplane ticket, room and board, and $150 a week for two weeks. It was my second airplane ride. I remember thinking to myself, 'I like show business.'

8

THE RHODES SHOW

On my return I rented an apartment near Madison and Tucker. It's still there. It had the look of a big house, but it had been made into apartments. It had two apartments upstairs and two down. I got one upstairs.

I took jobs playing anywhere I could, and I kept learning the guitar. I kept writing, too.

At that time in Memphis there were half-hour country music shows every Saturday afternoon on Channel 5. First up was the Rhodes Show, which was taped in the Channel 5 studio. Next was the Wilburn Brothers Show, then followed by the Porter Wagoner Show, the Flatt and Scruggs Show, and the Ernest Tubb Show. I may not have the running order right, but that's the gist of it.

I can't remember how or why I was there the first time, but I went many times to watch them tape the Rhodes Show at Channel 5. I met Dusty Rhodes, who was the show's main man. His brother, Speck Rhodes, played bass for Porter Wagoner in Nashville. Dusty's wife, Dot, would sing. And their daughters, Sandra and Donna, would sing. Sandra was also a great guitar player.

Dusty became my manager. He encouraged me to keep writing. I'd play him what I'd written each week. After he felt like I had enough songs, we made a trip to Nashville and I recorded 10 of them at Bradley's Barn. I had never played with professional musicians and

A VERY SHORT TIME

I was struck by how they could listen to me playing the song a time or two and be ready to record. Amazing!

We went to the Wilburn Brothers' publishing company and met the brother who ran the company. Their biggest writer at the time was Loretta Lynn. She was on the Wilburn Brothers TV show and one of my favorite country stars. Her records sounded so great with those clear tones, big bass, and her strong, confident voice, and those kick ass lyrics. I always felt better after hearing her sing. When I was in that office, amid these people who I knew so well from TV, and finding they are, well, just people, it blew my mind.

I knew we were in Nashville, but it was unlike the Nashville I knew. In this Nashville Don Everly might be walking across a parking lot. Or Porter Wagoner might be sitting at his desk in the RCA building. Just seeing the dog and megaphone statuettes at RCA was a trip in itself.

Mostly what I did on that trip was sit and listen to what they said, trying to figure out what they were talking about.

We rode with Teddy Wilburn from Bradly's Barn to get something to eat. The top was down, the weather was comfortable, the sun was fading, and I had officially recorded some demos. The breath of fresh air was everywhere.

Back in Memphis, Larry Raspberry taught me some songs to add to the 40 or so Dylan songs I knew. It really helped me get a handle on playing in a bar. I learned "By the Time I Get To Phoenix," "This Guy's In Love With You," "Everybody's Talking," "Poison Ivy," famous folk songs, and songs by Jimmy Reed. I should've kept one of those set lists. In those days I taped the set list to the top of my guitar, which may be why I didn't keep them. They seemed like old hat after a few gigs, and I just threw them away.

I was hoping to meet some people my age and into some of the same things as me. I found out about the Memphis Academy of Art and went there to maybe meet a kindred spirit or two and see about modeling. I was told they paid models, and I sure could use the cash. I did get a couple of sessions, but I think I overplayed my guitar. I was asked to play my guitar by one artist, and then another would ask me not to play. Truth be told I had never modeled, and the most I'd ever sat still was to watch TV or a movie. So my modeling career was cut painfully short due to my lack of everything it takes to be a model.

    I did, however, make some lifelong friends. Gordon Alexander, Ed Perry, Paul Mitchell, Ebet Roberts, and Kay King—who were all gifted in their chosen fields. Gordon Alexander and Ebet Roberts are still close friends.

9
BUFFALO

I got word I was booked to play all summer at the Holiday Inn in Buffalo, NY. That Holiday Inn was actually in Tonawanda, which is west of Buffalo. It was the last Holiday Inn before you get to Niagara Falls, and it had no vacancies all summer, which meant I would stay in a small motel across the street. I would still eat and work at the Holiday Inn but sleep across the street. Which was a wonderful arrangement.

Paul Mitchell, one of the guys I knew from the Art Academy, had a VW Beetle and drove Gordon and me to Erie, Pa., to visit Gordon's girlfriend, Jan, for a day or two, then he drove us to the Holiday Inn before heading back to Memphis. What energy we had.

Two of the big records at that time were "MacArthur Park" and "Jumpin' Jack Flash." Now, picture this. Paul Mitchell at the wheel of his VW with Gordon Alexander riding shotgun and me, scrunched up in the back with all the shit you have when three guys are driving to Buffalo from Memphis. I remember long hours with the windows down, the drone of that little air-cooled, four-cylinder engine, and the super tinny sound of the AM radio as it strained for a signal to give us a little auditory bliss. "It's all right now, in fact it's a gas."

Gordon and I met the manager of the Holiday Inn and got the lowdown on what we do, where we do, and when we do. We checked in to the motel across the highway, and the summer in Buffalo began.

We were there for 10 weeks or something very close to it. It's not that long, but we did meet some very cool local people we wouldn't have met if we were only there for a couple of weeks. I guess this is a recurring theme, but I wish I'd kept a diary. Shy of that, but still important, I wish I'd kept a ledger of names and dates. Just something simple. Oh, if I'd only a had a smartphone back then.

There were girls and guys who we hung out with. We all shared the same taste in music. We went to Toronto a few times where I bought an Indian shirt that had a thousand colors with a Nehru collar, and a pair of bell bottom blue jeans to go with it. My hair was not long when I arrived, but it was getting there.

The world was spinning, and I was too. And even though I didn't recognize it then I was having the time of my life.

Somewhere around the middle of our time in Buffalo I heard a song on the jukebox that was new to me. I thought I knew every song on that thing, so when I heard it again I went to see what it was.

Jukeboxes displayed the record number when the song was playing. If you wanted to know which song you were listening to, you had to go check while it was still playing. If you didn't do that, you had to wait until it played again to get the name of the song. The only other way to find the title of a song was to go through every title on the jukebox until you found it.

In my case, if I looked during the day, after lunch and before dinner when the restaurant was empty, I could spend all that time with my face down in that jukebox. Seems like I heard "Mr. Bojangles, Mr. Bojangles, danced." But I didn't really know. This jukebox had 200 songs, and when you pressed a button it made a roll of titles go from top to bottom, or vice versa. I had never spent much time up north, but they had a whole section of that jukebox that was dedicated to polka music. Well, I was no musical genius, but I knew the song I was looking for was not a polka song. So that eliminated maybe 30 or 40 songs. I knew the records that I liked, or at least had heard, so that eliminated maybe another hundred songs.

With careful attention I finally found that title, and it was "Mr. Bojangles." I dropped in my dime and pressed the associated buttons. As if by magic the sound of the descending bass line in 3/4 time filled up the speakers. When the voice began, I rode those words into a story that put me in the middle of the scene. I was in jail with a man who could dance with charm and grace and told his stories with shuffle-ball-step. By the time the dog died I was toast. I knew I had just discovered a masterpiece.

I knew so little about the music business that the thought of anyone else knowing this song never crossed my mind. But that's OK. There's no reason I would have known about record companies with A&R departments and a promotional staff. That stuff was still on Mars to me. All I knew was I found it, and now it's mine.

Gordon and I went to downtown Buffalo and stopped in a head shop. A head shop in those days sold hippie clothes, candles, that sort of thing. I met the owner, and I told her I was playing at the Holiday Inn and she told me about her son who played bass. A few days later Delmark Goldfarb came to the Holiday Inn and listened to me play.

We began meeting at his house to play some songs and listen to bluegrass music. At some point he told me about the College Coffee House Circuit based in New York City. I was rolling on some songs I had written that summer. Delmark played bass on a couple, and it felt good. He played a few sets with me at the Holiday Inn, and it got better each time.

He told me about Robin Polanker, a photographer he knew, and she became the first person to take promotional pictures of Delmark and me. I wore a turtleneck shirt, and Goldfarb looked very hip with his glasses, Van Dyke beard, and dark hair. Robin developed the film herself, and when I saw the pics I thought we looked the part.

10

THE COFFEE HOUSE CIRCUIT

After I played my last set at the Holiday Inn, Goldfarb and I bought plane tickets to New York and off we flew. We found accommodations at the Broadway Central Hotel, which had its heyday when Rembrandt stayed there in 1629. It had been deteriorating ever since.

About 6 a.m. the next morning some guy had decided our room was his room. He was pounding on the door with all his drug-addled might—which seemed considerable at 6 a.m. Goldfarb slid the chest of drawers against the door, and try as he might, the would-be intruder could not get in. It all happened so fast I never got out of bed. I sure as hell am glad Goldfarb did. I thank him to this day for his quick thinking.

Our audition was at 4 p.m., because you had to audition to get a spot on the real audition. I don't remember how many other artists were trying to get on the Coffee House Circuit, but we passed the audition to get an audition and were scheduled for 9 p.m,

Goldfarb told me that George Terry, the fellow who was running the auditions, told him we got the slot, but he couldn't put us on for another week. Goldfarb knew we couldn't afford to hang out in New York with nothing to do for a week, so he called Fred Weintraub, who owned the Bitter End and the Coffee House Circuit, and he got us the spot that night. Goldfarb said this pissed George Terry off. I didn't know about any of this at the time, and if I did, it flew right by me because all I was focusing on was the audition.

When we got on stage, I told a story about being at the Newport Folk Festival when the Chambers Brothers sang "Time Has Come Today." I liked that song. I just didn't think it was a folk song. They were a great soul band, but this was a folk festival. I told them I had written "A Very Short Time" in Buffalo that summer and while it didn't have anything to do with the Chambers Brothers, I said, "I'm gonna play it anyway." It got a little laugh, and I played my song. Then we may have played "Everybody's Talking" or maybe it was something else. When we left the stage, I had no clue if we would get on the Circuit or not, and I was too scared to hang around while somebody was making up their mind about it. If I was going to continue playing Holiday Inns or get the chance to play for sophisticated college students was news I'd rather find out later.

I walked around the Village checking out the head shops, people, and the traffic as cars crawled by. Every few yards someone coming from the other direction would lean over and whisper "grass, hash, acid?" I didn't know shit from Shine-o-la, but something in the back of mind kept saying "don't buy anything on the street even if I could afford it."

Finally, Goldfarb came bounding down Bleecker Street, turned up MacDougal and found me idling in front of some shop. He grabbed me and said, "We did it! We got on, and the people want to meet you."

Bryan Sennett was a tall, handsome man, who wore western-cut suits and cowboy boots right there in the heart of New York City, so I was immediately drawn to him. He had a management company with Fred Weintraub called Sennett-Weintraub, and they owned the Coffee House Circuit. He told us he missed hearing us play, but Janis Ian heard us and recommended us for the Circuit. Well, Janis Ian had just had a huge hit with "Society's Child," and she thought we were good. I remember saying to myself, "Shit man, this is cool."

Bryan walked with us to the Earle Hotel on Washington Square—the place I stayed the first time I came to NYC—and paid for a room for a couple of nights and gave us the address to his office and cab money. This was quite a step up from the Broadway Central. There were 8-by-10 black and white pictures of Stephen Stills, Jimi Hendrix, and other music stars on the walls, and I noticed my feet less and less attached to the floor.

Did I sleep that night? Who knows? Did I eat anything that night? Your guess is as good as mine. The thought that kept rolling through my mind was I'm going to play my songs for intellectual, mature, college students who would come to listen instead of drink and talk through the entire proceedings. Yes. I liked this very much!

The next day at Sennett-Weintraub, Goldfarb and I were sitting across the desk from Bryan. His secretary was there along with a couple of other folks who worked at the company. They asked us for background info—where we are from, how old we were, all the typical stuff you would expect. And then came a question I'd never been asked, at least not by anyone in the real music business. "Who do you listen to?" I have no idea who Goldfarb mentioned, and I wasn't thinking about it, so I was caught off guard.

Partly because I had my favorite song on my mind just about 24/7, and partly because I thought I could demonstrate how hip I was, I said "'Mr Bojangles' by Jerry Jeff Walker." Remember, this was my song I had found in the vacuum of my imaginary world, where I was the only person in the universe who ever heard this song.

Bryan looked at me then whispered something to his secretary, and she promptly and quietly left the room. We all kept talking about the music and songs we liked and which guitars were awesome and just general topics that pop up when music people get together. After maybe a half an hour I was thinking the meeting would be coming to a close when the door opened and in walked a tall, young, handsome man with a big smile. Bryan said, "Keith, this is Jerry Jeff Walker."

11
JERRY JEFF WALKER

I had an instantaneous reaction coalescing around disbelief and wonder all rolled up together. I can't remember what I said or if Goldfarb said anything. All I know is after the introductions, after the shock of learning Bryan was Jerry Jeff's manager, and after the meeting came to a close, Jerry Jeff said, "Let's go and have a drink and celebrate new beginnings." Or something like that.

Hot damn! The drinking age in New York was 18 and I was 19 so that meant I could legally have a drink with a real songwriter, who has a song that's the best thing I'd heard in ages. Oh yes. I'm in. Let's have a drink.

We were walking to some bar and came to a corner. For some reason I thought it was OK to continue walking, and I stepped down from the curb to the street when Jerry Jeff held his arm in front of me as a cab jetted by at what seemed like a hundred miles an hour. Jerry Jeff wrote the best song and saved my life. I have never forgotten it.

12

FLY TO MEMPHIS, HITCH TO NORTH CAROLINA

Goldfarb went back to Buffalo, and I was flying back to Memphis. My plane stopped in Chicago, and I was changing planes when the strap on one of my head shop sandals broke. I was flying on Delta, and the young guy I passed before I could get on the plane stopped me and said I couldn't board without my shoe on. I explained it had broken, but he would not budge. I had to spend the night and find a shoe store and get some shoes before I could go home. I was pissed. I didn't have the money to handle all that, so I called Bryan in New York and he wired me the money to get it done.

Believe me, that was the last thing I wanted to have happen, and I have always tried to avoid Delta Airlines ever since. It's funny how that works with me, but I must be hard wired that way. I thought that asshole could have handled it better than he did. I understand it now, but it didn't dawn on me at the time that a lot of people would freak out about a shoeless passenger going to the restroom. Oh well. I was a 19-year-old hitchhiker!

Back in Memphis I got my affairs in order so I could move to New York. I moved out of my apartment, took my records and turntable—which was just about the sum total of my worldly possessions—to my mom's house and hit the road hitchhiking to Fayetteville, North Carolina, to meet up with Jerry Jeff at a gig he was doing.

A VERY SHORT TIME

The Army guys there that night were looking at Vietnam as their next stop and didn't seem the least bit interested in hearing some folk music—not even played as masterfully as Jerry Jeff. So there was talking before, during, and after each song, and an artist like Jerry Jeff can't really deliver the kind of set he is beloved for in that situation. At least he had David Bromberg on guitar, and they could play off each other, but it's little consolation after playing the listening rooms Jerry Jeff was playing.

After they finished, the three of us got in the rental car and were off to the motel ... or so I thought.

On the way to the room we stopped at a 7-11 for some beer and Jerry Jeff decided to drive around for a bit. Before long we were lost in the North Carolina countryside. Beer was consumed in mass quantities—at least by Jerry Jeff. The amount of beer it took to get me buzzed was pretty small. I'm not sure about Bromberg. He may have had some beer, or maybe he didn't.

Anyway, somehow we ended up in a cow pasture listening to Paul Simon on the radio. The station was playing part of *The Graduate* soundtrack. It was a theme based on the song "Mrs Robinson" without the lyrics or any other instruments that are on the single. Bromberg and Jerry Jeff were talking about how great the guitar sounded as Jerry Jeff was increasing the speed of the rental car with every new donut he was doing. I was in the back seat leaning forward to hear the radio and just be part of the scene when the bumps began to get more pronounced. I felt my hands gripping the top of the front seat tighter and tighter, and I believe I was thinking something along the lines of, 'This is interesting and potentially dangerous.' Bromberg was getting perturbed with Jerry Jeff and had begun to reflect this with phrases like, "What in the fuck are you doing? You're gonna get us killed!" The car was fishtailing dirt from the back tires, and I think I got more beer on me than I had managed to get in me, but I couldn't help but think to myself, 'I enjoy hanging out with these creative types.'

FLY TO MEMPHIS, HITCH TO NORTH CAROLINA

As mysteriously as we found the pasture, we found a way out of it and were somehow on the way to the motel.

The next day Bromberg and I were sitting next to each other on the plane, and I began asking him a never-ending string of guitar, and other musical questions, that continue to this day. It may be years since we've seen each other, but it feels like not a day has gone by when we meet up somewhere. True friends make life worth living.

13
LIFE IN NEW YORK

When we got to Jerry Jeff's apartment, I met his wife, Janet. She was beautiful with long, black hair and dark eyes to match. She was quiet and seemed the exact opposite of Jerry Jeff.

It was early fall, and Jerry Jeff was about to record an album for Vanguard Records that became *The Drifting Way of Life*. It's still one of my favorites of all his records. It sounded like I wanted to sound. And I loved Vanguard Records, because they had Joan Baez, Mississippi John Hurt, Patrick Sky, Buffy Sainte-Marie, Eric Andersen and Ian and Sylvia.

I hadn't heard of Circus Maximus, the band Jerry Jeff was in with Gary White and Bob Bruno, but it was the connection between Jerry Jeff and Vanguard. He had to make one more record for Vanguard to have a clean break from the company so he could sign with Atco Records. Atco had the Coasters, and I was a huge Coasters fan. At the time I was learning about record companies and how they worked, but I really knew nothing about fulfilling contracts or any details like that. I just knew it was cool to be around people who did. This was my new world, and I was trying to soak it all up. But mostly I wanted to be around the artists who make the music, and I guess I'm still like that today.

Within a day or two, Jerry Jeff and Janet asked some friends over for dinner. That night I met Gary White, the bass player for Circus

LIFE IN NEW YORK

Maximus, Townes Van Zandt, Paul Siebel, and John Herald. We all played songs, and I wish I could remember which ones. Let me just say there were a lot of good songs going down all night.

I remember asking John Herald if he would play the amazing guitar part to "Four Road By" by Ian and Sylvia. He had played it on their record, and I couldn't believe he was sitting right in front of me. So I just asked, and lo and behold, he did it. I was in heaven. I was also intimidated because these guys were so damn good, had lived in the Village a long time, and their songs were awesome. I didn't know it then, but I would remain friends with them from that night on.

The office—that's what I called the management company—found an apartment where I could stay. I can't remember exactly where it was, but it was a place where I wasn't under Jerry Jeff and Janet's feet all the time.

I went to the Bitter End quite a lot and met Emmylou Harris there. I had never heard of her, but she could sing like an angel and had been in New York for a while. She and a friend of hers came to the apartment to hear some of my songs. I was so new I didn't know about such things, and it was another case of her being so beautiful I just couldn't collect myself enough to concentrate. I did better in this regard as time went by.

I was only at Jerry Jeff and Janet's apartment for a few days at a time, but I met a lot of his friends as they passed through New York doing gigs or business or both. Steven Fromholz and his partner Dan McCrimmon were there. Steven and I remained friends until he passed away in 2014.

My first tour for the College Coffee House Circuit was in upstate New York. Goldfarb and I would fly from the city to wherever we played. We usually stayed on campus in rooms they had for guests of the college. Sometimes they would have us a room off campus at a small hotel or motel. They provided meals and transportation to and from the shows, and we would practice wherever we could.

The gigs were usually at the student union or in small auditoriums. At every stop I tried to be better than the last. My repertoire was building, and I had collected jokes. I found if I told a story about the song I had written, it connected better with the audience. If I worked the mics — I always had two mics, one for vocal and one for guitar — by leaning back from the vocal mic a little, it kept the eyes on me and not on their watches. Anything I could put to use, I used.

The next tour was in Texas. We began in Commerce, then to Dallas, Ft Worth, and on to Austin. Goldfarb had never been to Texas, and after a few days he said he knew how to pronounce it. I said what do you mean? He said just say "taxes," and you'll sound like a native.

That tour was the first year of three years in a row I would play the University of Texas in Austin on my birthday. The first year the venue was called Le Potpourri. I didn't really know what that meant, but I didn't care. It was renamed the Cactus Cafe years later and that seems to fit it better.

We had the same holidays and seasons as the colleges did, so when they had a break for Thanksgiving or Christmas we did too. So those were times I went back to New York or Memphis.

Then came a day when I was asked to come to Sennett-Weintraub to meet with Bryan. I was still managed by Dusty Rhodes, and they wanted to formally take over. Still being a novice in this territory, I thought they would just tell Dusty they were my managers now and that would be all there was to it. In reality I believe Dusty may have been hurt by this, because he hadn't had very much time to do his thing with me, whatever that thing may have been. Now I was completely enthralled with folk music and playing on the Coffee House Circuit. As I look back on it, Dusty was going out on a limb for me, and I didn't even know what all that entailed. In the end, Sennett-Weintraub bought my contract from Dusty, and I never talked with him after that.

In 2006 when Dusty was dying, Chris Rhodes, his nephew, went to see him, and Dusty autographed his latest album for me. Chris also told me he believed Dusty just wanted me to do well no matter who helped me. How's that for a true gentleman?

In January and February of '69 the tour took us to upstate New York for two weeks and Minnesota for three weeks. In Minnesota, more than anything else, I remember how cold it was. When we left the room to go to a gig, it was so cold outside it took my breath away like it did when I was a kid and stuck my head in my grandmother's freezer in the summertime. The high temperature for the tour was 3 degrees.

Goldfarb and I spent so much time together, my cigarette smoking in our room was getting to him, and I was so stupid I didn't care. Everyone I knew smoked except Goldfarb. Hell, the whole world was smoking, and in my estimation he was being incredibly rude by burning this smelly incense trying to cover the exceptionally shitty smell of my cigarettes in our room. It all conspired to split us up. I wish I could have been more sensitive and realized it could have been solved some other way, but being that young, and so cold I didn't want to go out to smoke, just blew us apart.

We are still friends to this day. He has become a songwriter and rarely plays the bass, but I'll always remember that little Ampeg B-15 bass amp and the Gibson EB bass. We had a lot more fun than not, but our time playing together had come to an end.

14

SAN FRANCISCO AND LARRY BROOKS

I was so cold from Minnesota the thought of going back to New York was unimaginable. My friend Larry Brooks was living in San Francisco so I rang him to ask if I could come out for a while. Thankfully he was up for it because ... did I mention I was cold?

In those days if you wanted to fly somewhere you called an airline or went to the airport and told them your destination. You had a choice of airlines, times, and prices and you picked one. You gave them the cash, and they filled out the form by hand and placed it in this thing that cradled the ticket. Then they rolled the handle over it to imprint the airline name and other pertinent information via carbon paper onto the ticket. They took it out and tore your part off at the perforations and handed your ticket to you—no matter if it was round trip or one way.

After you were seated onboard, a stewardess—this was before flight attendants—would walk through and offer you a four-cigarette mini pack, usually either Winston, Marlboro, Salem and one other brand like Parliament or Viceroy. You could have more than one pack if you weren't too big of a pig about it. They gave you matches if you didn't have a lighter. Then another stewardess would come by to take your drink order. After all, who could smoke and not have a drink?

The seats were outfitted with a handy ashtray built into the arm of your comfortable seat. Just before takeoff you were versed on how to use your seat belt, and off you went.

When I landed in San Francisco, it was like the plane never touched down. Green palm leaves were swaying in the gentle breeze and people were walking about in long sleeves and unzipped jackets. 'Ah,' I thought to myself. 'I must be in heaven.'

In high school Larry Brooks was the drummer in a band called the Boys Blue. The band was fronted by brothers Mickey and Rickey Caughron, who were really great singers. They specialized in soul music, as did a lot of bands in Memphis at that time. They always killed it in the talent shows in the Treadwell auditorium. Larry had a love for folk music records too, and we spent many a night at his house listening to Dave Van Ronk, Burt Jansch, Furry Lewis, David Blue, and others when I was working at Sears and the title company.

After high school he bought a 650 Triumph Bonneville motorcycle and road it out to San Francisco, where he was friends with Joe Bauer, the drummer for The Youngbloods.

I stayed in the storied Haight Ashbury district with Larry, and we also rode his bike out to Marin County for a night or two at Joe's house. It was there that Joe played us a tape of the new Youngbloods single, "Darkness, Darkness," and I remember being blown away by how great it sounded.

One other memory from there; I was awakened in the morning by a loud buzzing. When I looked out the window it was two Ruby-throated hummingbirds flying in a horseshoe shape, with one starting on the right and the other on the left. They would fly down, pulling up just above the ground, then fly back up until the one on the right was on the left. They were doing this over and over. I couldn't believe how loud it was!

15
MICHAEL BROVSKY

Back in New York, Bryan Sennett was in the process of moving back to Colorado. And it was around this time I first met Michael Brovsky, who would become my manager. It was another new beginning for me and would be for Jerry Jeff, too.

I soon met Nick Holmes, who would become one of my all-time favorite people ever. We just clicked. He was in the ever-changing lineup of the Serendipity Singers and one of the best singer/songwriters I'd ever heard. Why he never became a household name is beyond me. He really was that good.

I spent many nights in his apartment listening to records, and one of those would soon become one of our favorites—Tim Buckley's *Happy Sad*. We would take a toke or two and go off into that world and stay there until both sides of the record had played. I had listened to Buckley's first two albums in Buffalo and very much enjoyed them, but this one was different. It had a free spirit that was unlike anything I'd heard in folk music. Maybe it was a mashup of folk and jazz, but whatever it was it sure spoke to me.

I was about to make a record in my pants! It was all I thought about. Every time I went to the office to talk about it, I was told making a record was two weeks off. "Keith," Brovsky would say, "we need to do — whatever it was this time — so let's give it a couple of weeks to work it out" and off I would go back to the village.

In the spring of '69 I helped Jerry Jeff load a U-Haul bob truck full of all his and Janet's belongings, and they made the move to Key West. They let me stay in their apartment till the end of the summer while I kept looking for a place of my own.

It was a really cool place and was right across the street from the Fillmore East. When bands played all you had to do was raise the window in the bedroom closest to the street and you could hear whoever was playing like they were in your living room. I heard the Who one night and never missed a note!

16
RONSTADT

I met Linda Ronstadt at the Bitter End in the summer of '69. She was, and still is, awesome. All the folkies around the U.S. loved her in the Stone Ponies, mainly because "Different Drum" was on the radio as much as any of the folk rock records in '67 and '68. I had a copy of the single — albums were expensive — and I remember hearing it on jukeboxes wherever I was touring.

When I met her and we began talking, it was kinda like talking to a record cover for the first few minutes. She was movie star good looking and could sing as good as it gets, and I'm just not around that particular combo very often. It was blowing my mind.

She loved "Mr Bojangles," and I told her I was staying at Jerry Jeff's so we walked to his apartment talking all the way. Just like regular people. When we got to Jerry Jeff's she told me Peter Asher had asked to be her manager and she was excited about it. I thought it would be the perfect situation for both of them because he was a great producer and she was a great singer.

Peter Asher managed and produced James Taylor and they were a huge success, so it seemed to me to be the very thing for him to have a woman on his roster.

We hung out at the apartment for a while then decided to go for another walk. This time we went back to the Middle Village, which is what I called where the Bitter End was. Jerry Jeff's place was in the East Village. Linda and I kept walking and crossed 6th Avenue and went into the West Village. I can't remember if we crossed on 3rd Street or some other street, but we were ambling along at 3 a.m. with no one on the streets but us when two guys came up behind us.

Now I'm not your go to fellow if someone is going to harass you, and I was a little scared, so I just stopped and looked in a store window, and Linda stopped with me. Sure as shit they walked by us then turned around and walked back, and I was shaking in my boots. Actually it was my sandals.

Linda was just Linda. She didn't let on if she was scared or not, but I think those guys and Linda knew I wasn't going to be able to do much of anything about anything anyway. It also didn't help that they were black. And that's what they came back to say. One of them said something along the lines of, "We see you're afraid of us, and we know it's just because we're black." Well, at least I knew that wasn't the case, because they could have been any color, and I would have still been just as much of a pussy. I'm an equal opportunity coward. Especially at that time of my life at 3 a.m. in New York City with a beautiful girl at my side I could not protect.

I've been embarrassed about it ever since, but I honestly can't think of another time anything like that has happened to me. Linda never brought it up again, and I'm glad about that.

Linda and I would hang out when we were in town at the same time, and we became good friends. She knew more about music than anyone I had met. She was a student of the art and knew what made a great song, as opposed to the ones that are just good. And she knew the minutia of music. What all the Italian words were and what they meant and why it's important. And she knew about the music business, too.

We were by Union Square one day and she was telling me I should sign with Capitol Records and not Vanguard because Capitol was bigger and Vanguard couldn't compete like Capitol could. All I knew was Mississippi John Hurt and John Baez and so many of the folk artists I was enamored with were on Vanguard at that time. The commercial part of the situation didn't register with me. That came later.

17

231 THOMPSON ST #12 AND GARY WHITE

I was looking for a place of my own, and finally found one that fall. Gary White still lived in the building where he and Jerry Jeff lived when they came to New York from Houston. I believe Gary told Janet Walker about a vacancy at 231 Thompson Street, and she told me. I went over to meet Norman Fayne, the apartment manager. He showed me apartment #12. It was maybe 200-300 square feet, I really don't know, with a shower and two rooms if you count the toilet room. I put a bookshelf between the sink, stove and refrigerator area to divide it from the sleeping/living space.

Michael Malone, who at the time was a carpenter, built a shelf for my record player, tape deck, and amp/tuner, on one side, and I put a nice sofa/bed on the other. About a year later he built me a loft bed that made things much nicer. It was home sweet home from the fall of '69 until I moved in '73.

After I moved in I'd go by Gary White's apartment almost every day. Gary is, all at once, funny, cynical, opinionated, benevolent, brilliant, wise, caustic, polite, and well, you get the idea. If you can't learn from someone like Gary then you may need help. I hung out there as much as he would allow and I learned something every day. We became lifelong friends—though he may not admit it.

He still played bass with Jerry Jeff occasionally.

A VERY SHORT TIME

That summer Jerry Jeff was playing the Newport Folk Festival and I got to tag along.

On the way to Newport, I heard the new Rolling Stones single, "Honky Tonk Women" for the first time on the radio, and it lit me right up!

I met James Taylor after he played a short set at the showcase for new artists. I told him he sounded great and his guitar playing should be more prominent on his next record. His next record would be "Sweet Baby James," and when I heard it I was delighted to see he took my advice. (I did say that to him, but I did not believe he listened to me, and I hope you don't either)

I got to meet Joni Mitchell and hear her play that night. She was incredible.

Jerry Jeff killed it when he played. Donnie Brooks played harp with him, and it worked like a charm.

The next morning I was with David Bromberg, and Harvey Brooks was with him, so I got to meet him, too. Harvey played bass with Dylan so I was floating on air. What a time it was for a young songwriter.

Touring never stopped when school was in session, and I loved it. In the fall of '69 I was playing the University of Delaware when I wrote "Rich Wayfaring Stranger." The lyrics came pretty quickly. I think I had the chords a bit before the lyrics. I was working on songs the whole tour, and this one seemed to be the best one. I thought it was anyway, and after all, if I don't like it, it ain't gonna ever see the light of day no matter what.

If playing at the University of Delaware wasn't my last date before school was out, it was close to it.

They didn't book me close to holiday breaks or the end of semesters, because that was usually exam time. I wish I'd have saved all my itineraries. I have one or two from the entire six years I did the circuit.

18

KEITH SYKES, THE FIRST ALBUM

The day finally came when I got a contract with Vanguard Records. I remember meeting Maynard Solomon in his office, and it all seemed otherworldly. I began playing guitar in '66—well December '65—and now, a few years later, I was a recording artist.

I had "Rich Wayfaring Stranger" and "A Very Short Time." I had "Edger Was a Worm." I had reworked an "Old Shep" type song into one I named "Gypsy." I had "Gifts," "Sad Song" and "Firefly," "The Wind," "You Were Going Crazy," "Anything Else" and "Ordinary Day." All together they made up my debut album. In hindsight I wish I had recorded "I'm Missing You," the song the Lonesome Rhodes, Dusty's daughters, recorded for RCA, to be a part of the album, but these were the ones I liked at the time, and for better or worse that was that.

Linda Ronstadt came to the studio when I was recording "Sad Song," and I was very nervous about her being there. I think she liked the essence of that song, but it has a wandering part that's not conducive to singing on in a natural way. It would have been very cool if I was working on a song she was into at that moment. But alas, timing has as much to do with things like that as anything, and she did not sing with me that day.

Keith Sykes, the album, came out in January 1970, and when it did I was introduced to the colossal feeling of how small I was. It happened when I went into a record store looking for my album. It didn't hit me when I first stepped in, it just kinda built a little at a time as I wandered down the aisles and began to notice how all these other artists have albums, too. How did I not notice this before? There must have been 5,000 artists' albums in this one store. And it wasn't even a big store. I used to go in a record store looking for a certain song or artist and never pay any attention to any records that weren't the one I was looking for.

On this day, looking for my record, all I could see was every record but mine. By the time I left I had a whole new outlook on what was going on. And it was an eye opener. I realized I was a comma in a sea of prose, and if I wanted to realize my dream I'd have to completely rethink everything I was doing.

Out on the road after the record came out, the crowds were beginning to swell and people just treated me differently than before. Mind you it was light years from anything like having a hit record, but at least I had a record. Once there was an ad in *Rolling Stone* for my album, and folks would bring copies of it for me to sign.

19

TOWNES VAN ZANDT

I was on a tour in Texas when there was a convention for the talent buyers for the colleges that were part of the circuit I played. I saw Townes Van Zandt hanging at the bar in the middle of this huge room. We hadn't seen each other in a while, plus we didn't know anyone else, so it was cool to talk to a kindred spirit.

After a bit he asked if I'd heard about his wreck. I said I hadn't. I'm paraphrasing, but here's the gist of it:

Townes was driving down a two-lane Texas road way out from anywhere, and the road has a 90-degree turn to the left. There's a bar on the side of the road, smack dab in the middle of the turn. Townes saw the turn, but due to the fact he was imbibing a bit, he didn't make the turn and headed straight for the bar instead. He crashed into the bar and came to a stop when the car lodged about half way in. He—with the help of the bartender—got the door opened enough for Townes to remove himself from the car. So what does he do first? He walks in, sits down at the bar and orders a Jack and Coke. The bartender obliged him and brought the drink. They talked for a bit when Townes said maybe he should call the cops and let them know what has happened. The bartender told Townes, "Oh, not to worry, the cops have been called, and they are on the way."

Now, to have the impact this story had on me, you would need Townes to tell it to you like he told it to me that night. And bear in mind this is from the man who gave us "Close Your Eyes I'll Be Here in the Morning."

Years later in the 1990's, I saw Townes in a Nashville bar one afternoon and we started talking. When it was getting late we walked out of the bar and he went to his motorcycle to ride home. He'd been drinking all afternoon so I offered to give him a ride home and he could get his bike the next day. I'm glad he took me up on it.

When we got to his house he asked me in and we talked for a bit. To my surprise he asked if I would produce his next record. I told him I didn't think I could do it justice because my head was all in commercial country and rock at the time. In hindsight I wish I'd said yes.

He would be gone in just a few years and I'll never have that chance again.

Such as it goes in this life we live.

20

KRIS KRISTOFFERSON

One of my favorite New York haunts was The Kettle of Fish on MacDougal Street. I used to have dinner there quite often, and one night a fellow with long hair, wearing a buckskin, or some other kind of leather jacket and pants, came over and asked I if was Keith Sykes. I said yes. He said he was Kris Kristofferson and he very much liked my album. I had never heard of Kris Kristofferson, much less that he was the hottest songwriter in Nashville. He looked just a little down and out, but nice, and it was always good to get a compliment like that. I thanked him very much, and that was about it.

A few months later he was back in New York and playing the Bitter End. After the show, back at the Kettle of Fish, one of his band members was leaning on a wall near a crowd of people surrounding Kris. I asked this fellow to tell me about him. "Well," he said in a Southern drawl, "he just had the last Johnny Cash single and several other country hits, and right now he has the number one song in the country with Janis Joplin. It's called "Me and Bobby McGee."

While I'm letting all this soak in, I'm thinking, why don't I know all this? I need to get on board and take a ride on what these guys have been doing.

I asked the fellow his name, and he tells me he's Donnie Fritts. I asked Donnie to tell me about the other guys in the band—who plays what, and what else they have done. He told me Billy Swan plays the organ and wrote "Lover Please" for Clyde McPhatter. Everything he said after that escaped my mind except "Lover Please" and Clyde McPhatter. If Billy Swan wrote "Lover Please" and Kris has the #1 record on Janis Joplin, that's enough to hold me for a while. You see, to me, Clyde McPhatter was one of those music people I thought was from some other world—a place where the music business, and the artists, and the songwriters, and everyone else, were from. It was just dawning on me that everyone is real people, even the people on the business side.

I guess when you hear songs on the radio when you're a kid you think of them as bigger than life. Still today, when I hear an old record I've loved since childhood, it has that effect on me. How could Clyde McPhatter be real and sound like that? How can a person write a song like that? Maybe it was because I was so deep into the folk world at that time that I never thought about the bigger world of music.

I was lost in the bottom of the songs that night in the Kettle of Fish with Kris Kristofferson and his band. I was, and I suppose I still am, lost in songs, but that night I was waking up to another reality.

21

DON NIX AND MUSCLE SHOALS

Early in 1971 I went to Memphis for a tonsillectomy, and I stayed with my mom for the week. I remember being very glad to get it behind me.

Before I went back to New York I went to hang out with Don Nix. Don was an original member of the Mar-Keys, and they had "Last Night," one of Stax Records' first worldwide hits. He was also friends with Leon Russell and told me about Leon and his duo, The Asylum Choir.

Don is a songwriter and made albums that sounded great. I wanted to make a record with the sounds he was getting. We talked about records and listened to records.

Don told me about Muscle Shoals and the players down there, about the records they played on and the hits they made. The only times I had played with a band was the demo session at Bradley's Barn, with Allen Taylor and Bubby in Johnson City, and when I made my album. Goldfarb didn't qualify as a band, so I didn't count him. So I had no idea of the value of musicians like that.

They could make the studio sound any way they wanted. I think I had six or seven songs I wanted to record. Maybe I'll remember them before I finish this book. I called Michael Brovsky to see if I could record with Don Nix in Muscle Shoals, and Brovsky sent a telegram to Nix saying to proceed. So we did.

I had been in over my head in other things and still came out OK. But this time was different. When I had only nine cents to my name it never bothered me. If I was on the side of the road all night long and no one stopped to pick me up, I didn't worry.

But now, I didn't know how to get a sound out of an electric guitar. I didn't even own an electric guitar. David Hood, Jimmy Johnson, Roger Hawkins and Berry Beckett knew music from top to bottom and back again. Don asked Wayne Perkins, the guitar player, to get me a sound. I played it like I would play an acoustic, and the sound it emitted was, let's just say, not there.

After I was back in New York the tapes were sent to Brovsky and Vanguard. Brovsky told me Vanguard would not pay for the tapes. I went into a funk. Not long after that, Nix called and asked me to do something about getting the studio paid, and I was as lost as humanly possible. I was also embarrassed and ashamed I was at the middle of it all. I believe it took a few years to get Nix, the studio, and the band any money. That's the first and last time I've been involved with anything like that.

I met Brovsky at Vanguard, where we met with Maynard Solomon. I said I liked tapes, and we should put the record out. Maynard didn't budge. Maynard said we could record in the city at Vanguard's studio, but he was not paying for Muscle Shoals. That left it to Brovsky to sell the tapes and give what he could to Nix. I asked Maynard if I could record an album solo and then be released from Vanguard. He said yes.

The engineer who worked on my first album was Jack Lothrop, and I asked Maynard if he could produce me now. Maynard was fine with it, and we began work not long after.

22
1,2,3

I went to the studio, and for the first time I had it all to myself. I looked around to see the layout in the studio and spent a little time getting a feel for it. I looked at the control room and asked how the console worked.

I had spent my advance from Vanguard on a record player, tuner/amp, speakers, a tape recorder, and two microphones, along with the associated wires to connect it all. That's the most basic rig you could have at that time and still record with a pretty good degree of clarity and low noise.

The studio, with the console and all the control it gives the engineers, was way beyond anything I knew. I asked Jeff Zaraya, Jack Lothrop's engineer, "How do I get me and my guitar to end up on a record?" He took the time to talk me through the process, even though I'm sure he knew I was not going to be able to repeat what I just heard.

I liked all the songs, except I believe I should have left out "Tell Me 'Bout College." At least I got Loudon Wainwright and Richard Brautigan in there, but the rest of it strikes me now as kinda silly.

"Mable and Henry" was my idea of a folk/soul song. Knowing there was no such category made me want to do it all the more.

I thought of "Pipeline Welder" and "Truck Driver Blues" as country songs. I believe I have an affinity for people who work at what are called blue-collar jobs. It must come from my dad being a plumber and me helping him during summers.

"The Diamonds" was blasted into my brain one day out walking. On one block I saw a woman with a little white dog sporting a jeweled collar, and on the next block I saw a down-and-out soul literally on the street.

Going to "Kentucky Lake" when I was a kid was the highlight of any summer. Blind Willie McTell and the McGarrigle Sisters influenced the music of this song. It's still one of my faves.

A lot of shit was distracting me during this time and "1,2,3" is the resulting song. It's kinda like listening to frustration.

I must have started "Country Morning Music" in Austin, because the lyrics and where I wrote each song are printed on the back cover of the album. But I'm sure I finished it in my New York apartment.

I had an idea about using Robert Browning's phrasing with music inspired from the opening song from the movie *Sergeant York*. If you check out those two things you might see where I was coming from. I named it "Country Morning Music" because I never use that phrase in the song. I thought that might be something Dylan would do. There I was—daydreaming about what someone else might do. But I still think the title fits the song, so I'm cool with it.

There was a girl who went to the Art Academy who inspired "About Her Eyes." To me she looked exactly as I described her in this song. It became the first song of mine that Jerry Jeff recorded.

"Daddy Raised Hell" was my song to my dad, or I should say the dad who was an alcoholic. He was incontestably a great dad when he was sober. One of my wishes that never came true was him being able to have a few drinks and then call it a night and go home, go to bed, and wake up the next morning and hit the bricks like all the other dads.

It is a point of pride that this song was one of Guy Clark's favorites of the songs I've written.

1,2,3

I reworked "Like A Candle" recently, and I believe it's better for it. Sometimes back then I was reaching for something I just couldn't grasp. If you listen you may feel what I'm talking about. If I go back and tinker with something it's because something is pushing me there. I don't do it for the fun of it.

I named the record *1,2,3* because I thought that crazy song summed up where my head was at.

23

LOUDON WAINWRIGHT III

I met Loudon Wainwright lll at the Gaslight before I recorded *1,2,3*. Sam Hood told me I should hear this guy's songs and see him perform. Intrigued, I went down the steps and took a seat. Before long, this fellow appeared on stage wearing regular-looking clothes. I mention this because most of the performers around this time wore things you'd see in the streets around the Village—anything from jeans, flannel shirts and jean jackets to total rock band stuff like outrageous '60s things the Beatles might wear. Loudon looked like he just finished work on Wall Street or maybe a lecture at NYU. No matter. Because when he began to sing, these lyrics and melodies sprang forth in the midst of these caricature-looking faces he made. It was one of the most original things I've ever seen, and it burned a place in me that's still charred and smoking.

We met after his set and talked a bit. He was living in the City and came to the Village to hear people play and/or just hang out. As time went by, we became good friends, and I was invited to his wedding to Kate McGarrigle, of the McGarrigle Sisters, at his parents' house in upstate New York. It was a fun night, and I got pretty drunk. After the party when Kate and Loudon were going to their apartment I went with them, completely oblivious to his parents asking me to let the newlyweds have their night.

The next morning it slowly dawned on me what a mindless thing I did, and I've like felt a heel about it ever since. Neither Loudon nor Kate ever said a thing to me about it, but I've never forgiven myself. I'd take that one back if I could.

24
SUMMER SOLDIERS

After a few tours that spring I became a regular back in New York. The office would send me out to audition for things like radio or TV commercials, or maybe a spot in a play.

The phone rang one morning, and they asked if I'd like to go to Japan and be in a movie. Whoa! They had me at Japan! I wrote down the particulars, and in a few short days I was walking to the West Village to meet with the people who were making the movie. For some reason I had a confidence that day, and I was not to be denied. I walked into the meeting with the attitude that I was the right one for this role, and I could do it. And to my everlasting surprise, a few days later I got the call that said I was going to Japan.

The movie people sent to me to classes to learn about Buddhism and become comfortable chanting, "Nam Myōhō Renge Kyō."

They were responsible for all the papers I needed to get a passport and to work in Japan, and it all arrived on time. I believe I had to have shots, too. And the main thing was I had to be ready to be gone for nine weeks. When the time came, I couldn't believe my luck as I walked out the door for Tokyo.

It's a long plane ride from New York City to Tokyo. We changed planes in San Francisco and again when we reached Hawaii. From there we were flying Japan Airlines, and we all were given hot washcloths to freshen up, and a big embossed card for crossing the international date line.

By the time I arrived in Tokyo I may as well have arrived in Oz. On the way from the airport to my accommodations, we passed by the Japanese Eiffel Tower. One of the movie people told me, with a smile in his eyes, that it's two inches taller than the original in Paris.

The movie people were so very polite and respectful. They helped me get checked in to my home for the next couple of months. I had a few minutes to collect myself, then we were off to have dinner with Hiroshi Teshigahara, our director, and John Nathan, the writer, and some more of the crew as well.

Dinner that night was sublime. It was my first time to use chopsticks, and I drank my first cup of hot sake. All this after a plane ride from New York to Tokyo.

John Nathan and I became friends pretty much right off the bat—which was a good thing since he spoke fluent Japanese, and most of the crew, including Teshi, as everyone called our director—could barely speak any at all. It was Nathan who helped me navigate this entire project.

And I needed all the help I could get. I had never even been in a school play and was as green as it gets concerning everything about movies. I had never felt a compulsion or even a connection to anything to do with acting. My only strong desire at that point was to go to Japan.

So here I was, among real actors, without any idea of what to do or how to act. If there was a saving grace in all this, I was told they wanted the movie to have the look and feel of a documentary, and my inexperience would help me reach their goal. Well, I thought, 'if they want inexperience I'm the man of the hour.'

The movie was called *Summer Soldiers* and I was only given enough of the script to shoot the day's work. When I asked for all the script they made it clear they weren't working like that, and I was to learn just what I was given. So, to add to my confusion, there was no way for me to get a real read on my character. All I knew about him was he had deserted from the Vietnam War and was being hosted for a few days at a time by an underground network of antiwar sympathizers. So I just did the best I could, and the rest was up to someone else.

Even though I couldn't speak Japanese, Teshi and I bonded well. I admired his aristocratic aura and gentlemanly nature. I didn't have to speak the language to pick up on things like that.

On a shoot one day I saw a beautiful girl, and we were introduced by the crew. Her name was Suiko. Of course we couldn't talk, outside of a few rudimentary words, but it soon became clear that was not going to be much of an issue and I suddenly felt I was not so alone.

We dated a few times, and it was always a hoot because of the language thing. We managed to enjoy each other's company by pointing at a menu and just saying "sake" or whatever would get us by in the moment.

Her hair was so black it shone with silver highlights in the sun, and her shy smile and her deep-as-a-well eyes kept me enthralled without words. Now and then I wonder about her and hope she's had a wonderful life.

After a few weeks we left Tokyo on the bullet train heading south to Kyushu Provence. We shot scenes near a U.S. Army base there. After filming was completed on a location it was off to another one. I enjoyed seeing as much of Japan as I could see.

When we went to Hiroshima I went to the Atomic Bomb Museum, and I couldn't sleep for three days after. The images burned in my mind, and all the descriptions I read on the placards walking through it would not stop flooding through me. The bomb that was dropped there was rated at one-fifth of a megaton. The smallest of today's bombs that are aimed at cities are at least 20 times that powerful. And I really can't fathom the power of hydrogen bombs. My takeaway from being in Hiroshima was, it is infinitely better to find a way to be a good neighbor and trading partner than be an aggressor.

About a week or so before the movie wrapped, *1,2,3* was released, and I saw the very favorable review Karin Berg had written for *Rolling Stone*. I was glad to have the record out amongst the world.

I met some soulful, beautiful people in Japan, and I was so glad I was able to go there and see as much of it I did. I never did pursue any further acting opportunities because it was never my calling. But I'll always have Japan.

25

IT TAKES A (GREENWICH) VILLAGE

Back in New York City a few months later a good review of *Summer Soldiers* was in *Newsweek* and a smaller, but still good one, in *Time* as well. I thought to myself, 'publicity is good.'

My friend Gordon Alexander, who I knew from the Art Academy, had moved to New York and taken the room right below mine at 231 Thompson St. With Gary White right there on the first floor I had a truly rocking bunch of folks to hang with. It wasn't too long before Gary's future wife, Annie, would move in with him, and suddenly we had a family. At least it was to me.

Kristofferson was coming up a lot. And out on the road we would see each other at festivals and assorted gigs. My community was growing.

The Philadelphia Folk Festival was one more center of gravity to look forward to each year. I met John Hartford there and heard the McGarrigle Sisters for the first time.

Any given night on a typical walk down Bleecker Street or MacDougal I might say hello to John Sebastian, see Eric Anderson or Dave Van Ronk at the Kettle of Fish, or talk with David Clayton-Thomas at Nobody's. I met Janis Joplin, Jimi Hendrix, and Jim Morrison within a three-month period. I only met them, I did not know them, but it was cool to be there.

Gary White had a song that was so perfect it was bound to be a hit. It's called "Long, Long Time," and every time I was at his apartment I asked him to play it. When he played it for Linda Ronstadt she snapped it right up and it became the lead single from her *Silk Purse* album. It went right up the charts, and suddenly Gary had it going on. He also had "Nobody's," the B side, so he got a double dose. It's still one of my favorite records, and to me that album combined country, rock, and pop so well it's really a landmark record.

I lost a notebook in the back of a cab one day, and I still feel totally weird about it. Gary White and I were going to the Philadelphia Folk Festival, and we were there before I realized it. It was a drawing book, a little bigger than a notebook, and I had some really good stuff in it. And I lost it and it bummed me out, but such is life. You can't fix what you don't have. So I started writing again.

26

ALEX CHILTON

Gordon Alexander wanted to go to San Francisco and soak up some up that vibe. He arranged to sublet his apartment to Alex Chilton. Everyone from Memphis knew of Alex because he sang "The Letter" when he was in the Box Tops. It became a worldwide success, selling more than 4 million copies and reaching number 1 for four weeks in 1967.

Alex and Gordon met in midtown Memphis when they lived next door to each other on Madison Avenue. So when he moved in to Gordon's apartment it was natural that we became friends because of our proximity and mutual love of music. Alex's tastes were as wide as mine. We enjoyed everything from classical to Bahamian folk and played records every day. I had a tape machine and two mics, and Alex was just beginning to write songs. I recorded him playing new songs so he could hear how they sounded.

He taught me about electric guitars. I would ask what guitar was on this or that record and he'd tell me about the guitars and the amps they were using and the differences between the pickups on each guitar.

My favorite electric guitarist was Steve Cropper, and I learned he used a Fender Telecaster. Alex introduced me to Eric Clapton as a guitarist, as opposed to being a member of Cream, which was all I knew. I was obsessed with the folk players, what guitars they played and how they were getting the sounds on their records, but I didn't know anything about electrics.

Over the next year I picked up the basic knowledge I needed to start learning and appreciate the electric guitar and the artists who used them so effectively.

I knew about Gershwin but nothing about Copland until Alex and I started hanging out. He knew about Robert Johnson but not about Blind Willie McTell. We traded information like baseball cards and had a great time doing it. One day he taught me "Sunny Afternoon" by the Kinks. This went on a lot. One day I showed him a lick by Blind Willie McTell. He used it in "In the Street," the song that was used as the theme song for the hit TV series, *That 70s Show*.

The Box Tops had toured with The Beach Boys, and Carl Wilson and Alex had become friends. When The Beach Boys came to play Carnegie Hall, Alex got tickets and took me with him. I couldn't believe how great they sounded. They were better than the records! Their finale was "Good Vibrations," and it just boggled my mind. The harmonies were to die for.

We went to their hotel after the show, and Carl left with us to go to my apartment, where we played songs through the night. I asked Carl if he would sing "Darlin,'" and when he did I was mesmerized. I still wonder how people can sing like that—full voice in that range in that key. Absolute perfection.

27

OFF TO THE LEFT COAST

After Ronstadt hit with "Long, Long Time," Gary and Annie went to California. They found an apartment and arranged for their belongings to be shipped. When they returned they made plans to drive back to LA. It was summer, and I was off the road, and I asked if I could make the trip with them. They were probably thinking, 'What could go wrong with Keith tagging along,' so they said yes. I think we all approached it with a spirit of adventure, but none of us knew what a wild trip it would be.

Gary and Annie had planned stops along the way, and the first one was at a model train museum in the Pennsylvania Dutch country. A collector and enthusiast had put together the largest model train display I'd ever seen. Of course I'd only seen a few setups at friends' houses, and maybe a big one at the Mid-South Fair or something like that. This thing filled up a huge barn and looked like an entire town, with the surrounding county and countryside all connected by model trains. You could see tiny men and women working in the fields or strolling down streets in towns, along with farmers out in the country loading their goods and livestock on a train when it stopped at the junction. I thought to myself, 'this cat must really like model trains.'

I didn't know how much Gary liked model trains until that trip, but I would find out over the years. He eventually became a dealer for actual steam locomotives that are about 12 to 16 inches long, with whistles and real steam coming out of the smokestack. He now has a room with nothing but model train engines in it. He was just getting into it when we made this trip.

As we wended our way south and west, I watched the scenery from the back seat of Annie's little gray, late-model Nash sedan, traveling through places I had hitchhiked through only a few years before.

The next time we stopped to do more than eat or rest for the night was Memphis. I introduced Gary and Annie to my mom, and Gary obliged when I asked him to play "Long, Long Time" on my sister's spinet. I could tell my Mom enjoyed it, and by the look on her face I could almost hear her saying, "Now Keith, why can't you write something like that?" Such as it is with young people and their parents.

Gary and Annie had met Alex Chilton in New York, so we went to see him at his family's midtown Memphis home. That day was the first time I had seen Alex's family home. It was a gray stone building that looked very substantial. It was beautiful without saying it out loud. This was also the first time I met drummer and recording engineer Richard Rosebrough.

Gary, Alex, and I traded Alex's acoustic around, but I can't remember if we played songs or not. What I do remember is I played a chord that Alex liked, and he turned to Richard and said, "Now there's a chord for you. That's what I'm talking about." Of course, when he said that I didn't say anything, but I was flattered. I got my "cool" cred for the day.

When we left Memphis we drove to Pasadena, Texas, to visit Gary's mother, and I think an aunt or two was there, also. I'm sure I was very economical with my conversation. I think it was a kind of defense mechanism. I figured if I said very little, older people might conclude I was smart. What I was really doing was trying to make sure my inner idiot didn't surface and blow my cover.

For one thing, Gary worked at NASA on the Apollo mission, so I knew he was smart. As a matter of fact, I thought he knew everything about everything, because no matter what I asked him he knew something about it and could explain it to me in a way I could understand. Or kinda understand — be it music or anything else. Even though you could make a case that he lost his marbles when he gave up NASA to drive himself and Jerry Jeff Walker, both over 6 feet tall I might add, in his Triumph TR 3 sports car, crammed to overflowing with all their shit including their guitars and associated paraphernalia all the way to New York from Pasadena, TX, to become rich and famous rock stars, he really was very smart.

Before Gary went to New York City, he and Guy Clark shared an apartment in Houston. Gary worked at NASA, and Guy was repairing and building guitars. They both played nights at the Sand Mt Coffee House or at Jesters. When Gary and Guy got an apartment Jerry Jeff would move in not long after — checkbook not in hand — according to Gary. He and Jerry Jeff were playing gigs with Bob Bruno, Peter Troutner, and David Scherstrom with Jerry Jeff and Bob Bruno doing the songwriting. Jerry Jeff had already written "Mr. Bojangles" by then.

When they made it to New York they got a gig the next night at Cafe Wah? on MacDougal, but within a week Gary's car was stolen. As Gary points out, he had insurance. It turned out to be what is known in some circles as "New York good luck" as cars can be more trouble than they're worth in the City.

So here we were in Pasadena, Texas, years later, at Gary's mother's house and about to hit the road to Los Angeles. What a world, what a world, as Teenie Hodges used to say.

We had been talking about going to Juarez from El Paso as a little side trip on our meandering land voyage to LA. Gary and Annie were a little apprehensive, but I assured them I was there on my 21st birthday and it was fine. I mean, it would be in broad daylight, so what could go wrong?

When we got there, the bridge was crowded and Gary and Annie were getting less keen about going with every passing minute. Still, onward we went. When we got over the bridge the traffic was miserable, and we all agreed this wasn't going as I hoped so we turned the car around. The traffic was so congested it took forever to move an inch, but inch along we did.

When we reached U.S. Customs the American border patrol took a look at our long hair and immediately judged us as drug traffickers and ordered us out of the vehicle and inside for an inspection. Just as Gary had feared.

We didn't have any grass on us, but there was an empty Sudafed bottle that previously contained some of the illegal substance. It still had a slight trace of the tell-tell aroma. They did the whole enchilada on Annie, cavity search and all. Eventually we made it away from there unscathed, but the good mood was shot. If it hadn't been for me, we would have been well on our way.

Driving out west back then meant driving on Route 66. As the sun got low in the late afternoon it could cut you right in two. With no trees as far as the eye could see and the desert sun directly in front you, it kept your eyes squinted almost shut.

We stopped in Gallup, NM, one afternoon. I loved seeing the natives dressed in fine clothes and turquoise and silver. We had a drink in a bar that seemed to be a mile long, and I felt like I was in a Western.

We were having breakfast somewhere along the way at one of those diners that were in the towns you passed through on 66. At a table near ours, some asshole was letting us know that hippies were not welcome in this place. Gary had taken all he could, and we were about to walk out when someone played the jukebox, and just as if it was planned, "Long, Long Time" came rolling out of the speakers. That's all it took to make it all seem worth it.

Gary's triumph was ours as we quietly reveled in the glory of knowing that dick would always be a dick, and we would have cool friends who are on the fucking jukebox, TV, and radio. All that jerk would ever know were shallow, small-minded people. Yeah us!

"Ointment or suppository?" I would ask from the back seat as we made the long drive across the desert. "What?" Annie would say." Ointment or suppository?" I would fire back. "What in the fuck are you talking about?" Annie would ask. "I just wanted to know if you would rather have ointment or suppository."

Those are the little questions in life that I like to torment my friends with. If I get on a roll, I can go on for a while. When I feel like I've dominated the conversion for too long, I let it go and things seem to slip back to reality. But if I think I can make someone laugh, I go for it.

We arrived in Las Vegas in the afternoon and found a reasonably priced room at a small hotel off the strip, got settled in, then went out for food and entertainment.

When we walked into a casino—I had never been to a casino—I got the feeling I just walked through the gates of hell. It wasn't a bad feeling per se, I guess it was a reaction due to my Christian upbringing and my naïveté from never being anywhere other than a coffeehouse or a bar. There was a one-armed bandit as big as an armoire, with a softball-size ball at the end of its three-foot handle. It had a sign over it saying you could hit a million dollar jackpot for $5. I declined the offer.

My entire life has been about taking chances and betting on certain outcomes, so I've always had trouble reconciling gambling. I mean it's like, "I bet this song will make some money" so my risk taking and betting goes on 24/7/365. Take that for a gambling problem.

Of course, Gary and Annie knew the ropes in Vegas. They made us reservations to see the Lido show. Before the show we had dinner in the Needle Tower Revolving restaurant overlooking all of Vegas.

The food was delicious, as was the view. After dinner, I found the view at the Lido was delicious, too. The girls—they looked like women to me—danced topless. And they were talented, full figured and beautiful, which is always a fetching combination.

As we were walking out, passing by the king-sized one-armed bandit, hearing a distant roar from a craps table, I heard that voice in the back of my mind saying, "It's OK, do anything you like," and I said to myself, "I like hell."

Gary and Annie had found a house in the Mt. Washington area of LA. It was a sweet little place with a yard on a nice street with houses all around. We were not in New York City anymore. The weather! Dammit man! How does it do it?

One morning we went to visit John Boland, who Gary knew through Linda Ronstadt. On another we went to the Griffith Observatory.

Going to Disneyland after we dropped a hit of acid was one of my favorite things we did. The LSD was on a very small piece of paper, and it dissolved in no time. Then we went into what was called the 360 Theater. It was round and there were handrails that went across in long rows. There was about 4 feet or so between each row, so you could hold the handrail and not intrude on anyone's space.

We ambled in with the crowd and stopped somewhere in the middle. After a few minutes it was almost full, and the lights were dimming. Then the doors slowly closed.

Movie screens covered the walls all around us, and then suddenly we were on a vast plain where you could see to infinity. A bird would fly by, and the wind would blow the tall grass. The calming scene was sharply interrupted by a movement such as an airplane banking on a steep angle, and everyone grabbed the rails with all their might. And when I did, It made me smile right out loud!

Next, we went to the haunted house, and we sat in a car that took you through the ride. As soon as it started, a hologram of this crazy little goblin flew over and sat beside me. It was great.

Disneyland was better than I ever expected. It was past anything I thought was possible. It's still a favorite memory after all these years.

It was getting close to time for me to go back to New York when the phone rang, and out of the blue Delmark Goldfarb was on the line for me. How in the hell did that happen? Turns out Goldfarb called the office, or my Mother, or someone, and got Gary and Annie's new number. It still makes me wonder how it came together.

Goldfarb was in the Army in LA doing whatever he was doing. I gave him the address, and he got a ride to Gary and Annie's house. Gary and Annie were meeting some friends for dinner, so it was fine if I hung out with Goldfarb for the evening.

We talked and caught up for a while, and as it was getting late we decided to find a liquor store. We walked down a winding street and finally came to one of those broad, flat, four-lane intersections. And wouldn't you just know, across the street less than a block away stood a small liquor store.

We decided on Janis Joplin's favorite spirit, Southern Comfort, and we each got a pint. It was 100 proof, and to our surprise, it was very sweet and went down as easy as you please.

We began our walk back when we were taken by the look of an old billboard. It had a permanent walkway built along the bottom of the huge advertising picture, and there were steps on the side you could walk up, so we walked up. And there we sat, talking about the view, about what's up next for each of us, and generally shooting the shit until the sun was going down. And all the while we were drinking the Southern Comfort, Janis Joplin's favorite spirit, and getting ass-blastin' drunk. I'm positive we did some grass, too.

By the time we got down from the billboard I think I can safely say we were, as Buffett would quote Lord Buckley, "God's own drunks." Getting up that hill took a long time. At one elevation I decided it would be a great idea to open car doors and take whatever was lying in the seat. Thank God it wasn't much. Folks, I'm a lotta things, but a thief ain't one of 'em. Except that night. Mercifully, we finally made it back to Gary and Annie's.

Here's the next thing I remember: Something hit my head really hard, and I tried to move out of its way by scooting across the floor. I must not have scooted far enough, because something hit my head really hard again. I somehow looked up, and there was Gary and Annie trying to come in.

The thing that hit me was the bottom of the door. I was in the way as much as a person can be in the way, passed out on the floor with my head right by the front door. When the door didn't open, they tried again. My poor head was in the wrong place at the wrong time. Not that there is a right time for this particular kind of thing. There is never a time you should be passed out with your head by the front door of your good friends' new-to-them house. Civilized people just don't do that.

But there I was in all my splendorous wonder.

All my polite upbringing by my diligent, single mom on full display—not. My sincerest humility, overshadowed only by my gentlemanly manner, was right there for all to see—not, again. To top it all off, I think Goldfarb passed out in Gary and Annie's bed. I had been sleeping on the couch during my stay, and I obviously wasn't there. It made no sense that Goldfarb should be in their bed, but neither did every other detail about that night.

Oh what a beautiful morning, oh what a beautiful day ... not, to the 10th power!

I don't have to tell you that my head did not feel its best when I awakened. Son of a bitch. That was, by miles, the worst hangover I've ever had. When Goldfarb left, he took the stuff I stole from the cars and tried to put it back. What a mess.

We've laughed about that night many times since then. And every time I recall that night, I think of something else that happened.

I don't believe Gary and Annie lived in that house for very long. They had one other place before they moved to Pasadena, where they have now lived for more than 40 years. The interim place had a redwood hot tub in the back yard, and Gary built model train tracks that ran from their kitchen window to the hot tub. The train had a flat car that you could set two glasses of wine on, and it would take them to the hot tub. Ingenious!

28

TRAVEL, PLAY, REPEAT

It seems like when I got back to New York I started touring and didn't stop. Northeast. Eastern Seaboard. Texas. South. Midwest. West. Northwest. Florida. Just going and going.

Most of the time I was a one-man band. The school would assign a student to the "singer-songwriter" for three days or so, and it was a break from their regular routine. They were always nice to me, but it's not like being with someone you know.

Sometimes Gordon Alexander would come out with me, and it was so nice to have someone I actually knew be there. We always managed to have a good time no matter where we were or what we were doing, but when he was on the road with me it was always a special treat.

The Coffee House Circuit flew me just about everywhere I went, which meant I was in airports a lot.

When the Boeing 747 was put in service I was among the first passengers to fly on one. I was just a singer-songwriter from New York City playing across the country. I just happened to be at the airport in Washington, DC one day when it was announced the plane we were scheduled to fly on had changed to a 747.

OK. Off we go. And off we went.

It was like any plane—but bigger. More aisles and more space between the seats. More everything. At first, the four huge jet engines under the massive wings pushed us a little slower than the 727s. And after liftoff the plane moved in bigger waves than the smaller ones. I could see the wing tips moving up and down, and then hear the gear coming up. After a minute or two I felt the plane cease any movement and a still came over and a calm prevailed. Then this thing had it going on.

We were encouraged to get up and go upstairs to enjoy a drink at the bar. Upstairs to have a drink at the bar! Indeed!

29

GUY AND SUSANNA

I was in Nashville either playing a gig or on my way to one somewhere when I met up with Jerry Jeff. Some of his old friends had recently moved there from LA, and he invited me to meet them. Guy and Susanna Clark were living in East Nashville in a tiny house with sparse furnishings and two big hearts.

We traded songs almost as soon as we sat down, drinking whiskey and smoking a joint or two over the course of the night. I can't remember what songs were played, but I felt a camaraderie between us that never wavered over the years. It was the beginning of lasting friendships I've kept in my soul.

From that night on, whenever anyone asked me about Guy and/or Susanna I replied with, "Yes, they are my friends."

One quick story. In the mid '70's, Guy and Susanna were visiting Jerene and me for a weekend in Memphis and on one of the nights we went to midtown for dinner and drinks. As we were leaving, Jerene and Guy were ahead of Susanna and me, and when we stepped outside I noticed a beautiful crescent moon and said, "look, a quarter moon" to Susanna. She—without a beat—said, "Quarter moon, in a ten cent town." And that's when that song was born.

30

JOHN PRINE

Kris Kristofferson played the Bitter End one weekend, and the place was packed for the Friday and Saturday night shows. On Sunday there was a much smaller crowd, so I went to that one. Kris was doing his soulful set when toward the end he paused and said he wanted to introduce his friend John Prine and asked him up to play a few songs.

Prine played "Sam Stone," "Donald and Lydia" and "Hello in There." I couldn't believe my ears! I sat there listening to his voice and guitar making a sound so intertwined it consumed me like that whale did Jonah. Nothing else existed for me in that moment as I was lost inside those words and music. I said to myself, "I quit!"

After the show I met John, and we talked a bit, and I discovered what a nice, unassuming person he was.

The next time I saw him was a couple of months later at the Kettle of Fish. He was across the room, and I guess we saw each other about the same time. He started walking over to me just as I started walking over to him. It seems like we became friends that night, and every time I saw him we became closer. I consider his friendship among my life's dearest treasures.

It would take another book to tell all the stories of our time together as friends and co-writers. Suffice it to say I've touched on some highlights I hope you enjoy. I truly believe there will be a host of books written about him and I can't wait to pore over every page.

31

KEY WEST AND JIMMY BUFFETT

I finished a tour in Florida in 1972. The office had opened a branch in Coconut Grove—which is basically in Miami—and I wanted to go to Key West, so I rented a car for the drive down. That day the traffic was light, and the scenery was phenomenal with the azure water and the horizon extending into infinity.

I got there and drove around a bit, and I think I may have even stopped for a bite somewhere, but that was about it.

The next year I had my van, and I decided to go again, but this time I called Jerry Jeff to ask about meeting some people. Jerry Jeff wasn't in, but Murphy, his girlfriend, answered the phone. She said I should to go the corner of Ann and Caroline and ask for Ashley Simmons, and I'd meet all the people I'd need to know in Key West. So, I did.

When I got there, there was a gorgeous conch house with a fellow sweeping the brick courtyard. I spoke up and said, "Does Ashley Simmons live here?" Without a beat he snapped back, "Who wants to know?" Whoa. He wasn't being an ass but just being cautious. After all, this was home to more than a few pirates, and it pays to be careful. I said, "I'm Keith Sykes, a friend of Jerry Jeff Walker, and got this address from him." I lied a little bit about that part.

He said, "Keith Sykes! I've heard of you. I'm Jimmy Buffett." To which I replied, "I've heard of you, too."

You see, I was in Canada on a tour with Jerry Jeff when he told me about this guy who had some trying times at gigs. The clubs would put his name on the sign and folks would come in thinking there would be a buffet. When they found out there wasn't an unlimited spread of food they would usually leave in search of another place to eat.

Buffett said Jerry Jeff told him about me when they were on the road.

I'm telling you, it's a small world out there sometimes. And this would prove to be a very auspicious day in my life.

I was invited to come in and to put my suitcase and guitar in a guest room and get ready to break some bread. During the meal Buffett told me about a party that was to start at 8 a.m. the next morning. "Hum," I said to myself. It had been a long time since I did anything at 8 a.m., and I was reluctant to commit, but Buffett seemed to not be taking no for an answer. Neither was Ashley. So, I agreed to go, even though I would not know one soul among the six boatloads of people leaving in the morning from a place called the Pier House. We were going to spend a day at a place called Woman Key.

The tour I just finished was long, and I thought I'd done well just to be in Key West. I really wanted to see some of the island. But I also wanted to meet some people, and this was staring me right in the face.

Woman Key, here I come.

The next morning everyone was up and cheery and full of pep and seemed so alien to me with their tanned faces and bodies and boundless energy. I felt like they were all looking at me like I was a zombie from the depths of New York City who hadn't seen the sun for centuries.

We walked down to the Pier House and the Chart Room Bar to find a commotion going on about the sangria that was supposed to be chilled in the bar's cooler. Turns out, the cleanup guy came in at 6 a.m.—6 a.m.! How do they do it?—and saw the barrel with the sangria in it and mistakenly thought it was waste from the night before. He poured it out, and cleaned that drum until it was Spic and Span.

Everyone had pooled their money for fresh fruit and red wine and made this barrel of really good sangria wine. And now it was toast! And no one had any money left. So, being self-starters and inventive, some of the guys did manage to scrounge up enough cash to get two gallon bottles of 190-proof pure grain alcohol, or PGA as it's known, along with a few watermelons, and that was the new sangria. It tasted a little stout, if you know what I mean.

With the sangria problem solved—well, kind of anyway—we set sail for Woman Key, about 6 miles from the Pier House. It was my first time in Key West—not counting that drive down, drive around, drive back thing I did—and the first time with this kind of sun, first time on this unbelievably beautiful water, and first time with almost all these people—I had known Buffett for going on a day—and I was beginning to wake up and see the world around me.

The guys with the boats all seemed like they were seasoned on the water, and the day was clear blue skies all around forever. When we reached Woman Key it looked like what I would describe as the quintessential desert island—palm trees and white sand beaches with mangrove trees in the middle.

There was one guy who looked as lost and out of place as I did, and we were drawn to each other like people do when they're out of their element and surrounded by everyone else who looks like they are perfectly at home. So while they were tanned and energized and in and out of the water, we were trying our best to get some shade from a palm tree that had about three big fronds to its name. It wasn't working well, but it did have about two square feet of shade. If we kept moving we could kind of not burn completely to a crisp.

"What's your name?" I asked. "My name is Greg Taylor, but everybody calls me Fingers" he answered. I told him mine and we decided to check out the "sangria." After a drink or two, it worked its magic. The third drink didn't taste as much like coal oil as the first one did. Well, it never really lost the coal oil taste completely, but I just didn't care anymore.

By noon the water was heavenly, there was a gentle breeze, girls were water skiing naked in the ocean, and I said to myself, "I like Key West."

Some of the people I met that trip would become lifelong friends. They had been around Jimmy and were aware he had a lot going on beneath the surface of his tanned exterior. I was just beginning to see it for myself. He gave me the impression he never met a stranger and would rather play tennis or surf than play guitar. I came to realize that yes, he loved sports and the competitiveness of it, but he also loved books of poetry and history and the sea and musicians of all stripes. He loved a good song. If it was a wordy folk song or an upbeat dance song it didn't matter. So long as it had the magic, he was a fan.

I found out his kind of friends weren't random people he met at a late-night bar—although that wasn't a deal breaker—or a producer or publisher from the music world, or anyone in particular. It was people who were driven to be good at what they do, who worked hard, played hard, and taught their children right from wrong. Pretty much the same ethos as mine and most everyone I've been friends with.

That trip to Woman Key introduced me to Tom and Judy Corcoran, Phil and Pat Tenney, Benjamin "Dink" Bruce, Chris and Sonia Robinson, Vaughn and Cydall Cochran and more. These folks, along with Buffett and Ashley Simmons, made me feel welcome and at home, and I became enamored with them and Key West for life.

As John Lennon sang, "Some are dead and some are living," and it breaks my heart every time I get the news one of us has passed on, but I keep them living in my heart.

KEY WEST AND JIMMY BUFFETT

I stayed in Key West at Ashley's house for a few weeks writing songs. Several have been recorded. "Train to Dixie" was born on that trip and has been recorded by Marcia Ball, McKendree Spring and even Buffett, although he never released it. In 1979, "Right Or Wrong" became the title of Rosanne Cash's first American album. She also recorded "Take Me, Take Me" for that record. "Only Human," was written on that trip, which Rosanne recorded later.

32

RECORDING WITH A BAND IN NEW YORK

I got home from Key West and was sent on a 10-week tour. That amount of time alone on the road can make you crazy, and I just about lost my marbles. That's a long time to be alone in a crowd!

When I finished the tour, Brovsky set me up in a small studio to work on songs in hopes of getting me another record deal. I can't remember the name of that studio, but I was told it was where "Dancing In The Moonlight," a pop hit that still sounds good to me, was recorded.

I reached out to Murphy Odom, my friend from Memphis, to play bass. I also recruited Ken Woodley, another pal from from Treadwell who played several instruments, and I asked him to play organ. Lastly, I got in touch with Mike Gardner, one of the best drummers in Memphis at that time, to be our drummer. We flew them to New York and put them up in the Chelsea Hotel.

Because Brovsky got a really good price from the studio, we started at about 1 in the morning and recorded until about 8 in the morning. We cut 10 tracks.

It was my first time producing, but of course I didn't look at that way. I was simply recording. I hired the musicians, set the arrangements, and picked the keeper tracks. Still, to me, producers were people who knew what they were doing. I was simply an artist trying to make a record. I also went to Jimi Hendrix's Electric Ladyland studio and recorded one of the tracks with New York musicians. Brovsky got some interest from Capitol Records, but nothing worked out.

One morning I woke up and took a shower, drank myself a cup of instant coffee, and walked downstairs. Once outside, I felt something wash over me like an ocean wave that left a feeling of it's time to move on. I didn't think too much of it at the time, but it stayed in the back of my mind all through that day.

33

AUSTIN AND MARY LOU

I was in Austin, but this time I wasn't playing at the University of Texas. I got a gig at a cool place called Castle Creek. I saw a pretty girl, and Michael Murphey, who for many years has gone by his full name, Michael Martin Murphey, introduced us. Her name was Mary Lou David, and she was what I thought of as really sharp—a most excellent smile with a little bit of mischief in her eyes, and carried herself with confidence. She told me she played bass and had a rig, and if I wanted a bass player to look no further.

Over time we were together more and more. She learned my songs, and before long we started gigging together. I had a show in Mobile at the University of South Alabama, and after that show she went with me to New York.

The office had set up a new company called Directions Unlimited, and she worked there for a time. Terre Roche worked there too, and they became friends.

Mary Lou and I played college bars and folk clubs in the Northeast. She liked New York, but she loved Austin, and since I was ready for a change we packed up and left New York for good this time. Well, not for good because I've been back many, many times, but I decided to live in Austin.

I had bought a used 1969 Dodge van that Elroy co-signed for. I had worked for years but had never bought anything on time but my

Martin D-28 guitar, so I'd never established credit. After this, I would have credit. Whadayouknow—a folk singer with credit!

Working out of Austin, Mary Lou and I were gigging in Dallas at the Rubaiyat, which was *the* place for touring folk acts to play. I had been going there for a few years to hang out after my El Centro College and SMU shows, and had met a few of the people who played there. One of these people was Mickey Raphael.

Mickey—who would become Willie Nelson's harmonica player—was playing with Chuck Stevenson at this time. I was sitting beside Mickey when Stevenson walked on stage. He was wearing overalls, with his long hair in very small ringlets underneath a Hoss Cartwright cowboy hat. I turned to Mickey—this is before I knew he played with Chuck—and I said he looked like Buckwheat. I didn't think anything more of it. I sure didn't mean it as a cut or being derogatory in any way. He reminded me of Buckwheat, and that was it. He sang and played masterfully. I thought that look was a good hook and he did it very well.

The next time I saw Mickey he said Chuck was using Buckwheat as his stage name and got a record deal with RCA. As they were about to release the record they found out there was another act named Buckwheat and he couldn't legally use that name. So they were forced to use BW. Ain't it wild how things go around?!

After our gig at the Rubaiyat, Mary Lou and I heard about a small music fest at SMU. It started the next day and we went to check it out. While we were there we heard a band called Uncle Walt's Band, and they proceeded to blow our minds with their songs, harmonies, and musicianship.

They were so good! Their sound transported us back in time to the 1930s. The songs were so original and performed so well we had to talk to these guys. We found they were sincere about their music and dedicated to their craft. No one else was doing anything like the songs they played. No one looked like them, either. It was eerie being in the same room with them because they had a certain electricity we could feel; a feel that emanated from the sound they made. What a lovely thing music is.

Back in Austin, we rented an apartment at the Rio Grande Apartments on Rio Grande. I know. They named apartments after the street they were on. Jerry Jeff had moved to Austin from Key West a year or so earlier and Murphy—the girl who gave me the lowdown about Key West—was living with him. So that made three people I knew, and there were a few more I had met.

My time in Austin was highlighted by the musicians I got to know. It began with Jerry Jeff's band.

They may have had the Gonzo name. If not, it wouldn't be long until there was a Lost Gonzo Band. There was Bob Livingston, who played bass, and Gary P. Nunn, who played bass and keyboards and drums and the fuckin' kitchen sink, I guess. They could all play each other's instruments. John Inmon played as good electric guitar as anyone I've ever known. Kelly Dunn playing organ was like hearing a spirit flying through the room. And Michael McGeary was a drummer who played with just the right dynamics. Together they were exactly what Jerry Jeff needed. They could play, they were creative, and they were there at just the right time. Together they helped create what is now known as Texas Music.

Mary Lou knew people from all walks of life. She knew politicians, musicians, and club owners. She introduced me to the legendary University of Texas football coach, Darrell Royal, and his wife Edith—two of my all-time favorite people.

I can't say why, but Darrell thought I was a cool guy and invited me to their house whenever his music friends were coming over. Darrell and Edith both loved music and would sit and listen to songs in their living room as long as anyone would play. A few times Darrell and I sat up real late getting down to the bottom of the music and the ones who write and play it.

If it wasn't for Edith, I would've never known Darrell was the football hero he was. He sure didn't talk to me about it. She's the one who told me he was an All-American player at the University of Oklahoma. Of course I knew he was the football coach at UT. I didn't know a thousand other things about his football career. The stadium where he took me to see UT play Wake Forest opened in 1923 and in 1996 it became Darrell K. Royal-Texas Memorial Stadium. That's a big deal. They don't name stadiums after folks they don't care much about.

Uncle Walt's Band moved to Austin to work with Willis Alan Ramsey. Willis lived in the same apartment building as Mary Lou did before we lived together. He gave me a copy of his album and it was one of my pride and joys. I lent it to a guy in the early '90s who never gave it back. Some people ain't got no class.

I met Willie Nelson, Johnny Rodriguez, and more at Darrell and Edith's. Kristofferson would come when he was in Austin and I enjoyed many good nights filled with songs and stories. One night, after a lot of great songs had been sung, Willie sang the melody to the "Truck Driving Man" with these words;

"I stopped at a whorehouse in Texas
The name was Nose Bugger Dan's
I throwed a waitress through the jukebox
When she played the Truck Driving Man"

And I said to myself, "I like Willie Nelson."

After a few months at the Rio Grande Apartments, Bob Livingston told us about a house that was coming up for rent out by Lake Travis. He was living next door to it and said we should check it out. After we did, we made the move from town to country.

I always felt a connection with Bob Livingston, and I consider him a friend to this day. He's got a lot of music in him, and I felt comfortable around him when we'd see each other. You could say we could talk. So when we lived next door we would do a little grass now and then and listen to music.

I went over one morning, and Bob asked if I'd like to try hash oil. I'd never heard of hash oil, but once in a while Gary White would have some hash, and I liked that, so I said sure.

He had this little glass pipe—that was the first time I'd seen one—and a glob of this black, shiny paste that was wrapped in aluminum foil. He had it in the refrigerator. I knew nothing. I watched curiously. He took a butter knife, or something like that, and got a little of the paste and put it on a piece of foil. Then he put a flame under the foil, and when smoke bellowed up from the paste he drew it in through the glass pipe. 'OK,' I thought, 'I've got it.'

He put the flame under the paste, and I took a deep pull, and almost instantly my lungs felt like they were going to explode. I coughed violently. I kept coughing. And I coughed some more. When things finally settled down I realized I'd never been high on pot. This high was God's own high, and I was out of my league.

Bob talked, and I kinda sat there and nodded occasionally, but I knew nothing about what he was saying. Or anything else.

Mary Lou and I had a gig at Castle Creek that night, and I foolishly thought I'd be down from my high and ready to do my show by the time I was supposed go on. Well, let me tell you something. Nine hours later I was still on Mars. I had never played stoned or drunk or anything but stone cold sober until that night.

As it happened, we were opening for Robert Klein, a new comedian, who was in town touring on that album with the pictures of record covers on the back. I always loved to see Sam and Dave and the Stax label in that picture.

The placed was packed to the rafters, and I was still as high as a Georgia pine trying my best to keep from completely blowing this gig. I can't say if I did a passable show or not that night. I do remember

Robert Klein was "on" and so good I don't think it made any difference what I did.

I've seen Klein a few times since, and it always surprises me that he remembers me. Some people are like that. I wish I had that gene.

Mary Lou played her last show as my bassist one night at the Rubaiyat when we opened for Jerry Jeff. We got up to jam on the last song, and she lost all her confidence and turned her amp down. The guitarist reached over and turned her back up. She turned it back down and left the stage, never to return.

In the fall of '73 I put a band together for what would be my last extended tour for the College Coffee House Circuit. Layton DePenning was on guitar, Don Fischer on bass, and Jimmy Marriot on drums. We went all the way to Virginia and came back through Kentucky, Tennessee, Alabama, and Louisiana in my Dodge van. It was a wild ride, and we played very good together. OK, I admit it. It would be almost impossible to sound bad with those players.

As much as I remember the music being tight and exciting, I remember two things that are part of the American fabric that happened when we were on that tour.

Billie Jean King defeated Bobby Riggs at his own game and, sadly, Jim Croce lost his life in a plane crash not far from where we were in Louisiana.

When we were in Virginia, near DC, to my surprise Emmylou Harris came and brought a bunch of her friends with her. She did then and still does have the best smile in show business. I say this because everyone knows she has a voice that's beyond compare.

Elroy came to see us when we played Lexington, and it was so good to see him sober and really enjoying himself.

When we finished in Baton Rouge we piled in the van and went to New Orleans for the night. We had dinner al fresco at Pat O'Brien's, and the waitress offered our drummer a light when he asked if it was

OK to smoke a joint. I don't know if you can get away with that, even now. But it was all OK that night.

Mary Lou started working with Uncle Walt's Band and soon became their manager. This meant going on the road to make sure the band got as good a shot as possible with the club owners and various PAs that all bands have to deal with. It wasn't long before Mary Lou and Walter fell in love, and I became all heartbroken and went to Key West.

34

KEY WEST, NASHVILLE, MEMPHIS

Buffett was out of town, so he let me stay at his place. I had everything I owned in my van and just parked it and walked all over Key West. Or should I say moped all over Key West. Poor ol' heartbroken Keith, back in Key West and all blue.

After a few days I went to the Chart Room at 10 in the morning, and lo and behold there were five or six people already there — all drinking their first of the day just like I was about to do. I took great solace in this. That's the stuff that makes me feel at home in Key West.

Chris and Sonia Robinson had the apartment on the ground floor on Waddell Street right beside what is now Louie's Backyard. Above their place was Buffett's apartment.

It was not unusual to start the day with a dip in the ocean, which was conveniently located just out the back door. The water was healing and made even better when Sonia would make a batch of frozen mango daiquiris and we would bob in the ocean, drink those mango daiquiris, and repeat. Those idyllic days in Key West mean so much as I think back.

Jimmy had finished his second record for ABC Dunhill and came home with a test pressing. When he played "Come Monday" I knew within the first few bars he had nailed this song. By the time it was over I looked at him and said, "Man, that's a hit."

A VERY SHORT TIME

Later that night we went to the dog track on Stock Island. Dog racing didn't have the horrible stigma it would have in later years, and we went just for fun. We stayed for a few races and bet on the second race we saw. I bet on the number 2 to place and Jimmy bet on it to win. It won, and we cashed in and left soon after. It's always nice to stop when you're ahead.

I stayed at Ashley's for a bit, and a few places here and there, but I had gigs to do, and I wanted to go to LA and see about living there. I knew Gary and Annie, Linda Ronstadt, and had a few connections in the record business. I was thinking I could base there for a while and keep doing the coffee house gigs.

If I could have stayed in Key West bobbing in the ocean, sipping mango daiquiris, moving from one friend's place to another, I think I would have stayed forever. But alas, I needed to be where the music was. I was an artist and wanted more than playing in bars, even if the bars were in Key West.

I was getting ready to go when Key West had a cold snap like it hadn't seen in years. I think it went down to the mid 40's and everyone froze. The next day I went to the army surplus store and bought a sleeping bag to use when I wanted to sleep in the van. When I made it to the top of Florida, the cold snap was more pronounced than in Key West, and I froze again. That sleeping bag sucked.

I made it to Nashville to visit Guy and Susanna. They were living near Vanderbilt by this time, and there were coffee shops and a few bars nearby where people could play.

Guy and Susanna had settled in the neighborhood, and their apartment had become the de facto place to gather and swap songs with some of the best writers in town.

This is where I met Rodney Crowell and Mickey Newbury. I take that back. I met Newbury when Guy and Susanna lived on the Cumberland River and Newbury lived next door. No matter. I met Skinny

KEY WEST, NASHVILLE, MEMPHIS

Dennis and other friends of Guy and Susanna, and I always had great fellowship with those writers. I heard a ton of great songs.

I stayed a week and had such a good time. The day would go like this: get up and cook some breakfast. That could be any time of the day—just whenever we woke up did the trick. A few songs were played after breakfast. Then Guy and I would walk to this liquor store that had a huge Palomino horse statue in front and we would get a fifth of Palomino Whiskey. The whiskey would be communal, and it would be gone by the next morning. So, a repeat of yesterday was always on the agenda.

Most nights I would hear Guy play "Old Time Feeling," "L.A. Freeway," "She Ain't Going Nowhere," and more. Rodney would play "Bluebird Wine," "Leaving Louisiana in the Broad Daylight" and more. I played "Country Morning Music" and "Daddy Raised Hell" and whatever else Guy wanted me to play.

It was song heaven, and in its way was as good as anything I've ever done in any place I've ever been.

After a week I heard that highway sound and got in my van to make a stop at Phillip Rauls' house in Memphis on my way to LA.

No matter where Phillip went to live, sooner or later I could be found knocking on his door. He was married to Phyllis in those days, and I always found open arms when I came to visit.

Memphis was still a powerhouse music city when I got there in April 1974. Liquor by the drink had become legal a few years earlier, and clubs were opening that catered to a younger crowd. An area in midtown called Overton Square was hopping like Bugs Bunny going after a bag of carrots.

TGI Friday's opened its first franchise there, quickly followed by Bombay Bicycle Club, Hot Air Balloon, and a host of others. The main music club was Lafayette's Music Room, and it was buzzing all the time. The hottest band around was Larry Raspberry and the

Highsteppers, and when they played Lafayette's it was full tilt boogie and packed to the rafters all night.

Raspberry was a force of nature. He played every set like there was no tomorrow. He played until the fans had to have an energy drink to drive home. I never saw Bruce Springsteen when he was playing clubs, but when he played Memphis a year or two later I saw that same kind of lightning in a bottle that the Highsteppers had every time they hit the stage. I always wished I had the same kind of music adrenaline those guys were working with.

Phillip was working for Atlantic Records and had the best record collection ever. I had some good records, but he had me beat times 10. I'd spend a lot of afternoons browsing his trove with my mouth watering. Professor Longhair to Yes, he had it all.

I went to Lafayette's to hear whoever was playing one night, and across the room I saw the girl I had been drooling over since I was in the fourth grade.

It's true. On rainy mornings Treadwell School would put us in the auditorium to sit until class started. Each grade had its section, and I was in the fourth-grade rows. I looked to my right one morning as this girl walked by and sat in the fifth-grade seats. She had very dark hair, and I thought I had never seen a prettier girl. After a time or two I began to love rainy mornings when I'd get to see her. I found out her name was Jerene Rowe.

All through school I considered myself lucky if I chanced to see her. Since she was a grade ahead of me, I only saw her occasionally, and of course I was too shy to ever say anything to her. I would hear about her dating an older guy from another school, or she was seeing some fraternity guy, and I always thought I'd never get to know her.

On this night she was right across the room, so I went over to her and told her about the rainy mornings, and I think she believed me.

It was true, but I admit it did sound a bit like a come on. I got her number and called her the next day, and we talked and made plans to meet for a drink or whatever. Day by day we became closer. I would go to bed at night thinking about her. Wake up thinking about her. Spend all the time in between thinking about her. This is when my plans to go to LA began to fall apart.

Phillip told me about Big Otto's, a club near Memphis State—now the University of Memphis—and I got a gig there. I asked Murphy Odom to play with me, and he became the first Keith Sykes Band member.

Murphy had played bass with me on the sessions in New York, and now he turned me on to Don McNatt. I knew about Don from school, but I didn't know him personally. He was in many talent shows at Treadwell and could put you in a spell with his acting. Murphy said he could sing and play guitar, and when we rehearsed it worked very well. We became a regular act at Big Otto's.

Jerene worked for Earl Daly, a lawyer and CPA whose clients included all the members of Booker T and the MG's, Al Green, Don Nix and several other artists who recorded for Stax Records. When she came to see me at Big Otto's, it wasn't unusual for Duck Dunn or Don Nix to be in the crowd. Once Nix brought former teen sensation Brian Hyland with him. Aside from his teen hits he recorded "I'm Afraid to Go Home," which I knew from Gene Pitney. It's still one of my favorite songs.

I needed a place of my own, and I found a little storefront on Merton Street in the Binghampton part of town. It had a small office in front and a bigger room in back, and I rented it. It was a great place to do my thing in Memphis.

With the help of my old friend Johnny Webb, who lived across the street since I was 12, and a few other souls who gave up some personal time to help me, we knocked the plaster off the walls of the back room to expose the bricks, and put up some sound-absorbent material here and there. After we painted the ceiling black, I had a nice little rehearsal space and an office to keep my records and tape recorders. I bounced around to shower and wash clothes, and slept at Phillip's or where ever I landed on any given night

After a couple of months Jerene said I could stay with her, so of course I did. I was riding high!

Dane, Jerene's son, was 5 years old at this time, and his dad lived in Memphis. This put me in a bit of an awkward position. I was always missing Elroy when I was a kid, and I didn't want to be in the way of Dane having a relationship with his dad. I just wanted to love him without hurting anyone. He seemed to like me, and who can't fall for a 5-year-old?

In the meantime, back to the band, I had Ray Barrickman on bass, Don McNatt on guitar and vocals, and Chi Howerton on drums. In the fall of '74 we got a gig in Key West at a place called the Lamplighter on Stock Island.

It was a cool club with an adjoining two-room mini motel that worked out great for traveling bands when they played nights in the bar. The band and I drove down in my van, and Gordon Alexander, who was now my manager, rode down with Jerene in her car.

Gordon did everything. He went to the store and made sure we didn't starve, kept the club owners happy and out of my hair, made calls to book gigs, and most importantly kept things light and funny. He was just sarcastic enough to make fun of everyone who wandered into our sphere.

We played nights, and we had some regulars we became familiar with. One of these guys called himself Mark Star Guitar. He was in his late teens or early 20s and was the boy toy of a woman who was at least in her 40s. They would come in around the middle of our set and ask if he could sit in. I would say "OK, one song. Two tops." He would play, and his cougar would applaud and scream for him like he was Eddie Van Halen—this guy could play but he was not a pro—and Gordon would have us in stitches. It was hard to keep from laughing, but as soon as Gordon cracked us up, he'd say, "Don't laugh, she's gonna tip us like crazy."

During the last week we had company from Memphis. Gordon's girlfriend, Paula Townsend, Don's girlfriend, Ellen Tolleson, and Ray's girlfriend, Raynor Sessions, all arrived and suddenly there was a lot more happening at the old Lamplighter. This is how Gordon remembers it:

> Dee Delmar owned the bar and juiced us up for free after the gigs were over. At one point during our stay he invited us all over and his mom made conch chowder and a bunch of fresh seafood. Besides "Mark Star Guitar," there was a fat dentist who would come to listen to the band some nights, and we would let him get up there to do a lame version of "Cocaine." He looked silly in his white shirt and trousers, singing "Cocaine, running 'round my brain."
>
> Ray, Chi, Ellen, Rayner and Don had to share a room, and Keith, Jerene, Paula and I had to share a room. There was a tree behind the motel with huge avocados, and when we heard a "thump" on the roof we knew one had fallen. We would run get it and make guacamole.
>
> Phil Tenney took us out on his boat one day. We went to an island, and everyone took off their clothes. When we got back, my entire body had turned salmon-colored — the sunburn was so bad that I couldn't wear clothes, so the girls took turns rubbing lotion all over me. My fever was probably over 100.
>
> Of course when Jerene hit her head on the air conditioner and had to go to the hospital, that was a bummer. If I remember anything else, I'll let you know. signed, G-man.

Buzz Cason came in on the last couple of nights we played the Lamplighter and introduced himself. He told me his ex-wife lived in Key

West, and he came to visit his daughter from time to time. He also told me he was a publisher and songwriter.

I asked if I might know anyone he works with, and he said he had a pretty extensive catalog of Jimmy Buffett songs and also most of the songs by Bobby Russell. I told him I knew Buffett, but I didn't know Bobby Russell. That's when I found out Russell wrote "Honey," one of the most successful songs of the '60's. It sold 7 million copies the first few weeks after its release. And "Little Green Apples" was another huge song Russell wrote around the same time.

I take any info like this with a grain of salt, because I've heard so much BS from strangers who approach me when I'm working.

Buzz was very nice to me and said he owned a studio in Nashville. If I was ever in the neighborhood I was welcome to come in and record some songs. Just demos. No strings attached, and no charge. He did it because he enjoys helping songwriters when he can. He gave me his number, and I earnestly thanked him.

On our way back to Memphis I remembered a little club I was taken to see when I played the University of South Alabama in Mobile. It was called Thirsty's, and it was not far from USA and on the way back home. We stopped by in the afternoon and no patrons were there, only the staff. Being in need of work I asked if we could play a few songs and audition. If they liked what they heard, then we could talk about a booking. They were sufficiently impressed, and we did get a gig out of it. It would be a while, but they would let me know as soon as they had an opening.

We weren't home very long when we got a booking in Louisville. We had to pass through Nashville to get there, so I called Buzz Cason to see if this was too soon to take him up on his offer to cut some demos. True to his word we were welcomed, and Buzz set the date. It would be at 11 at night on the way back to Memphis after the Louisville gig. The studio was, and still is, named Creative Workshop, and it's in an area known as Berry Hill. At that time it was only the second studio there and would remain so for many years. If you happen to go there now you can't turn around without bumping into studios in any direction.

We were a band with very little studio experience. When we played we sounded like we just come in off the street. Or, in our case, right out of a club. The results sounded like it, too. But for demos it would pass.

We recorded 12 songs that night, all in one or two takes. Among them were "Sooner or Later," which was called "Jerene You Are My Woman" at that time. It ended up on *The Way That I Feel*, my third album. "Right Or Wrong" became the title song for Rosanne Cash's first U.S. album. "Rainin' in My Soul" was also on that album. "Just Wanna Dance" was on Rodney Crowell's third album, and "Oh What a Feeling" was on *But What Will The Neighbors Think*, his second album.

This demo session is also where I met engineer Brent Maher, who had recorded Ike and Tina Turner's "Proud Mary," and would go on to record, write, and produce many pop and country hits, most notably all the Judds records. The date on the tape box says it was Oct. 29, 1974.

35

THE HIGHSTEPPERS

1975 came along and the "new" had worn off me in Memphis and I was going nowhere fast. I opened a lot of shows solo at Lafayette's and I relished those gigs. If I happened to get a gig that paid enough I would occasionally hire the Dixie Dawg Band to back me, but mostly I stayed home on weekends with nothing to do but hope something would work out.

To my everlasting appreciation Larry Raspberry hired me to be in the Highsteppers. I toured most of that year with them and learned a lot about what it takes to front a band. I think I had good instincts, but to make it work night after night is an art, and Raspberry was Van Gogh. I watched and let it soak in as much as I could. Some of those songs had me holding on for dear life, but I was determined not to let Raspberry down.

One night before we played in San Antonio, Raspberry was going over some changes to a song at sound check. He was telling me he wanted this lick in, another lick out, sing this instead of that, and make sure I do a triplet on this part, when Jerry McKinney said, "And go ahead and put that broom up your ass and sweep the stage while you're at it."

During my time with the Highsteppers I got to know these great musicians by listening to them play. After the shows I listened to what they had to say about playing. The saxophone player, Jerry McKinney, was one of those rare musicians who never played a wrong note and had the feel and tone to make each solo intoxicating. David Broussard, the bass player, was from Louisiana, and he carried that feel with him everywhere. Mark Sallings, from McCrory, Arkansas, was another gifted sax player. If it weren't for McKinney having seniority, he would have been playing those sax solos. Bill Marshall was born sitting behind a drum kit and could keep any time signature Raspberry might toss his way. He went on to play with Hank Williams, Jr., for more than 20 years. Joe Mulherin was on trumpet, and he was the one who taught me some music theory; how harmonies worked with horns, and how sections made unisons and chords, all depending on the arrangement. And with Carol Ferrante singing harmonies on most songs and lead vocal on others, the lineup of the band was complete. I was a lucky man to be in the company of these great musicians.

I know I'm gushing about the band, but I have to say it all came together by the means of James Russell Goforth, our roadie and tech. Without complaint he put the sound system together every night and packed it up after the show. He could fix anything that was broken and build whatever was necessary to keep us on the road.

We had an off day in Tulsa and were in the room watching TV when I said out loud, not thinking anyone would answer, "I wonder how TV works?" For the next 30 minutes Goforth explained the mystery to me. I sat and listened, and in my typical fashion I could not make heads or tails out of anything he said. I thought to myself, 'at least somebody knows this stuff.'

36

JERENE

Jerene took a job working for FM 100, the most important station in the area. FM 100 was where Jon Scott made a name for himself before he was hired by MCA Records in Los Angeles to be head of album promotion. He gave the station the street cred it built on during the early days of FM rock. He was the one who would play a record all night long if he loved it. He helped bring David Bowie to Memphis for what was only his second show in America. When AM radio was king, Jon was the one in Memphis to buck the system and play album cuts and new bands. And it didn't take long until every 18-to-30-year old in Memphis was listening to FM 100. Plus FM 100 was in stereo!

By the time I moved back to Memphis FM 100 was the hip station. So when station manager Bill Hays hired Jerene as his assistant it was a big deal. It meant she would meet all the major artists who were in town promoting a new record. And even though broadcasting was on its way out and narrowcasting was on its way in, it was still a thing when she was there. She met Kenny Rogers when he was struggling to get airplay for "Lucille," and newcomers like Olivia Newton-John and Barry Manilow when they came to town. Billy Joel had one hit and was bucking for more when he played the 300-seat Ritz Ballroom and FM 100 promoted the show.

Since FM 100 was the station the concert promoters used for their main radio marketing, Jerene, and by extension, I, got to go to

JERENE

all those shows and after-parties where we met all the artists. Station manager Bill Hays knew if he had a knock-out looking secretary, the male artists were more than happy to have her in their pictures.

There is no way I can overstate how important Jerene was, and is, to me. She's a Memphis girl through and through, born and raised.

She became my manager in 1976, and together we have made it work through all the good stuff and the bullshit the years have tossed our way. And folks, it ain't always been easy. But whatever I am today I owe as much to her as anything I've done myself.

37

THINGS GET ROLLING

By the beginning of '76 things were turning in my favor. Lafayette's was hiring me to do shows with a band and I was still opening solo for almost every act that came through. I did Bob Seger, Barry Manilow, Minnie Riperton, Maria Muldaur—which was the first time I met Stephen Bruton—and Larry Raspberry and the Highsteppers, and I just can't remember them all.

Bill Murray, an architect friend of mine I met through Don Nix, had designed Onyx Recording Studios and later designed a club on Madison Avenue called The Black Dog. I played there once over the holidays in '71. A few years later it changed its name to Procape Gardens. In '76 they brought me in on a regular basis, and I finally had a place I could count on for some steady income.

During times when it seemed like no one was listening, I made up songs on the spot. One night I was trying to get through to the crowd and I thought of a bluesy kind of rhythm—eighth notes in the key of E—on my Telecaster. Off the top of my head I sang "Lord, how I love to ride." A few people looked my way. So, I went to the four chord and sang the same thing. A few more heads turned. Then I just trusted my muse and went to the five chord and sang, "over the prairie, across to the mountain side."

So now, rather than everyone playing pool or standing at the bar talking, I had a crowd within the crowd listening to me. I borrowed the next verse from Blind Willie McTell and sang "Went down to my praying ground and fell down on my knees, I ain't crying for no religion Lordy gimme back my good gal please." That gave me time enough to think of the next verse. "I wish I had a nickel, Mama wish I had a dime. I'd give a thousand dollars if I could get 'em at the same time." In the time it took to sing it, I had a new song. It was just a little blues, but people stopped to listen, and that made my night.

Another night I did the same thing with another song. The crowd was hardly noticing me so I started playing music that was kinda like a song my mom would sing to me when I was a little boy. "Down in the meadow by the itty-bitty pool swam three little fishes and a mama fishy too"—don't even ask me how that popped in my tiny brain—and I sang "I'm not strange I'm just like you." Then I did it again and asked the crowd to sing it back and I'll be damned, they did! So "I'm Not Strange, I'm Just Like You" was born that night in that place.

Between Procape and Thirsty's I could work again under my own name and that felt good. It also gave me time to write in my little office/rehearsal place on Merton. I had put together a solid band as well. I had met Joe Gaston in San Francisco after my freezing tour in Minnesota. Joe was a great bass player for me, because he loved the simple music that has always run through my style.

I can't remember how I met Tom Jansen, but all I can say is he was the exact right drummer for me at the exact right time. He was "not too soft, not too loud, just enough to draw a crowd."

Ray Barrickman had come back to Memphis to play with me, this time without Chi. Which was a good thing. Chi and I had never really gelled, whereas Tom and I did immediately.

38

CHRIS BELL

Here's another curiosity. I can't remember how Chris Bell and I got together, but I don't care. Alex Chilton and I became friends when he lived in Gordon's apartment in New York. When he went back to Memphis he got in a band that became Big Star. When Alex sent me their record I became a Big Star fan right off the bat.

I'd heard fragments of the songs that are on their first album, *#1 Record*, bubbling just under the surface of the songs he played for me in New York. That's when he was working on finger picking and using it in his songs.

Of course, the first thing I do when I get a record is check out who wrote the songs. The name Chris Bell is prominent on both sides. And that voice. He's the only person I'd heard at that point who could keep up with Alex. Say what you want about Alex, but that cat was a singer with a capital "S."

Chris was a rock singer who also appreciated The Carpenters. We were in my van one day talking about the Eagles and he was going off about Joe Walsh, who had just joined the band. He thought that Walsh's singing couldn't keep up with the other members of the Eagles. I kept thinking to myself that Chris Bell and Joe Walsh were very similar rock singers. Of course, I didn't say a thing. At that time, I would have given anything to sing like either one of them, but alas, I'm gonna sound like me no matter what.

CHRIS BELL

Chris Bell loved a wide range of styles. Led Zeppelin was a huge influence on him. When I gave him a copy of Uncle Walt's Band he loved it. Like me, as long as it was good he could get into it.

When we played Thirsty's, we'd play two consecutive weekends from Thursday to Saturday. The roads were not as developed as they are now, so it was impracticable to drive back and forth. For that reason, we would find the cheapest place we could and stay nine days.

We would arrive early enough to set up and play on the first Thursday, and the last Saturday we would pack and drive all night back to Memphis. Chris did this a few times, but the last time he played with us we were in for a shock.

He was sharing a room with Jerene and me and we checked in. Jerene and I went out to take care of something—who knows what—and when we got back Chris was gone. He left a note with a number to call.

Chris was a devout Christian but never preached or got in your face about it. It is just who he was. Jerene called to see what was up and Chris told her he booked a room at a Holiday Inn. He would be staying there this time. He said he prayed about it and not to worry. He would still be playing the gig. When Jerene asked why, Chris explained that he had talked with Jesus. Jesus told him it was OK to do it. I, of course, didn't know what to do or think because this was the first time, and so far, the only time, anyone I know has ever talked to Jesus about the accommodations.

Sadly, it was the last time I ever played with Chris. He was a gifted musician, and his body of work gets more accolades with time. He died well before the cult around Big Star began. I surely wish he could have enjoyed the success of having co-written the theme to the hit TV show *That '70s Show* that ran eight seasons and is always on the air somewhere in the world.

He is one of my favorite memories. RIP, Chrisman.

39

KEITH AND JERENE

The best thing I did in 1976 was marry Jerene. We had been living together for two years or so, and I had told her I was ready anytime she was. One sunny day she said "Well, you wanna get married?" and I couldn't say yes fast enough.

In those days you had to have a blood test to marry, although I don't quite know why. When we went to get ours, I remember as soon as the needle went into my arm, I looked at Jerene and said, "Till death do us part."

We had the ceremony in our front yard, and my mom, grandmom, sister and her family were there. Jerene's family was there, and a bunch of friends came, and that was it. Larry Raspberry was my best man. No big anything, just a small service with friends and family.

The next day we went on our honeymoon to the Spring River in Arkansas and camped in our van. We rented a canoe and were driven a few miles upriver, where we put in. We'd made lunch and had plenty of snacks packed in the canoe. We began rowing downstream.

Almost as soon as we started, we hit rocks that stopped the canoe dead. We banged our chins on the cross bars and of course all the food, cigarettes, matches, us, and everything else was soaking wet in the bottom of the canoe. We were told there are 27 rapids on the river, and we didn't really know what that would entail until we found out.

KEITH AND JERENE

One of the rapids made us overturn, and we got separated. We had to try to catch the canoe as it drifted happily along with the current. We ended up cracking up on 25 of the 27 rapids with our bloody chins, wet clothes, and all. We realized by the time we got back to camp that it was the end of June and the river was very low, which is why we wrecked on almost all of the rocks.

We were lying there in our van when I said, "You wanna do anything?" Even though I knew the answer. "No," was her single-word reply. "Me either" was my two-word comeback.

Jerene and I were tired of renting, borrowing, or finagling, a PA every time we did a gig and needed to buy one. We asked Raspberry what he did for stuff like that. He introduced us to Waite Ligon, who worked at the Bank of Bartlett and had financed several things for Raspberry. He was used to working with musicians and let us borrow $2,000.

Murphy Odom built the PA for us. He recommended we get a Tascam board, because we could record rehearsals, make demos, and do live shows with it.

The monitors were quite possibly the worst monitors known to man, but it was better that what we had, which was nothing.

Now all we had to do was rent a trailer.

40

THINGS TAKE OFF

Jerry Jeff did an album around this time called *It's A Good Night for Singing*, that included two of my songs. "A Very Short Time" and "Someday I'll Get Out of These Bars," which I co-wrote with Richard Gardner.

Gardner was a photographer with the *Commercial Appeal*, Memphis' morning newspaper. He would come by my office on Merton to hang out and pitch me lyrics for songs.

One day I told him I was hoping to get to where I could play gigs in concert spaces rather than the bars that I was doing. I'd tell him, "I'm gonna get out of these bars someday and play where people sit and listen like they did when I was on the Coffee House Circuit."

Imagine my surprise when he came in with the lyrics to "Someday" almost completely fleshed out. All I had to do was write the music, add a line here and there, and poof, we had a song.

I made a demo in the office and sent it to Jerry Jeff and what do you know, he did it. He'd told me for a long time he would record "Short Time" one day, and he did that one, too. That album sold about 150,000 copies in the first few months, and I thought to myself, 'I like writing songs!'

There was a studio around the corner from my office named Shoe Studio. I was friends with Jim Cotton, one of the engineers. Jim was a stellar engineer who later moved to Nashville to work with Harold

Shedd, scoring 40 number one hits and selling 75 million records with the band, Alabama. He also co-produced "Achy Breaky Heart," the first Billy Ray Cyrus hit.

Jim fronted me some studio time. I used my band and we recorded about 10 songs. As soon as I could I planned a trip to New York in hopes of getting a record deal.

Tim Riley was working at Ardent Studios in Memphis and I called to see if he knew any record company people in the City. He gave me a list of six or eight people. One of them was Bob Reno, who had worked for Vanguard and believed in me. Bob once sent me to Jackson, MS., to cut two songs with Huey Meaux, the so called "crazy Cajun." Vanguard didn't release either of the songs, and I can't even remember what they were.

When I called Bob at his new label, Midland International, he asked me to come and see him. Not long after that he offered me a deal.

The record we made sounded softer than my dance band gigs. Some of the people who came to my shows thought it should have been more rock 'n' roll than it was. I understood their point, but the record was where my head was at the time, and I thought it was pretty good.

I normally don't listen to my records, because all I hear are the bits I don't like. Sometimes, if it's been a long time since I've heard one, I'll hear one by surprise and think it's better than I remembered it.

Keith and Jerene 1976

From top; Baby Keith, Kentucky, 1949; age 5, Murray, 1953;
with Paul Mitchel, Gordon Alexander just before Buffalo, 1968;
Holiday Inn sign, Charleston, SC, 1968 ~Gail Blair; 1st promo pic,
with Delmark Goldfarb, 1968 ~Robin Polanker; First NYC gig,
Izzy Young's Folklore Center, 1968 ~Ebet Roberts

From top, with Linda Ronstadt in NYC on the subway, 1969; with John Nathan and Hiroshi Teshigahara during filming *Summer Soldiers,* Tokyo, 1971; with John Prine, Loudon Wainwright and Steve Goodman backstage at the Bitter End, 1972; with Alex Chilton at Big Otto's, Memphis, 1974 ~Bernard Denima

from top; with Chris Bell, Joe Gaston, and Tom Janzen, Keith Sykes Band 1976 ~Jerene Sykes; with Jerry Jeff Waker and Steve Goodman at Thirsties, Mobile, AL, 1977 ~Jim Williams; with Loudon Wainwright backstage at The Bitter End, 1977 ~Ebet Roberts; with Tom Janzen and John Prine at Thirsties, Mobile, AL, 1977 from top; The day Elvis died Emmylou opened for Willie in Memphis; with Jimmy Buffett and Jerry Jeff Walker, 1978, Miami ~Tom Corcoran; with Jimmy Buffett in San Antonio, 1979, ~Jerene Sykes; with Kris Kristofferson in NYC 1979, ~Jerene Sykes; on stage with Buffett, 1979; ~Jerene Sykes.

from top; at Air Montserrat with Jimmy listening to playback of "Volcano" ~ Jerene Sykes; Jimmy listens to playback of "Survive" ~Jerene Sykes; with Jimmy at Montserrat airport ~Jerene Sykes; at Air Montserrat with Hugh Taylor, Russ Kunkel, Fingers Taylor, Buffett, and James Taylor ~Tom Corcoran; on Euphoria ll with Jimmy's little Martin; ~Jerene Sykes. All pics from 1979.

from top; This is where the *Changes in Latitudes, Changes in Attitudes* cover with Jimmy's inscription should be; with Joe Hardy recording the *I'm Not Strange* album, 1979 ~Jerene Sykes; with Buffett, last night as a Reefer, Birmingham, AL 1979; Playing *Saturday Night Live*, 1980.

from top; Picture I took of John Fry in Saint Martin, Lesser Antilles, 1981; with Rodney Crowell, Nashville, 1984; with Kelley Bass, my first house concert, 1984; with Paul Seibel, Gary White, and Jessie Walker McLarty, in Austin, Jerry Jeff Birthday Bash, 1985 ~Jerene Sykes.

from top; at Kilzer's album party with John Hampton, Jim Zumwalt, Jack Holder, Kim Denny, Dave Smith, and John Kilzer at Justin's, 1988; with John Prine as we relive our finger print night, Kiva Studio, 1990 ~Sheila Lewis; playing with Todd Snider, Memphis, 1992 or '93.

from top; the first Songwriter Night with Bob Cheevers (not pictured), Spooner Oldham, and Dan Penn, Joyce Cobb's, Beale St Memphis, 1993 ~Anita Webb, 1993; Various postcards from the Songwriter Nights.

41

THE WAY THAT I FEEL

"Sooner or Later" had finally solidified, and it's the lead song on the *The Way That I Feel* album.

"Just As Long As You Love Me." I asked Bob Reno to produce one song. He was reluctant, but after some coaxing he got on board and we went to LA to do it with Jim Ed Norman arranging. I believe Jim Ed actually did the producing, but I really wanted Bob to be invested in this record. We chose "Just As Long As You Love Me," and it was the single from the album.

I wrote "All I Wanted" with Carl Marsh. Carl had done fantastic synthesizer work on the Cate Brothers' "Union Man," and he did the string arrangements for this album.

"They Take It" was the first time I worked with Willie Hall on drums. Willie was Isaac Hayes' drummer for 22 years and played on "Shaft," which is still one of my favorite records.

"Coast Of Marseilles." I started working on the music to "Coast" while I was in Mobile. I'd sit by the bay and run those chords. That diminished chord, which comes second in the opening progression, comes via an old Burl Ives record of folk songs. One of those songs is "Go Away From My Window," and he used that chord to great effect in that song. I thought it fit well with this one.

I've told this story many times over the years about when I played *Austin City Limits* with "Rodney Crowell and Friends." Talk about a song swap. Here I was with Rodney, Guy Clark, John Prine, Billy Joe Shaver, and Billy Caswell on national TV, and I'm telling how on Sunday, Thanksgiving Day, I was coming in the kitchen way too often hoping for a bite to eat when Jerene said, "Just go write a song. The food will be ready when it's ready."

Someone in the audience shouted, "Thanksgiving is always on Thursday!" Well, I've been embarrassed before but nothing quite like that. It got a terrific laugh, but I'm still embarrassed by it.

I did leave the kitchen and wrote the lyrics for "Coast" that Thanksgiving day. I came up with Marseilles by way of Country Joe McDonald. Country Joe was on Vanguard, and I was asked if I would like to go by the studio where he was recording. He played a few songs he was working on, and one was about smuggling drugs and mentions Marseilles. He sings about it being a place where the merchandise can be shipped around the world.

I loved the way the word sounded and decided this song is where I'll use it. And so it is.

Buffett always said I wrote it in a brief moment of sanity. He also said it's one of the most beautiful songs he'd ever heard.

"I Feel So Good." Bob Wray came from Muscle Shoals with Roger Hawkins to do this record. Roger is a world-class drummer, and I was hoping he had forgotten about my failed attempt at recording at Muscle Shoals Sound. He hadn't forgot about it but assured me all was OK on that front. He was there after all.

Wray was gently hitting the bass strings with a drumstick and getting this wonderful sound when I asked if it was a part of anything. When he said no, I said we have to do it in this song. And that's how that cool bass part came to be on this song. I still like it.

"Sounds Like a Hit" was my attempt at going for a hit record. Looking back I worked a little too hard on it, but I like it. If I play it now, I usually leave out one of the parts, and I think it tightens it up quite nicely.

"What's Different About Her" was written after "Sooner or Later," and I kept it in the same vein. Those chords are influenced by Walter Hyatt. I loved how he could put a jazz chord in a folk song and have it come out so good.

"Call It Love." I wanted something I could play solo acoustic, and this one fit the bill.

"The Last Line" was something I kept going for, trying to tell in a song what it's like being on my side of the microphone.

When *The Way That I Feel* came out it got a very favorable review in the Memphis Commercial Appeal from Walter Dawson. He said it was a "small but nevertheless real masterwork." I'm very proud of that.

Wayne Crook and Warren Wagner, the producers, did really good work on the album. They were right there with me at every phase of the record and always were honest with me. You can't really do more than that for an artist.

One afternoon in Mobile, we went looking for a van we could convert to a travel van. My Dodge van had been a good workhorse but was getting long in the tooth. We needed something new we could make more comfortable for us and the band. We wanted to stay with Dodge, and we found a dealer with a B-300. It was green, long and strong.

Jerene's brother, Bobby Rowe, had been a funny car driver. After that he opened a shop making crankshafts for drag racing cars. I asked him how he went about buying a car. He said take 20% off the sticker price, add $200 and make an offer. That's what I did and left the rest to Jerene.

I walked around the showroom looking bored, and after a while she made the deal. The salesman came out to hear us one night and told me when I left the office to walk around the showroom he truly believed I wanted to leave without buying the van.

Jerene had to keep at it, but we did get it for the price I offered.

Back in Memphis, we had a nice interior installed, and we were off and running.

We toured for *The Way That I Feel* and did a lot of gigs. When we found out we were doing a few dates opening for Jesse Winchester in Louisiana, that was really cool.

I met Jesse in Montreal when I was on a tour with Jerry Jeff and staying a few days with Anna McGarrigle. Anna and Dane, her soon-to-be husband, were friends with Jesse and invited him over. We spent the evening listening to his spectacular songs in his distinctive style, and I was in seventh heaven. He played everything with such a great feel. When he played his version of "Lavender Blue Dilly Dilly," it sounded like it was one of his songs, even though it's a folk song that's been covered many times. I knew it from Sammy Turner's hit in the early '60s.

A few years later, I was working shows with Jesse Winchester. Sweet.

42

BOB KELLY

Around this time I met a man who would become a very important person to me over the years. His name was Bob Kelly.

Kelly was an imposing figure, over 6 feet tall and looked like he was a body builder. Jerry Jeff was playing in Memphis at the Xanadu Ballroom — I could be wrong about the venue — and there was a large crowd trying to get in. Kelly was leaving the front of the line saying something I couldn't make out, but he sounded pissed. I'd only seen him a few times and had not met him, but I knew he was promoting concerts in and around Memphis, so I asked him what was wrong. Words were said — not to me but over my head — to someone and I surmised that he was having trouble getting in. I said Jerry Jeff is a friend and I could get him in. He said no, he could get himself in, and whoever he was pissed at was an asshole. I'm paraphrasing obviously.

This doesn't sound like the beginning of a long friendship, but it was. For years to come Kelly hired me to play any number of concerts as the opening act, and when I began to draw he promoted shows on me.

43
BUFFETT DOES COAST

In 1975 Buffett recorded "Train To Dixie" and Don Light, Jimmy's manager, asked me to come to his office to hear it. As I listened I could tell they had really put an effort into it and the singing and musicianship was spot on.

When the song ended Don asked if I thought it was a single. Well, I thought to myself, 'Jimmy had just hit with "Come Monday" and this record didn't sound anything like that.' And considering the two records were so different, I said, "I didn't think it did."

We were listening to a vinyl test pressing, not a tape copy that people usually played in their office. So I figured I had an album cut for sure. But when the album came out the next year "Train" wasn't on it and the reason was that they didn't want another album cut. They wanted a single.

So I learned an important lesson that day. If you're asked if you think the song is a single, the answer is - you guessed it - yes. With a capital "Y"!

Buffett came out with *Changes in Latitudes, Changes in Attitudes*, in '77 and it hit like a ton of bricks. He was suddenly everywhere all the time playing the big rooms all across the country. "Margaritaville" became an instant classic. It was just like Sam Phillips, the record producer who helped usher in the age of rock 'n' roll, had said in many interviews, "It's got to be different if you want to get anywhere." I'm paraphrasing but that's basically it.

And Jimmy was different. In the middle of the heavy rock, disco, and hugely produced ballads, there was little ol' "Margaritaville" kicking major ass with its acoustic guitar and marimba fills. Everyone who liked their music less intense and more story oriented embraced that record. Soon they would be into the lifestyle that Jimmy embodied. I thought it was awesome and always will.

After Jerene and I got married I gave up my office/rehearsal place and cleaned out the garage at our house. It was smaller, but workable, and we were playing enough so we didn't have much time to rehearse anyway. Our best stuff seemed to come in the heat of the moment, and we were getting good enough to talk through the changes and go out and play it. Playing was really fun when we were hitting on all eight.

We were rehearsing one afternoon when Jerene came out to tell me I had a phone call. I went to the house and it was Buffett. He said he was going to record "Coast of Marseilles."

Over the phone I told him in a calm voice and collected demeanor that it was great news, and I couldn't thank him enough. But in my mind I was doing cartwheels, screaming in ecstasy to the top of my lungs. We chatted a bit more and that was it. I told Jerene as soon as I hung up the phone, but I couldn't bring myself to tell anyone else in case everything fell through. I didn't want to jinx it.

Buffett had played Memphis a few months before, and we went to the concert at Memphis Ellis Auditorium, the same place I first saw Bob Dylan play on February 10, 1966. After the show we exchanged albums. I gave him *The Way That I Feel* and he gave me *Changes in Latitudes, Changes in Attitudes*. I signed mine for him, and he signed his to me with a loving inscription saying how he doesn't get to see some of the people he cares for very often, even though they are the ones who mean the most to him.

Years later Todd Snider suggested I get it framed and I did. Why didn't I think of that? (As I write this it's at Ardent Studios and I'm not allowed to call there, much less pick up any of my belongings. I'm still not sure why.)

Buffett sent a rough mix—the basic recording without the finishing touches and final mixing—of "Coast" and at the end there was a recitation of him telling the world about Keith Sykes. My mind was blown again.

Not long after he called again to ask if I had any more tunes. They were short a song and still looking. I suggested "Last Line."

Butch McDade, the drummer for the Amazing Rhythm Aces, had played on my version, and his feel made it come together. When I put it to Jimmy that way I think he knew what I meant and maybe that's why he recorded it, but I don't know for sure.

I do know I was excited to have two songs on his new record because first, he was a great artist, and second, his last record had sold through the roof and everyone knew this one would do well. It was exciting times for me.

When *Son of a Son of a Sailor* came out in 1978 and I could buy one at the record store and hold it in my hands I went from being a songwriter guy to a Songwriter Guy right then. I thought to myself, 'they can't take this away from me.'

44

STEVE GOODMAN

I first met Steve Goodman the same night Kristofferson introduced John Prine at the Bitter End. I'm sorry to say I don't remember much about Steve that night because Prine had slain me.

But over the years we became friends from playing the Philadelphia Folk Festival along with other gigs here and there. He was so quick witted, a badass guitarist, and a great writer who liked what I was doing. Imagine that.

When we hung out I could count on hearing a good joke and a pile of wicked songs.

One time when I was playing Thirsty's, Steve was also playing in Mobile and came over to hear my last set. After I finished my gig I went to see him at his hotel.

He had just finished producing John Prine's *Bruised Orange* album. He was playing me the mixes when "That's the Way the World Goes 'Round" came on. When it got to the line that said, "I was crying ice cubes," Steve stopped the tape and looked at me with that unmistakable sparkle in his eyes and said, "It must get really cold at John's house." Those are the times that keep me writing this book.

45
AND THE HITS JUST KEEP ON COMING

That fall Jerry Jeff asked me to come to Miami to record "I'm Not Strange, I'm Just like You," the song I wrote on stage at Procape. He was signed to a new label, Electra, and went to Bayshore Studios in Coconut Grove to record.

Bayshore had great equipment and vibe, and was owned by Bill Szymczyk, the Eagles producer. Coconut Grove was the Greenwich Village of Florida, and I loved hanging out there every time I went to Miami. The Coconut Grove Hotel was walking distance from the studio, and Jerry Jeff had the whole band staying there. This was gonna be good.

One afternoon I came to the studio and Jerry Jeff was with a fellow and said, "Keith, this is Fred Neil. Fred this is Keith Sykes." 'Damn,' I thought to myself, 'Fred Neil!' I was a fan of Fred because he wrote "Everybody's Talking" that Harry Nilsson recorded and had a huge hit with. I had been playing it since my first gigs and never stopped loving it. Now here he was sitting in front of me.

He was very impressed that Jerry Jeff had all this going on. He kept telling Jerry Jeff he wished he could get a record deal with a handsome budget but hadn't been able to make it happen. I kept thinking how cool it was that he was sitting right there in the room talking like a real person, instead of the songwriting god that he was to me.

46

THE YEAR OF THE CHILD

Kris Kristofferson and Rita Coolidge had married and were touring together. Kris was in the hit movie *A Star Is Born* and Rita was always on the pop charts, and their concerts were selling out all over the country.

Their bass player, Tommy McClure, was a friend of Bobby Grace, one of my high school buddies, who Jerene and I saw regularly. Bobby would get tickets from Tommy, and the three of us would go to Kris and Rita shows if they were anywhere nearby. Driving a few hundred miles was a breeze for us, and we did it whenever the stars lined up.

During all this Jerene and I got to know Billy Swan and "Funky" Donnie Fritts and his wife Donna. I had met Fritts and Swan with Kris in NYC but really didn't get to know them. I had met Stephen Bruton, Kris and Rita's ace guitarist, when he played for Maria Muldaur. And now we were introduced to Sammy Creason and Michael Utley. All the players in Kris and Rita's band were among the best musicians in the country.

At the end of '78, Kris invited Jerene and me to New York for the "Year of the Child," a TV special put on by the United Nations' UNESCO. It was held in January, and all the huge stars of the day were set to perform.

It was insane backstage. The Bee Gees, Henry Winkler, Donna Summer, Gilda Radner, and anyone you could think of were all acting like regular people. Just sitting around waiting for their turn to do their thing.

All the music artists were asked to give something to the foundation to help underwrite the charity. When we went with Kris to do his sound check with Rod Stewart, he found out that Rod had given them "Maggie May." Kris said he gave them an album cut and was blown away by Rod's generosity.

After the big night, Kris and Rita took us to Studio 54, and it was everything it was cracked up to be. What a night!

We were staying at the Waldorf Astoria, and our room was elegant. It made us wonder what kind of room the stars were in.

The morning after the show the phone in our room rang and I answered. It was Buffett. He asked if I'd like to be in the Coral Reefers. It was one of those times again. I thought about saying something like "Let me check my busy schedule," but I was truly stunned. And how did he know where I was? No matter. I said yes, and he said we would rehearse in Miami and hit the road right after. Eureka!

Later that day Mike Utley and his girlfriend Fran were getting married in the hotel, and we went down to the reception. Stephen Bruton was playing classical music on an acoustic guitar when someone finally asked me what's going on. For the first time I could say I just joined the Coral Reefer Band.

47

CORAL REEFERS

The Reefers were staying at the Coconut Grove Hotel, the same place I stayed when I was with Jerry Jeff working on his *Jerry Jeff* album. We would hang loose during the day and rehearse at Criteria Studios in Miami starting in the afternoon until 10 or so at night.

I had the *You Had to Be There* album that Jimmy released between the *Changes* and *Son of a Son* albums, and I felt pretty versed in how things might go down. And once we began rehearsals, I felt good about my end of the bargain. "Dixie Diner" was always a stretch for me, but at least I had done it every night when I was a Highstepper. It was different than anything else in Jimmy's set, and after I settled in I loved playing it.

Jimmy's players were among the best, and I knew I always had to be on top of my game. Harry Daly could play bass as good as it gets. Barry Chance had come from a musical family—his dad was legendary Nashville bassist Lightnin' Chance. I think Fingers Taylor was Coral Reefer #1, because he and Jimmy had played gigs since they were in college at the University of Southern Mississippi.

You could hear Fingers' soul when he played the blues. He could listen to Little Walter for hours on end and did so on a daily basis. But, at least when I was around, he played it on a boom box turned way down low with the box resting on his shoulder, cradled up by his ear.

He also played the organ and piano really well. His harp solos on Jimmy's songs became transcendent when he was at his best. "A Pirate Looks at Forty," is just one example of how he could play straight harp, and then shine playing draw harp on "Dixie Diner."

Keyboardist Andy McMahon was on the first tour I did. Then later, when Utley came with us, they made a big, luxurious sound together.

My first show with the band was to be in Charleston, SC, the place I played my first gig back in 1968, but at the last minute a show was added in Oxford, MS.

Jerene came down, and in the morning before the show she, Jimmy, and I went to Rowan Oak, William Faulkner's home, that had just been acquired by the University of Mississippi. We had the whole place to ourselves. One fellow was there to watch over it, and that was it.

We went all through the house, and one of the things that caught my eye was a phone book, about a quarter inch thick, hanging on a string by the wall phone in the kitchen.

I went back to Rowan Oak about 20 years later, and everything looked the same as it did the day we toured it in '79, but you were no longer able to go through the entire house like we did.

That night we played at the coliseum in Oxford.

When Jimmy introduced the band, and my name was called, I got a pretty big ovation. Jimmy turned around to me and said, "They know you!" I beamed a bit, but I knew that was not going to happen every night.

We were traveling in that plane you see in the movie *The Rose* starring Bette Midler. It was a 54- passenger Viscount airliner with four big Rolls-Royce turbo jets that had been converted to an 18- passenger touring plane. It was a long way from the "Green Bean," the nickname for my Dodge B-300 van.

Next stop, Charleston. This was, for me, my first gig with Jimmy Buffett. Even though we had just played Oxford, this was the one when I knew I was in the band, and it was time to pull it all together. I'm not sure why I looked at it like that. I just did.

We had fun. We made great music. We were traveling first class, staying at first-class places, and the hardest thing I had to do was to be in the lobby at 10:30 for an 11:15 takeoff. Which is to say, it was the easiest job I ever had.

The luggage was in my room by the time I got my key. It was collected the next day after I went to the lobby. Our road manager, Bobby Lieberman, and his crew took very good care of us, always. The plane was a great place to hang. There was always someone interesting to talk to, or you didn't have to talk at all.

Jimmy had a stateroom in the back to rest, think, or whatever. But he would usually hang with us. But it was there when he needed it.

When we touched down there was a car, limo, or van to take us to the hotel. At the appointed time we had a lobby call to meet up for transportation to the venue. At the venue, food and drink would be provided—M&Ms included, but no one gave a shit about the color of the individual pieces. We seldom did a sound check after the first gig because the roadies were pretty good musicians, and by the time we got on stage it sounded exactly as it did the night before. Repeat until the tour was over.

All I cared about was doing the best I could every night. I got better with each passing show. I tried to find something in every song to accentuate at just the right moment. It may not have been anything more than raising the neck of my guitar at a certain place in a song. Or looking for a better tone if I thought it might help. Every link in the chain counted.

48

MONTSERRAT

We got word we were going to the island of Montserrat to record Jimmy's next record. George Martin, the Beatles producer, had built a studio there named Air Montserrat, and Jimmy booked it. We were only the second act to record there, and everyone was excited to be going.

We flew commercial to St Croix, U.S. Virgin Islands, and spent the night there. We took smaller planes from there to Montserrat.

That was my first time to play with Mike Utley, the only musician to have played on every Jimmy Buffett album. Hey, all you record keepers out there. If I'm wrong on this, I ain't wrong by much. I may be leaving out the first two albums Jimmy did for Barnaby Records. But I'm pretty sure he did all the albums from the first ABC Records forward. Utley is a master musician and has played with so many artists I bet he doesn't remember them all.

Our drummer for the first few days was Kenny Buttrey, the legendary Nashville drummer. Fingers, Harry, Barry, Andy, Deborah McColl, and I, were the Coral Reefers who made the trip.

The studio was something out of the clouds as far as I was concerned. Just the view was enough to make me happy. But the gear would make any studio jealous with its Neve console, Neumann microphones, and every piece of outboard gear imaginable at your fingertips. It was the first time I used an individual headphone mixer.

They were stationed around the studio so each musician could adjust the volume of the vocal and instruments to his or her own needs. It defined state of the art at the time.

After Kenny Buttrey left he was replaced by Russ Kunkel, one of every musician's favorite drummers. I personally couldn't believe I was getting to record with him, but Buffett never failed to surprise me.

In the beginning we were using Geoff Emerick, who was George Martin's engineer. He went about his business in a way that reminded me of several rock 'n' roll engineers I had been around. If a guitar didn't sound right to him, he left the control room and made adjustments to the musician's amp. He also played back the takes so loud it was hard for me—and I believe others as well—to hear it. It was that loud. It was also the opposite of how things worked in Nashville. Touching an amp or any piece of the musicians' gear was taboo. When producer Norbert Putnam brought in Gene Eichelberger, his engineer from Nashville, I believe all of us sighed a bit of relief.

Emerick did stay on with us even after Eichelberger came on board, and from then on, we got on very well with him. After all, if you engineered Sgt. Pepper's, you may have a different style, but you earned the respect of everybody in the entire music world.

After these adjustments were made the band began to gel, and the tracts are the results. I'm proud of everything I did on that record except for my playing on "Sending the Old Man Home." I thought I did well at the time, but I should have redone my part. As a matter of fact, I should have just sat back and enjoyed James Taylor's performance. He was outstanding as always.

Speaking of James, when we were close to finishing the record James and his brothers, Alex and Hugh, came to Montserrat to spend a few days. It was a joy to meet the three of them while they were on their mini vacation with their friend Jimmy Buffett.

We had our evening meal each night in a large room in the studio building with food prepared by a local chef. These meals were always special, because invariably someone would say something that would crack everyone up, and that would go around until someone else followed up with another outrageous comment, until it would climax with us all completely laughed out. That's how Johnny Montezuma came to life.

I was sitting next to Jimmy one night and for some reason turned to him and said, "Do you think I could make it if I changed my name to Johnny Montezuma?" And that's all it took. Before I knew it Fingers changed his name to "General Tom" and became Johnny's manager. An entire fictitious underworld sprang up around us.

When the tracks were recorded we all went into overdub mode. Some of us might have a day off while others would be working. On one of my days off I commandeered a golf cart and Andy McMahon and I went looking for the volcano we had all heard about. We got a map, and off we went.

Passing though Plymouth on winding roads we made it through the jungle, up the mountain to Soufriere Hills. There was nothing in the way of signs, or an interactive tourist museum, or anything other than the volcano. Steam was leaving the earth and headed for the heavens in the middle of what I thought looked like the surface of the moon. It was yellow and gray barren earth in the middle of the lush, verdant jungle. We looked around for a while and then made our way back to the studio, talking about the contrast we witnessed and how wild and free things are on Montserrat.

If this was in the USA it would have a chain link fence around it with plenty of "Danger, Do Not Enter" signs everywhere.

I told Jimmy about our trip as soon as I saw him, and he said we were going back the next day. Cool with me.

On this trip—and I'm not making this up—I saw a woman with a stack of bananas on her head walking on the side of the road. When Jimmy and I arrived at the volcano, he was as taken with it as I was. I guarantee you that if you saw it, you would be taken as well. We were exploring the vents—the steam I mentioned before are called vents—and how the water condensed and made a creek that meandered down the side of the mountain to the ocean. Right where we stood the water was very hot, but down 30 or 40 feet away it cooled off enough to feel like it was about the temperature of a hot tub. We grabbed some of the clay dirt and dammed up a skinny part of the creek. Our "tub" was three feet wide and three inches deep at most, but we splashed the hot water on us, and it was all quite enjoyable.

As we made our way back to the golf cart, I swear there was a five-foot iguana as colorful as you can imagine not 10 feet from where we were. It didn't seem to be afraid of us as it moved slowly off the road into the jungle. What a day! It was absolutely like something out of National Geographic magazine.

When we got back to the studio we realized we smelled like two 150-pound gobs of sulfur. We didn't care. We sat down and started writing "Volcano."

I had been going to see these musicians play in this tiny bar, and I told Jimmy everything they played was in F. I said we should write in F. So he began to strum in F. I sang "I don't know." Jimmy seemed to like it. So I said it again. I was trying to think of what might come next when he sang, "I don't know where I'm'a gonna go when the volcano blows." I very much liked that. I sang "Ground is moving under me." Jimmy sang "Tidal wave out on the sea." I sang "Sulfur smoke up in the sky." Jimmy sang "Pretty soon we learn to fly." And on it went for about 15 minutes and we were done. Wow!

The next day everyone was talking about how to cut this song. I saw Kunkel across the pool and yelled out "Straight fours on the kick" which means play the kick drum once every beat. I thought it would ground the whole song. He did and it does.

That afternoon Jimmy hired the three guys I had heard in that tiny bar, and they played on the intro and it just made it happen. One of them had a three-inch diameter bamboo stalk about six feet long that he blew into. Another had an acoustic guitar, and the other had a homemade looking ukulele. Kunkel played the chimes on the intro, and it was coming together really well.

That night Jimmy asked everyone to come in and do something at the end of the song. I think it was Lieberman who sang the "he don't know" and started the "no no no" on the ad lib part, and the party was on. When it was over we had a song that appeared out of nowhere, and it was truly a magical, lightning in a bottle thing that only happens when you are really lucky.

Jerene was coming down to spend the last week with us, and I drove a golf cart to the airport to pick her up. The airport consisted of one room with a counter on one side where the radios were, and that's about it.

I arrived about 20 minutes early, and to my surprise there sat the studio owner, George Martin. Sir George these days. I was keeping my cool, looking out the window for the plane, and checking out a map on the wall. When I couldn't go any longer I looked at George Martin and said, "Tell me everything about the Beatles" with enough insincerity that I hoped he knew I was only breaking the ice. To my everlasting relief he smiled, and we began a casual conversation.

We talked, but always in the back of my mind I'm thinking, 'This is fucking GEORGE MARTIN.' If there was a picture under the word "gentleman" in the dictionary it would certainly be his.

I told him I was waiting for my wife to arrive, and he said it must be the plane he was leaving on. I thought to myself, 'GEORGE MARTIN is talking to me!' It was another amazing thing that happened to me because I knew Jimmy Buffett. When the plane arrived, George—I called him George now—said his goodbye to me and hello to Jerene, and that was it for my time with a living legend.

Tom Corcoran sailed Buffett's boat, the Euphoria ll, to Montserrat. After the album was recorded and our time at Air Montserrat was up, we set sail with Captain Tom heading for St. Barth's. Rain was starting to fall on Montserrat Bay as Geoff Emerick, Gene Eichelberger, Jerene, me, and a few others, all took Euphoria's dingy to the boat. We settled in for the night sail.

It was choppy, and some of us fared better than others. Emerick was a bit seasick, and Eichelberger had an issue with diabetes, so their trip wasn't ideal. After a while I went below and fell asleep and didn't wake up until morning.

When I made my way to the deck it looked picture postcard perfect with the sun rising and St Barth's silhouette cutting over the sea. We anchored in the harbor and walked to a restaurant where the tables were in the sand and clothing was optional. We lunched on shark grilled to perfection, served with lovely condiments and mimosas.

We were almost finished with our meal when Corcoran looked at his watch and pointed across the water. He said keep an eye out over there. Right on cue we saw a private jet about 200 feet above the water headed straight for us. It closed in on us in no time, then went straight up with a huge roar and we all yelled as it did. Corcoran said Buffett told him to tell us when he'd be buzzing us. He said the pilots were Vietnam vets, and in this part of the world, if asked, they loved to do this kind of thing.

Everyone flew to St. Martin to get a flight home except for Jerene and me. We stayed on to hang out on the Euphoria ll for another week. After a day we were surprised to hear Deborah McColl and a friend calling out to us on the boat. Turns out they stayed on for a while too, but soon went off again to wherever they were staying.

We met Jerome, a friend of Jimmy's, whose parents had a home on St. Barth's. He befriended us and showed us all over the island. Jerome met Elizabeth Ashley a few years later and worked for her for many years. He was a young, French, handsome man, so I wasn't surprised by that.

I also met Dr. Kino on this trip. He was from Guadalupe and was with us on Montserrat and worked for Jimmy for many tours to come. One evening he came over to The Euphoria and asked us to come with him see the boat where he was cooking that night. The boat was 80 feet long with an elegant blue hull, and we had never seen anything like it. The hall was wide and led to the staterooms. It seemed like it had everything any world traveler could want. I wish I could remember her name.

We met a lot of the boaters who were anchored in the harbor. They were from everywhere. Most of them were as curious about us as we were about them. At night we would take the dingy to shore and walk around or go with Jerome somewhere. Once we went to a nightclub where I heard the song "Just A Gigolo" by Louis Prima for the first time. Talking to the people there was so cool and just being there was … I don't know how to explain it! We loved it.

One afternoon this old wooden boat sailed in. There were two sailors on board, and we got to know them. This boat was built in 1909, 60 feet long, no lifelines or other such things. The captain was from England and told us he had sailed her across the Atlantic several times, and she never let him down. He was somewhere in his 40s I guessed, and his one-man crew was in his 20s.

When our week was over, we told our new friends we were leaving for St Martin. They said they were sailing there and we could go with them as long as I helped. That was another one of those "Let me check my busy schedule" things. To put it bluntly, we jumped on the chance to do it.

After we loaded our bags and settled on board, I was asked to steer the ship through the harbor. The engine was started, the prop was engaged, and the boat began moving. I took the wheel while they were hauling up the anchor, moving this thing there, and tying that thing to the deck, and before too long we were just about into open water. I kept at the wheel. We went into open water, and I was still at the wheel. It finally got to the point I no longer knew where to steer the boat so I asked what I should do. The captain pointed, and I followed orders.

A VERY SHORT TIME

The day, the weather, and the water. It was all beyond any sailor could hope for. The mate dipped a bucket over the side and hauled up the water and poured it over his head. He said the water is salty but so fresh he used it to cool off.

A tiny island protruded over the horizon, and the captain told me to sail to it. He asked me how I was doing, and I said fine. "Do you want to keep at the wheel?" he asked. "Yes," I said.

The boat would ride up to the top of the waves and then gently slide into the troughs. The waves, and the sun, the wind, and the world, held steady. Jerene and the sailors talking, me at the wheel. I've never had a day quite like it.

The sun was sinking low when we made it to St. Martin. We bid farewell to our new sailor friends and got a room for the night at a small hotel right where we came ashore. That room had the most wonderful ceiling fan, and we slept under sheets.

It was a most unforgettable trip. One last thing. I asked Jimmy for the little Martin guitar that was on the Euphoria, and he said I could take it for a while but I could not keep it. It was a little 0 size, maybe smaller, with a '40s style head stock. I know most of you don't know what I'm talking about, but let me just say it was extraordinary. I took very good care of it. I'll tell you how we parted later.

49

I'M NOT STRANGE, I'M JUST LIKE YOU

Back in Memphis, Jerene and I were talking about what to do for my next album. Jimmy had paid me 20 sessions for the Air Montserrat sessions, and my royalties for "Coast" and "Last Line" were coming in. We had the month of June off, so we decided to talk with John Fry, the owner of Ardent Studios, about recording there.

I'd met John with Alex Chilton years before, but I really didn't know him. Joe Hardy was working there as manager and chief engineer, and we had been getting together from time to time to talk about music and just hang out.

I was still gigging with my band when I was home, and I was going to use them on these recordings so everything seemed all set. Here's the thing: When I was touring with Buffett they would gig on their own as Uncle Tom's Jam Band and were doing quite well. They were making about the same money as when I was playing but didn't have me to pay. So they had decided they were going to split from me.

That left me without a band for the studio. When I told Fry and Hardy about it, Hardy said he could play bass. I knew he could because I'd heard tapes of songs he worked on in the studio and they were quite good. They also told me John Hampton, the new night guy, was a very good drummer, so why not give him a try. I said OK, and we booked the studio.

We didn't have the money to pay all at once, but Fry said we could pay after the record was out with the receipts from sales at gigs and distributors. He was like that. He made deals with artists he thought were in it for the right reasons to give them a chance. When it worked, he made out well. If it didn't, he lost the studio time, but it was time that wasn't booked anyway. Not a win-win, but not a lose-lose either. We paid Hardy and Hampton a fee for each song, so Fry didn't have any out-of-pocket expenses.

Hampton and Hardy turned out to be a blessing, because the tracks were really good.

"B I G T I M E." I wrote it with the idea of making a record you can dance to. All the songs I'd written before were songs to listen to, but this song made your feet happy. At least that's what I was going for. I was inspired by New Wave artists and used "Summertime Blues" as my muse.

"Love To Ride." I'd been playing it since I wrote it on stage at the Procape. Mary Martin was working for Warner Brothers Records and gave us a little money to record a few songs, so we went to Jackson, MS, at Malaco Studios, and did it with James Stroud and those kick-ass players down there.

This time, Hardy's bass track was much more basic than the Malaco track, but the feel was right in the pocket. I put that Creedence tremolo guitar part in it—I should have worked up a part that was more original but I was pressed for time and that lick worked—so there you have it.

"When My Work Is Done" is my homage to Buddy Holly. The movie, *The Buddy Holly Story*, came out the year before, I was playing his records more than usual, and his songs were running through my mind a lot.

"Ain't That Some Loving" is me trying for a Memphis soul song. It's maybe my favorite song on the album.

"928." I needed a very fast song, and I was a fan of the Porsche 928 sports car, and "928" is a product of that.

"I'm on a Roll." I remember finishing this one in my garage. Mirrored sunglasses and "all my friends are telling me I'm a rock 'n' roll star" seemed to fit the motif I was going for. It was the first song that Redbeard, the famed "air personality" on radio station Rock 103 played from the record, and thus was the first time it was played on any radio station.

Redbeard became a great friend to Jerene and me and was instrumental in the success we had during that time.

It also makes me think back to the days when radio played local bands and gave them the exposure they needed to become a draw. I believe it's a real shame that no longer happens. It helps the stations and the artists.

There are many stories of a band or an artist getting local airplay that led to a major label contract. And I guarantee that the fans are listening to the stations that get behind local talent. Like I say, good for the stations, good for the artists.

"If You Said Love." I never meant to rip a song off, but this got too close for comfort. I knew it, and everyone else did too. But you can make your own call if you happen to have the Memphis Records version.

"Smack Dab In The Middle." When Jerene and I were staying on the Euphoria ll, I went through every drawer and cubbyhole on the boat until I finally found what I was looking for. The music! Buffett had a plethora of cassettes, and the one I listened to most was a Mills Brothers collection of some of their best. "Smack Dab In The Middle" hit the spot for me. I copied down the words and found a riff that approximated what the big band horn section was doing, and I've played it every time I've had a band since then. You can't beat a shuffle beat to get people up and dancing, and those lyrics are just heaven.

You should look up songwriter Charles E. Calhoun sometime and check out his songs and contributions to American music. You'll be surprised!

"Maybe I'm A Mockingbird" is one of those songs I worked on for a long time, maybe two or three years. And that's not anywhere as long as I've taken on other songs, but since I was a young man then, and time is relative, it was a long time. When I finally settled on the lyrics, I knew I had one I'd always feel proud of. The very sparse arrangement still intrigues me.

"I'm Not Strange, I'm Just Like You." After all the work I've put into songs wouldn't you know the one I popped off on stage is the one people, especially the ones from Memphis, know me for more than any other song. "I'm Not Strange" is synonymous with partying hard, up all night, and screaming at the top of your lungs crazy. Hey, I'm not gonna look a gift horse in the mouth — or any other bodily part — but sometimes even I can't relate to me being the same guy who wrote that song and "Coast of Marseilles."

Jerene kept after me to record it. I really didn't want to. When it came down to the last song, I relented. She wasn't going to take no for an answer anyway.

We had recorded everything in Studio B, which is the smaller studio, then moved to Studio A to mix. But because we needed just one more song, it wasn't practical to move back to B so we did the session in A. John Hampton left after he played drums so A was clear and totally open.

I deliberately played the lead guitar as loose as I could get away with.

Jerene called as many people as she could think of on such short notice, and they met next door at Trader Dick's to wait until we were ready. When it was all set, I went over and said, "Anybody wanna be on my record?" and everyone followed me to Ardent.

We ran the tape to the last part of the song. I was in the control room for the first take and thought everyone sounded a trifle laid back. So I went into the studio, and like an orchestra conductor, I prodded them on. We recorded it three more times. Each time they got more into it, and we finally got the effect we were looking for — a rowdy, half-full bar, way after midnight.

50
BACK TO MY REAL JOB

In July I was back on the road touring with Buffett. This was my first tour on a bus. The tour was in the Midwest and Southeast ending in Chapel Hill, North Carolina at the UNC football stadium in the great outdoors. All the audience was on one side, and I was told there was 25,000 people there. During the intermission, Jimmy asked me to come out with him so the two of us could do a James Taylor song. We played "Carolina in My Mind," and the sound of that many people going batshit crazy for a song still reverberates in me.

The next tour was on the West Coast. We rehearsed in San Diego and stayed in nearby condos.

Sammy Creson was fast becoming one of my favorite drummers, and we were staying in the same unit. I remember asking him about all the records he had played on. So many hits! He said one of his favorite artists was Tony Joe White.

When Tony Joe first came out with "Polk Salad Annie" Sammy said just the two of them would tour. It sounded strange to me, but I get it now. After playing in so many configurations of my own bands, I've found if it feels good to you, people are gonna feel it, too.

During the last rehearsal, the galleys for Jimmy's new album were brought by, and I checked them just like everyone else. Right there it was: *Volcano* was the title cut. I looked at the credits and there it was: under the word "Volcano" were two names, Jimmy Buffett and Keith

BACK TO MY REAL JOB

Sykes. A few minutes later I was called into a small dressing room and Jimmy was there with Harry Daly.

Before we left Montserrat Jimmy told me we would split the song 50/50. Somehow, Harry thought he was supposed to have credit on it, too. Jimmy was perturbed, I was surprised, and Harry was saying Jimmy had promised him writing credit on the album. Jimmy said Harry would get 10% of "Volcano" and it was coming out of my half. I didn't say a word. Well, I said OK, which was all I could muster under the circumstances. I thought Jimmy had written all the ad lib stuff at the end. I wasn't there when that was going down, so I assumed that's the stuff Harry must have participated in. In any case, I was glad to be part of the song even though I would have loved to have been credited as the only other writer. I know what I did, and I know what Jimmy did and that was enough for me. I have lived with it that way and don't have any animosity toward Harry. It just is what it is.

One thing for sure, I have done very well with "Volcano" ever since it was released. It has sold a mountain of records, and it's always playing somewhere. And one other thing. Jimmy has played it at every concert he's done since the album came out. Yes, I'll concede an exception to that, but I bet you could count on one hand the times he didn't include it in the great 8—the songs he's included in every concert since then.

When rehearsals were over, Mike Utley and I took the train from San Diego up to Los Angeles. It was my first chance to talk with him one on one, and I enjoyed it very much.

He told me he was talking with some A&M Records executives who told him they were being ripped off to the tune of $10 million a year by pirates in Southeast Asia. Wow! And that was just one record company. I also found out that Steven Bruton was Utley's roommate. Both of those guys are such tremendous musicians. He also said he and his wife, Fran, were moving to another place. It was just a casual conversation and these were things we wouldn't have shared if not for this day off.

A VERY SHORT TIME

When I arrived in LA I went to see famed manager Irving Azoff, who managed Jimmy, the Eagles, and a host of other uber-successful artists. Irving listened to "Love to Ride," and told me he loved it.

I'd heard he negotiated contracts for artists he didn't manage — Bob Seger to be precise. But when the time came when I could have called to see if he was interested, I didn't. So I'll never know what might have happened. Irving was, and is, a very busy man.

We were about to do a three-night stand at the Universal Amphitheater, and we were staying at the Chateau Marmont.

Jerene came out and we got to spend some fun time together. When we went to L.A. to record "Just as Long as You Love Me" we were together but we didn't have time to do much. This time was just the opposite, and we were loving every minute of it.

Rodney Crowell and Rosanne Cash were living in LA, and they came to the hotel to see us. It was the first time I met Rosanne, who was pregnant with their first child. She was quiet and seemed ready to be a mom that day.

I don't know how you girls do it. If men had to have the kids I doubt if there would be a population explosion anywhere.

Backstage at the Universal Amphitheater is *the* place to be if Jimmy Buffett is in town. We met so many people it was hard to wrap my mind around it. Jack Nicholson, Jane Fonda, Peter Fonda, Elizabeth Ashley and Bonnie Raitt all were there. I knew Bonnie from shows with John Prine, but the movie stars were new to me. Turns out they are regular people, too — except they're really talented, good looking, rich, and famous. You just don't see them in Memphis very often.

Every time I looked around for Jerene, I'd see her and Jack Nicholson for a second, and then they'd be gone. Hmm. They seemed to have a lot to talk about.

We loved these occasions, and they only happened when Jimmy was around. People just love his music, and of course we did, too. LA was a fun trip that time.

BACK TO MY REAL JOB

At some point around this time we played a two-night stand at Red Rocks, the stunning outdoor amphitheater outside Denver. Jimmy was living in Colorado, so he was no stranger there.

Jerene came and brought Dane and John and Stacy Kilzer with her. They had driven out in the green bean, our Dodge B 300 van. Large mountains and large times.

I remember there were tall oxygen bottles stationed around the backstage area. You could have a hit anytime you felt a need. I never really felt the need, but I took a few hits just to see if it made me feel any different. It didn't.

After the tour Jerene and I would try to find ways to promote *I'm Not Strange*, and a curious thing happened. Somehow a distributor in Europe found out about the record and ordered a hundred. He sent the $500 in U.S. funds and we sent him two boxes with 50 copies in each. The next month the same thing happened. "Damn," I said to myself, "I like European record distributors." This carried on for several months, and we paid John Fry the $500 every time.

The last tour I did with Buffett was in the early fall of 1979, and it was called the *World Tour of Florida*. Thirteen of the 15 dates were in Florida. One was in Baton Rouge, on my birthday. The Coral Reefer band was very kind to me that night.

Jimmy let me open this tour—something he rarely did for anyone—because my album was out and we could sell it at the merch booth. He let me bring my band to play my set with me. I had Jody Stephens on drums, Mike Crews on lead guitar, and Brad Webb, the mighty, mighty blues guitarist, played bass.

The last night of the tour was in Birmingham, AL. It was on a Sunday, and when I played "I'm Not Strange" Jimmy came out and sang it with me. How cool is that!

My life as a Coral Reefer came to a close .

51
LIFE IN A WHIRLWIND

We were packing 'em in at Trader Dick's in Memphis, knocking 'em out in Mobile and making pretty good money doing it. John Hampton was playing in my band by this time, and Mike Crews was on guitar. Mike Briggs was on bass, and suddenly I had a great band. About a month or so into his time with me, Briggs became Mike Brignardello. So, if any of you know one and not the other, now you know them both.

We were getting gigs at theaters opening for stars, and doing as well as we could as independents. Redbeard continually played the record on Rock 103. There were a few stations here and there giving us some help, but we were really buzzing in Memphis.

John Prine had moved to Nashville so we were hanging out a lot. He would come to Memphis or we would go to Nashville. Sometimes Jerene and I would take a little time off and spend the weekend at the Spence Manor in Nashville. We always enjoyed that so much.

We would see Guy and Susanna, visit with Mary Martin, meet other songwriters and have a great time. We were at a point where we had a little money, and we savored the fruits of our labor. I was becoming known as a songwriter. Life was good.

That December we got a call from Jon Scott, the wild Memphis radio DJ who had moved to L.A. to work for MCA Records. He was fired from that company and hired by ABC Records. His triumph at the time was Tom Petty and the Heartbreakers.

It seemed the record company couldn't figure how to get them on the radio and were about to drop them when Jon found a copy of their first record in the back of a closet. He pulled it out of there and took it home and played it 300 times in a row. Or something like that.

He went to see the band at a gig and tried to gain their favor, but by this time they didn't want anything to do with anyone from the record company. But Jon persevered. He told them to listen to a certain radio station at a certain time the next Monday and they would hear their record on the radio. According to Jon their reaction was, "Sure, we'll listen," in a decidedly unenthusiastic reply. If you want to know this story in depth you need to get a copy of Jon's book, "Tom Petty and Me." It's a really good read about Jon and one of America's greatest rock bands.

They did listen on that Monday and heard their record at the appointed time, and the rest, as they say, is history. "Breakdown" became their first hit, and Jon became their treasured friend from then on.

So imagine my surprise when we got a call from him. He wanted to know if we would fly to LA to hang out at his house and meet Tom Petty and all the Heartbreakers with no strings attached. Just a get together to meet each other kind of thing.

When we were there Jon said he loved our record and wanted to know if he could try to get us a deal. Of course, we said, absolutely.

He set up a meeting at Columbia Records in New York where we met some guys in the A&R department. I always wanted to do something with Columbia because of Bob Dylan. We were excited to be at the famous "Black Rock" building walking the same halls that Dylan and Paul Simon walked.

I picked up a little blue book from a coffee table as we waited for our meeting to begin. It was a book of all the artists who were currently on the label. I said small book, but the print was tiny, and I'll bet there were 50 names on each page. It had at least 50 pages, maybe more. Every genre imaginable was represented by those names in that book. How could this be!?

The A&R guys were nice, but they didn't have the same enthusiasm that Jon Scott had. That, along with the fact that no one could possibly know all the artists they already had didn't leave us with much enthusiasm either. So back to LA we went.

MCA Records bought ABC Records, and Tom Petty didn't like the fact that he had nothing to do with the deal so he wanted out of the contract with MCA. MCA asked what would make him happy, and he settled on getting a label of his own. Backstreet Records was born out of this.

Jon wanted to work our record and had invested money in us—all that airfare and lodging wasn't cheap—and we wanted a deal with a major label. So here it was. We could be with Backstreet Records and have Jon Scott working for our team, and that sounded good. We met Danny Bramson, who founded the label, the contracts were drawn up, and the deal was made.

We got a two-record deal. The numbers were good and we paid what we owed John Fry. We also paid Hardy and Hampton through the union this time. In addition we paid Jon Scott a fee for getting us the deal and still had money left as an advance. "Yes," I said to myself, "I like record deals!"

Ronny Blair, my brother-in-law, whose father owned a house in the Raleigh area of Memphis, was selling his home. With Ronnie's help, his brother, Bobby, made a deal with us to buy the house. It had two acres with a spring-fed pond in the back. It also had a large garage that Ronnie's dad, E.L. Blair, had built that was 40-by-30-by-16 feet that I could use as a rehearsal space. For many years to come that house would be the center of our universe. Jerene and I loved it dearly. Dane felt at home almost immediately, so we were all set.

LIFE IN A WHIRLWIND

From the time when we made the record deal to the time the album came out is a blur to me, because so much was going on all at once.

John Hampton became my go-to studio man at Ardent. We became fast friends and gigged together, recorded together, and hung out together. Joe Hardy was working all the time, so I don't believe he felt slighted when I started working with Hampton. It was something that just happened.

Jerene was doing the sound for all our shows. She was also my manager and spent all her time on the phone. I kept trying to make our new cordless phone become a cellular phone. This is way before cellular phones. I ran antenna wires from the garage to the pond to get a signal from the phone base station down there. It never really worked. At least my hookup didn't work. The result was Jerene was stuck in the house on the phone every day. No rest for the weary!

That summer Jerene and John Hampton went to LA to remix the album with Greg Ladanyi, so Ladanyi's mixes and the substitution of one song were all finished out there. Here's the story about swapping the songs.

"Making It Before We Got Married" was written after the original version of the "I'm Not Strange" album was released. When we signed with Backstreet, Danny Bramson wanted to know if I had a song to replace "If You Said Love," which we all agreed sounded too much like a Buddy Holly song. I played him this one. I wanted to hold it for the next record, but Danny and Jon Scott thought we should do it for this album. So, there it is.

Tom Corcoran came up from Florida and shot the cover pics for us. And the Backstreet Records version of *I'm Not Strange* hit the streets.

We were gigging all around, and I remember one night in Colorado Springs we were opening for Poco. After my show John Mellencamp (then going by John Cougar) came backstage to see us. He hadn't released this breakthrough "American Fool" album yet, but "Nothing Matters and What If It Did" would be out that September. I loved his records and his voice. John's a natural-born rock 'n' roll singer if there ever was one. That night he said he enjoyed my show, and I felt like we made a connection. It would be a few more years before I got to see him live, but when I did it was crazy good. All I think of when I think of him and Tom Petty in those days is what great bands they had. No wonder they both made it to the Rock 'n' Roll Hall of Fame!

We were on a tour in the Northeast and had a night off in Syracuse and went to see Rockpile, the great but short-lived band that both Dave Edmunds and Nick Lowe were in.

Nick Lowe and I were talking about him producing my next record. He seemed willing, but I wasn't ready to leave our team at that point. I've wondered many times how that would have played out, but I'm not one to look back very long. No one can tell the future and you sho can't do nothin' about the past!

5 2

SNL

We played the last night of the tour in Boston. Liz Welsh, one of the talent coordinators for *Saturday Night Live*, came to see us and evidently was impressed enough to invite us to play the show. Jerene always told me I was gonna play it one day. I thought to myself, 'Is this really happening?'

A few weeks later we were in New York. On the Thursday before *SNL* we went to the studio for camera blocking, which is the techs watching you play to get the cameras set up.

On the Friday before *SNL* we recorded the *King Biscuit Flower Hour* show. Guess who the host was for the *King Biscuit* show? Robert Kline! He's the fellow I had opened for in Austin. When he saw me he said, "Keith, how's it going my man? Glad to have you here." It sure made me feel good to know there are people like that in the world. It set me at ease, and we did a fine show.

Phil Lynott of Thin Lizzy was there and looked like a million bucks in his white jacket and black spandex pants. And I was so excited to meet Rodney Dangerfield. "Caddy Shack" was a huge hit that year, and I had been a fan since the '60s when he was a staple on the *Tonight Show with Johnny Carson*, *Merv Griffin*, and *Mike Douglas* shows, and we all knew "I Can't Get No Respect." When Robert Kline turned to Rodney and said, "Well Rodney, your movie is a blockbuster, your shows are drawing the biggest crowds of your career, and you own three clubs that are packed every night. What are you going to do next?" Rodney said, "At my age, if I take excellent care of myself, I expect to get sick and die." I still use that line and a couple more he did when I'm on stage.

The *SNL* cast on this night, December 6, 1980, was Eddie Murphy, Joe Piscopo, Denny Dillion, Gail Matthius, Ann Risley, Charlie Rocket, and Gilbert Gottfried. On Saturday the entire show ran at 9 p.m. before a studio audience. The writers and actors were still working out parts of the skits. We played our song—"B.I.G.T.I.M.E."—and Aretha Franklin, who was the headline musical act that night, played hers. The 9pm audience leaves and another audience is seated for the live show at 11:30.

If you're a fan of the show you know there's never been a musical act that hasn't received a huge ovation after their song, and we were no exception. I can't begin to tell you how cool it was to go on, do the song, and hear that crowd after the song is finished.

When we went to the after-party I learned there was an estimated 11 million people watching that night. Ellen Burstyn was the guest host and Aretha was the musical guest, so what was I, you ask? Well, at that time they were doing a trial with new musical acts who had never been on national TV, and I was it for this show. But back to the after-party.

Out of the blue Jane Buffett walked in with Ed Bradley, the *60 Minutes* TV journalist. My mind was blown all to pieces!

All the people, the crew, the actors, everyone, were so good to us and very professional in every way. *SNL* will always remain one of the highlights of my life.

53

AND THEN IT HAPPENED

I was lying in bed the next Monday evening, December 8, when Dane came into the room and told me John Lennon had been killed. Disbelief. Shock. Sadness. All the above and more. We were flying so high, and then a complete and utter crash. The wind went out of my sails so fast I couldn't catch my breath.

I became so benighted I couldn't bring myself to brag about the triumphant last few days without feeling shitty and guilty about it. The momentum we created was turned into molasses, and the morass that seemed to cover the entire world was palpable. I resigned myself to sit and go inward for the immediate future, and I think a lot of the rest of the world did, too.

A week or so later I played a sold-out show at the Orpheum Theater in Memphis and the first song I did was Lennon's "In My Life."

Rosanne Cash's *Right Or Wrong* album was released in September of 1979 and I had the title cut. Now it was 1981 and her new record, *Seven Year Ache*, came out in February with two of my tunes on it. And with it I began to get out of my funk. Life has to go on, and this record was so good it was bound to do well. I didn't get a single but the album went gold, and I felt good enough to work on my new record.

54

IT DON'T HURT TO FLIRT

I had been in the studio to try out some new songs, but I didn't feel like I had a winning combination yet and kept writing. We toured and toured, and someone was always telling me what I should do. I listened, but I just wanted to figure it out myself.

When Jerene and I had a plan, we went to LA to talk with Danny Bramson. As soon as we got to the office, Ronald Reagan was shot. Danny and I looked at each other and said, "What in the hell is going on? We've got to stop meeting like this."

The last time we were together Lennon was killed. And now this. Insanity.

We still managed to set a time frame to record, and we went about getting it done. We were staying in Studio City, and one evening we were riding the elevator up to our room when Telly Savalas got on the elevator. I told Jerene we were safe because we had Kojak with us.

We recorded *It Don't Hurt To Flirt* in 1981 and it was released in '82. I really believed it had a lot of promise. It was the first time we had used automation on one of my records, but I didn't like doing it. The technology at that point was 8-bit. So, when you moved a fader, it really didn't respond in real time. There seemed to be a lag between when Hampton would make a move and something in the mix would take place. I don't want to get too technical about such things, but suffice it to say I missed mixing the way we used to do it.

IT DON'T HURT TO FLIRT

Before, three or four of us would crowd around the board, and we each had a few faders to make moves on. It was fun, exciting, and when you screwed up you had to do it all again. If we had had today's technology, I'd be singing a different tune. But it was primitive then.

"Hangin' Around" has a great track, and I sometimes wish I had written a love song lyric for it. Hey, you never know. I still might do it.

"Don't Go Away" was one I had been going over in my head for a long time. It came together at the last minute.

I wrote "In Between Lies" with John Hampton. He had a track he was working on and played it for me. I asked if I could co-write it with him, and he agreed. It was the only single to chart, but just barely. It made it to number 3 on the Billboard's Bubbling Under the Hot 100 Chart.

"In My Hideaway" was a finger picking song that I arranged for the band. It still has some of that folkie feel to it, and I like the message it has—especially for me at the time.

"Love Shines Bright." A few years prior, Memphis firefighters were on strike when we were playing Trader Dick's and the building across the street went up in flames. Turns out, a lot of buildings burned during this time. I used that and other images to give this song a feeling that all wasn't right with the world. I think it brings some rock to the album.

"Secret Life." I worked out the bass part for this tune around 1975, but by the time we were recording it, a similar bass part was used on a Steely Dan record. Mike Brignardello refused to play the part I wrote which confused me. I should have brought in another bass player to play what I asked Mike to play, but I just didn't reach that conclusion at that time. The track is OK, but I wish it was like I originally conceived it. After all, it was me who wrote it, and if by chance Steely Dan said something about it, it would be me to answer for it. Such is recording.

"Tell Me When It's Over" is a fun song to play. It makes me wish I had a band for all my gigs!

"It Don't Hurt to Flirt" was inspired by a girl in Trader Dick's who passed by me when I was on a break. She was a fan and was very shy. I said, "It don't hurt to flirt," and the idea stayed with me.

"I Couldn't Love You Better" was my idea of a love song. Rodney Crowell always liked it, and that made me like it, so I recorded it.

"Buying A House" came about because Jerene and I found out very quickly that the powers that be don't trust music people very much with their money. We got the house and never missed a payment. I'm very proud Rosanne Cash sang the background vocals on it.

"Let's Drink, Let's Dance, Let's Rock" was me stringing three songs together. I really got into it after I got started and just couldn't stop. At the time I thought I created a masterpiece, but there's not all that much to it. Oh well. I guess it was a "disasterpiece."

The record company dropped me not long after this record came out, so my memories of it are bittersweet. After so much going on with *I'm Not Strange* I was disappointed that this one didn't do as well. But I learned fast to keep on truckin' and let things go when I need to.

In May I was invited to play the Memphis Music Fest and drew 17,000 to our show. It was a high-water mark for me, and I'm still proud of it.

55

THIS WAS THE BEGINNING OF THE END OF MY EARLY LIFE

I began to realize I had gone up the pop chart about as far as I was going to go. I just couldn't stop trying for it. That's the paradox of those situations. It's like being a young man and an old one at the same time. I was thirty-one when things started happening with the major label deal, and thirty-four when it was over. We were back to playing clubs like we did before that big ride, and I didn't like it. I set out to put myself in the best situation I could to stay in the game and get to the next level.

I bought a bus. I wanted the band to do all the tours and dates we were offered. Sometimes they paid very little. But if we could hold out and do that for a year or so I believed we would get a reputation as a band that would play whenever for whatever and build a following without the big labels.

I thought if we had a bus, even an ugly one like the one I bought, some people would be swept away by that think you must be doing well.

All that doesn't matter. All that matters is you're playing real music real good. That's it. When people find out about you, they come to see you play for themselves to hear the stuff you do. If you give your best every night, people will find you and pay you to do it. I'm an antique now, and I still believe that.

The gigs we were playing averaged about $2,500 a night. We weren't getting rich, but we kept playing because a lot of bands would love to be in that situation, and we knew it.

Jerene got along with almost everyone she dealt with, but sometimes there was someone who wouldn't pay. They thought she'd go away, but she hung in there until it was settled. She did all that and the sound, too.

I had some talented players with me in those days. Hampton would play drums and sing when he wasn't in the studio. Mike Crews sang and played lead guitar. Mike Brignardello left shortly after *Flirt* was released so David Cochran took his place on bass. Jeff Klaven was a great rock drummer, and I always enjoyed playing with him. He stayed until he got a gig in California. It's hard to remember all the players, and I know I've left a lot out. I apologize.

We asked Terry Manning if he wanted to do some projects with us, and he seemed happy we asked.

For some time we had been wanting to produce a record on Mike Crews, and this seemed like a good time to start. Mike had some really cool songs, and we cut 12. I thought they all stood up well and the record sounded really great. It's hard not to sound great with Terry Manning. From ZZ Top and Led Zeppelin to the Staple Singers and Lenny Kravitz—he always made great-sounding records.

Jerene and I went to England, Belgium, the Netherlands and France, pitching Mike's album to record companies and trying to meet distributors for our fledgling Memphis Records. But their offices are full of the same kind of people who are in the offices over here, and we didn't meet the right people. In hindsight I think we should have only talked to the indies.

56

PLAY X PLAY

In the fall of '82 we started recording an album that would become *Play x Play*. Terry Manning recorded, overdubbed, and mixed it, as well as co-produced it with Jerene and me. It was also the first time I used a drum machine in place of a drummer.

We had Dave Cochran on bass, Robert Gladney on sax, and Mike Crews played guitar on "Too Close on the First Date." Mickey Raphael played his fabulous harmonica, and Jimmy Griffin, who was in Bread, the band that ruled the airwaves throughout the '70's, sang backing vocals.

I'm not going to get into the songs on this album other than to say I was going for a more commercial sound and failed. Some of the songs were written with the radio in mind, and I can't think of a worse reason to write songs. Plastic. Phony. Contrived. Those are the adjectives that come to mind when I think of this record. Still, there are a few songs I think are quite good and stand up over time.

"Bachelor Blues," co-written with Mike Crews, I believe is a very good rocking blues even though the lyrics are filled with images that could be looked down on by members of any number of women's movements today.

"Trash" still tickles me. It's about those newspapers—if you want to call them that—that were sold in the racks in the grocery stores all around the country. If you can get past whatever I was trying to do with my vocals, and forget about the synthesizers, and just listen to the lyrics you might be able to enjoy it.

"When I Close My Eyes" is a good one in many respects. John Kilzer always loved the line "my thoughts have a mind of their own," and that was enough for me.

"Play x Play" ended up being the least accepted record I've ever done. OK. I'll say it. I'm sorry. I must have gotten lost on the way to the studio.

Except for *Austin City Limits* with Rodney Crowell in 1983, I didn't have much of anything to call a lasting contribution to the world of music that year. On that show, which was called "Rodney Crowell and Friends," I was among some of the most talented songwriters on the planet. I was playing with Guy Clark, Rodney, John Prine, Billy Joe Shaver and Billy Caswell—some of the best writers there are.

In some ways it was a wake-up call for me to get back to my roots, which was writing songs first, singing them later. Not that I started doing it right away. There were still some twists and turns to make my way through before that would happen. But it did get me thinking about what I was going through, where I was, and where I was going, and if it's something I still wanted to do.

57

FUN ROCKIN'

One thing I wanted to do was record another stripped down, raw-sounding record. I'd been playing electric guitar for a while and I knew a lot more about how to get the sounds I wanted than I did a few years earlier. I had also become more experienced and learned more about recording during those years.

I went into Ardent with John Hampton and Joe Hardy, and I told them what I was looking for.

I wanted to record a take that had energy and spirit and forget about everything else. I had some crazy ideas. Like asking Hampton to double the drums on some tracks while adding a few licks to make them really big.

I still had my 1956 Stratocaster, which was a badass guitar and the only thing I ever regret having sold. And my Tele. And my Guild Acoustic 12-twelve string. That was my arsenal. Hamp always had his Gretsch drums, and Hardy used a Steinberger bass that was perfect for this project.

I had written most of the songs while Jerene and I were on vacation in Destin, Florida, with our friends Lou and Kathy Loeb. When they all went to the beach, I stayed behind on the balcony looking out at the Gulf and hearing the music in my head, writing the lyrics in my notebook.

When we started recording, I felt like something good was happening. Hampton and Hardy were such great musicians, it made it difficult for me to not end up with something cool. *Fun Rockin'* was the result.

"Say I," like all these songs, was a simple rocker. I was really feeling it at the time, and it still comes out of the speakers like gangbusters. "If you want me say I ... love you."

Without wasting any time we went right into "Think About Love." Just fun. Just energy. Don't overthink — which, it could be said, I have always had a knack for doing — just dance, and drink, and relax!

"Hello Memphis" is a blues with a twist of Memphis barbecue and spirit, folded with bass, drums, and guitars.

"Do You Wanna Go Home, Rubin?" Our first Great Dane was named Rubin. He was a very unusual dog. He was bred to be a harlequin but came into the world almost all white with pink eyes, bless his heart. Jerene used to take an eyebrow pencil and draw a circle around one of his eyes so he looked like a very large version of PD from the Little Rascal shows.

One morning when I was particularly hung over, he came prancing into our bedroom all joyous and everything, and I became very jealous of him because he was feeling so good.

Anyway, when I was on that balcony in Destin, I was thinking about him and this song popped into my head. He is woven into the song, but it's not about him.

"Didn't I Love To" is another piece of the rock 'n' roll pie I was baking.

"Fun Rockin'" describes the record so well you might think I wrote it to be the title cut, but I didn't. It was just a cool happenstance. The intro is real.

Hardy and Hampton were both studio dogs who lived and breathed the studio. They could play it like Johnny B. Goode played his guitar. Hardy was messing with the Fairlight — an early music computer—and was playing phrases backwards. He found if you said the word "spaceships" into it and played it backwards it still said "spaceships." It blew my mind, so much so I had to put it on my record. I don't know if anyone ever tried it, but if you do you will be as stunned as I was. The rest of the song continues the dance to a rock beat motif.

"She's My Girl" is one of the many songs I've written with Jerene in mind. While most of them delve into my love for her in a more cerebral way, this record is talking about her legs!

"You Don't Say" is a blues I wrote with my Blind Willie McTell influence showing. I'm playing my 12-string, and Lyn Jones is playing his harp. I was listening to the playback, and I wasn't getting what I was going for. So I asked Hampton to slow the tape recorder down. And there you go. That was it. I can't really sing like that—well maybe I could now, with me being this old and all—and if you try to find the key it will not be the one we recorded it in.

After the record came out I got a call from Jim Dickinson, the widely respected, legendary Memphis musician, songwriter, and producer. When Jim called it always meant something even if he just wanted to say hello and see how I was doing. But this time he called to tell me he thought "You Don't Say" was one of the coolest things he'd heard in ages. Needless to say, that's among my favorite memories.

"Tall and Lean." It's never really mattered that I'm not tall and sometimes I haven't been lean either. I try to stay lean, but I can't do anything about my height. Still, in this song, I sing about being Tall and Lean. I even mentioned my Japanese movie experience.

"Glowing in the Dark" is a reference to imbibing on the excessive side. I heard the record on the radio in Hot Springs one afternoon and went straight for a beer.

Fun Rockin' was the fastest-selling record I had recorded up to that point. We were sold out in a few weeks, and because we didn't get a label deal from it we didn't pursue it any further than the one pressing.

Of course we would have felt differently about it today. It was also the last record I did that was on vinyl. Vinyl was on its way out, and cassettes were the biggest sellers. CDs were still in their infancy.

This release also marked the closing of Memphis Records.

I began feeling like I was spinning my wheels doing the same gigs at the same places night after night. Then the day came.

We were playing in Little Rock one weekend at a place called SOB's, and some switch in my mind flipped.

I went to Main Street in downtown Little Rock on Saturday to Mr. Cool's, a place that had clothes like some of the black artists would wear, and I found a suit I liked and bought it. I wore it that night, and Jerene and the band were wondering why I had it on. Somewhere in the night I announced from the stage I was closing this chapter of my life and going on to something else. I don't believe anyone thought much about it, but I was serious.

58

PUBLISHING, PRODUCING, AND WRITING

I'd had my publishing company since 1972, and at first I didn't really know what to do with it. Michael Brovsky told me I should have it, and so there it was. When I moved to Memphis and opened my little storefront I began to try to get a few outside songs, and I managed to get "Some Day I'll Get Out of These Bars" recorded. That was the first time I had a song I didn't write by myself in my own publishing company.

I got a song called "Fallin' Out," written by Denny Lile, a friend of Ray Barrickman, but it took 10 years to get it cut. More about that song later on.

I wrote to the Library of Congress and requested everything to do with copyrighting songs and publishing. Within a few weeks I received a package about six inches thick filled with all the government brochures, articles, and pamphlets I believe you could get that dealt with music publishing. When I read all of it I discovered it wasn't in Latin nor was it from Mars, and I could understand what all this stuff was saying.

Sometimes it seems like lawyers put shit in contracts because they know it's so convoluted and repetitive no one will understand it. That way they get paid to tell you what it says. For instance, you read a paragraph that starts with something like "the record shall contain one song, hereinafter called the song, embossed on a contrivance hereinafter called a mechanical reproductive device now known as a 45 (forty-five) RPM record, but not limited to 45 (forty-five) RPM, or any device now known or devised in the future." And it keeps going for what seems forever. The lawyer will say "This is referring to how the record will be reproduced." And most artists will say, "Ah, OK. Sure." By the time you get to the part that says you will never be fully able to make money doing this stuff you're ready to say, "Great! whatever." After all, you're getting to make a record!

When I read the Library of Congress stuff I learned I could be a publisher. Of course, there's a lot about being a publisher you don't get from the Library of Congress or anywhere else for that matter.

You need to have that intuitive thing you either have or you don't—that musical thing that lets you recognize a great song from a good one. Not after it's on the radio or when it's at a record store, but when you hear it played by someone who can barely sing or play. Or someone who plays and sings famously well. And conversely, you have to know when that person who can play and sing better than all get out is playing and singing a song that just doesn't have it. Let's face it. If you could do it every time you'd be rich as Croesus. Nobody can do it every time, but some people are so good at it you think they can.

59

LOVE, LOVE, LOVE

Jerene and I drove to Nashville to fly to Key West from there. I was booked to play a month long gig at Pepe's. On the way home we had plans to see John Prine and spend the night at his house.

Of course, the plane was delayed, and we were late getting to Nashville, and by the time we made to John's it was midnight.

Jerene had said goodnight, and John and I were still talking, laughing about whatever it was, when it dawned on us we had never written together. We had known each other for 15 years, and I guess we were having such a good time it never crossed our minds to give it a try.

I played him a verse and chorus from a song I started working on in '76 and asked if he wanted to write it with me. Within about 10 minutes he had written the two verses that had eluded me for 10 years. So came the birth of "Love, Love, Love." He recorded it on his *German Afternoons* album later that year.

60

JOHN KILZER

I met John Kilzer when he was playing basketball at Memphis State—now the University of Memphis—when Phillip Rauls took me to a game in 1974. The entire conversation was "good to meet you," and that was it. After John finished college, we got to know each other well. He and his girlfriend Stacy Park went with Jerene and Dane to meet me in Denver when I was playing Red Rocks with Buffett. But it wasn't until one night when Jerene and I went by his apartment across the street from Overton Park that I heard one of his songs.

We were about to leave when Stacy said "John, why don't you play Keith one of your songs?" I didn't even know John was writing. I knew his major was English literature, but I didn't equate that to him writing songs.

John played a song called "Clever Undercover," and I was slain. I asked if he had any more and he said yes. "Why don't we get together and you play me more?" I asked, so we made some time to do it.

When I hear songs that ring that bell in my mind, it tells me this writer has a great knack for doing it. He wasn't playing country or folk. To me, it sounded like intelligent, well crafted, rock music. I thought I could help him get a record deal that could possibly lead to a career.

In short, I was excited. He was tall, good looking, had a great voice, and his songs were absolutely solid.

I drew up the first contract I had ever written from scratch, we signed the agreement, and I went to work. That was in the middle of

1986. I met with John Fry and worked out a deal with him, again on "spec," meaning Fry would defer the studio costs until we landed a deal with a major label.

We went in to Ardent and recorded every song Kilzer had written to that point on a cassette. This way the recordings would have a professional sound, but we didn't incur the high price of 2-inch tape.

Fry heard the results, as did Hampton, and we made arrangements to book the studio and musicians. We recorded four songs. "Green, Yellow and Red" was the first one. I can't remember the others, but every one turned out very good.

Hampton engineered and played drums. Dave Smith played bass, and Jack Holder played guitar. This was Kilzer's first time in a studio, and he was amazed by the way he sounded. I was thrilled and Hampton was too. We all knew we were on to something.

The next thing I did was call Rodney to ask if there was any room on Rosanne's next record, and there was. Rodney and Rose recorded two of John's songs. One, "Green, Yellow and Red," made the record and was Kilzer's first cut. The other one, "707," was used for special projects. The album earned Rosanne a gold record, and John was very proud to be a part of it.

I went to New York to shop Kilzer for an album deal, and on two different occasions I heard "Tennessee Flat Top Box" on the radio when I was in a cab. And both drivers were from foreign countries. How about that.

I met with Karin Berg at Warner Bros Records, and she was interested and wanted her counterpart in LA, Roberta Petersen, to come on board. I was excited and left New York that week thinking something good was on the horizon.

In Nashville, I met with music attorney Jim Zumwalt, and he was very interested in working with Kilzer.

Things fell into place so perfectly it seemed unreal.

A VERY SHORT TIME

Jody Stevens was working for Ardent shopping acts that Ardent had a vested interest in. When he went to LA and played Kilzer's tapes for Geffen Records they became interested. Zumwalt negotiated the deal, and by the fall of '87 we were in the studio recording what would become *Memory in the Making*, Kilzer's debut album. It took 13 months from signing the publishing agreement to signing a record deal.

By the end of the sessions, I thought Hampton had done such an excellent job engineering I asked Zumwalt if it would be OK if I listed him as a producer along with me. He worked it out, so it became Hampton's first producer credit. It was also my first major label production credit. We were all thinking this would be the record that paves the way for Kilzer's career.

"Red Blue Jeans" was the first single and video—videos were a huge thing at the time—and it went Top 10 on Billboard's Top Rock Tracks.

"Memory in the Making" became the song he was most appreciated for and a variety of radio stations played it. It's such a great song and loved by a lot of influential music business people. Hampton often said he got almost all the production work he did later because of it.

I got a little production work from it as well. I produced four songs for B.J. Thomas that included "Memory" when he was with Warner Bros. But my main thrust was publishing. Well, it was publishing and writing. Okay, it was publishing, writing and producing. But publishing was big in there.

61

HIPBONE

After Kilzer's record was released, John Hampton, Jack Holder and I formed a band called Hipbone. Those two guys were tremendous musicians, and I was a fairly good bass player. I guess you could say I played bass as a hobby—especially compared to John and Jack.

We played for fun, and fun was had by all. We played mostly cover songs, and the bar bill was usually more than we made. Our wives would come and have as much fun as we did, if not more fun. As people say about such times, those were the days.

Our first gig was at a place in east Memphis called the Cruel Shoe. I was nervous because this was my first time playing bass in front of strangers. Hampton and Holder were the pros from Dover.

We went on stage, and before we played the first song Duck Dunn walked in. Crap! Here I was, already nervous as a cat, and one of the best bass players of all time just sat down at the bar. Jack and John didn't care. They could hang with Duck or anyone else. If I had been playing guitar, I wouldn't have thought anything about it either. But I was on bass.

It went like this; John counted the song off, and every note I played sounded worse than the one I played before.

Finally, Duck left, I settled down, and we had a rather good first gig after he was gone. But what a way to start my professional bass playing life!

A VERY SHORT TIME

People often ask if there is anything I would have done differently, and my stock answer is no, since I can't do anything about it anyway. Why bother even pondering it? But as I write this I'm thinking about Hipbone. Because there was so much talent that went untapped I can't help but wish we had gone into the studio and recorded some things we played in our sets. Hampton and Holder made me reach to the top of my bass playing ability, and I got really good at it in the context of our band. If we'd gone into the studio I bet we would have begun to write, and then the sky would have literally been the limit. Oh well. I'll shut up about it.

62

PITCHING AND WRITING

I'd go to Nashville for a week at least four times a year. This helped me maintain visibility, and I was able to get meetings with many of the major country producers and record companies. I owe a big thanks to BMI for helping me. Jody Williams introduced me to a lot of folks in Nashville who always took the time to hear a few songs.

I got a few covers. Stephony Smith wrote jingles at an ad agency in Memphis, and I made a deal with her on a song called "Cowboy Man." I pitched it many times, but no one wanted it.

One day I was in Bob Montgomery's office at Columbia. Bob was from Lubbock, Texas, and was in Buddy Holly's inner circle. I'm always swept away a bit when I meet people who are so important to music, particularly those in early rock 'n' roll. I thought I had it together when I handed him a cassette with a song I was crazy about. He listened to the traditional 20 seconds and stopped the tape. He tossed—or pitched if you prefer—the tape back to me and said, "El Paso."

I thought to myself, 'does he want a song like "El Paso"? Hmm.' I looked over the tapes in my case and picked out "Cowboy Man," and handed it to him. He played it, and it actually made it all the way through. When the song ended, I could see him reaching to get the tape out of the deck, and just before he did another Stephony Smith song began to play. It was called "Thinking About You Again."

It's a lovely ballad, had a great feeling demo and Bob let it play all the way through. He looked at me and said, "I'm producing Shelby Lynne, and we've finished the record, but I'm gonna scratch one song and put this one in its place."

So there you go. Sometimes you just have to get out of the song's way. If this song wasn't Stephony's first cut, I bet it's one of them. She's gone on to write some of Nashville's best in my opinion.

In '76 I pitched "Falling Out," by Denny Lile, to Mary Lou Hyatt, my old girlfriend from Texas. Mary Lou had been working for Waylon Jennings for years and kept his office in very good working order.

About every two years she'd call and tell me Waylon really liked the song, but he had lost the tape and needed another copy. I'd send a fresh one right away.

This went on until 1986, when I got the news that he had recorded it, and it became a single. Eureka!

It went to number 8, and Denny and I were so glad it did! It just shows you persistence is a good thing to have in your arsenal.

I still thank Mary Lou, and I thanked Waylon before he passed away.

63

PETER ASHER

Kilzer needed to get a manager, and the first person he asked was me. I told him I didn't think I could do it. He needed a manager who had an office in a company town, who had other clients who are successful so he would have more possibilities than I could provide. In hindsight, I should have taken him up on it. But at that time I was trying to help him be successful, and I wanted someone who could really help him reach his audience.

It finally came down to Peter Asher and Al Bunetta. Peter Asher had James Taylor and Linda Ronstadt. Al had John Prine. He was also Steve Goodman's manager until Steve passed away. In the end John picked Peter Asher, which I believed was an excellent choice. Actually, I believed either one was fabulous.

Kilzer started touring and had a truly great band with Harry Peel on drums, Jack Holder on guitars, Dave Smith on bass, and Freddie Kirksey on keys. That's a lot of horsepower right there, and those were some high-octane songs.

I was in Nashville one night when they played the Exit In, and I was blown away by the performance.

After the show I went backstage to say hello and gush over the show, but I felt the strangest vibe. Everyone was nice enough, but I have always been able to tell when I'm not wanted.

When I left I still felt excited about the next record, because they played arrangements that had the songs sounding most excellent.

I called Hampton and told him this would be the breakthrough. The first album had made so many inroads that every door was wide open, so if we nailed it—and I thought I'd heard the songs that night that would do the trick—Kilzer would have some hits.

In short order I heard that Kilzer wasn't happy with our publishing arrangement and had decided to get another producer, too. I got one of those, "will you hold for Peter Asher?" calls. "Yes," I said. We talked for a bit. I asked him if Hampton and I couldn't do the whole album couldn't we at least do four songs? No was the answer. The result of all this was it ended my relationship with Kilzer, and it ended the roll we were on.

Kilzer's second record came out and sat there. We did get a placement in one episode of Beverly Hills, 90210. I'm not aware of any radio play like we got on the first record. It was so—all this is my opinion, which is admittedly prejudiced—stupid and so easily fixed that I still hate to remember it. But that's the way it went.

64

TERRY MANNING, PUBLISHER

I wanted to have a better chance at pitching tunes, and Jim Zumwalt told me Terry Manning was looking to buy a catalog that had a variety of songs he could use for some of the artists he was producing. Of course, I knew Terry well and knew his work ethic, so I said I was interested in selling my catalog for the same reason Terry wanted to buy one. Zumwalt laid out favorable terms for both of us, and the deal was made.

The songs in that catalog included 60 songs I wrote and/or published, were recorded and released, and generating income. It included my Buffett songs, Rosanne songs, and songs that were on my albums.

Just a year or so into that deal Terry and his wife divorced, so he sold his studio in Memphis and moved to the Bahamas. As a result he was no longer in a situation where he was working with artists like he did when he owned his studio. The opportunities to use these songs were more limited now. But that's a chance I took, and still I believe it worked in everyone's favor—all things considered.

65
BUFFETT'S LITTLE MARTIN

In July of '89 Bob Kelly hired me to play a festival on Mud Island in Memphis headlined by Buffett. I thought this would be a cool time to give Jimmy's little Martin back to him. He had lent it to me as we were leaving the Euphoria ll back in '79 after we recorded the *Volcano* album. He wouldn't be expecting it, and I knew it would surprise him.

He was in high spirits when we got together that afternoon, and we had a good time catching up, telling jokes, and just hanging out.

I wish I had a picture of his smile when I handed the Martin to him. It was priceless. He actually hugged it. It was one of those times that can only be fully appreciated by the people involved.

I loved that guitar and hated to say goodbye to it, but I would have hated myself if I didn't give it back.

What do you give a person who has everything? Something special. In this case I didn't give him anything, I just returned something he loved. It was a special moment.

66

YOU GOT GOLD

One late summer evening I got a call from John Prine. He told me he had an idea and wanted to come to Memphis to write with me. Over the phone I was cool, calm, and collected, saying, "Oh, yes, my man, that's great," but in my mind—yes, you got it—I was jumping up and down yelling "I'm gonna write another song with John!"

He got to our house that night and played the part he had. "You got gold, gold inside of you" and I said to myself, "How lucky can one guy be?"

I said we should put it to rest and get up in the morning and work on it when we're fresh. He agreed so that's what we did.

The next day we got up, had a bite to eat and then went to my "shop," as I called it, and went to work. He didn't have a verse, so I started singing what would become our melody. I don't know what words I may have thrown out, but he came up with, "Is there ever enough space between us to keep us both honest and true?" I'm thinking, 'Shit man, this guy's on fire!' I may have said, "Why is it so hard," but before I could really solidify anything, he had "Why is it so hard to sit in the yard and stare at the sky so blue?" All the first-verse lyrics are essentially his doing.

There was a little lull when we started the second verse, and then I got, "Life is a blessing it's a delicatessen," and John came up with, "of all the little favors you do." I'd toss out an idea, and he'd take it all the way home.

Then the killer line. We had the verses and choruses and we were singing them when we got to the last line of the chorus and John sang, "And I got some gold inside me, too." I looked at him, and he knew what I was going to say. We both knew this one was special, and we nailed it.

Well, he nailed it, and I helped. I've always been satisfied thinking, 'If it wasn't the two of us that day that song would not have materialized.' But to me, John was on fire, and I'm glad he was. We were finished within an hour and had this most wonderful song.

"We should go out tonight and celebrate," I said just minutes after we were done. "Yeah, let's do it," John replied.

We ate at a restaurant that overlooked the mighty Mississippi. We had drinks with our meal, and we saw the stars on the water as the boats passed by.

We left there for Midtown Memphis to hear a band that was akin to The Quintet of the Hot Club of France and was fronted by Peter Hyrka. The bass player's last name was Papajohn, and he played the upright bass so well I still wish I could play with him to this day. It was a fine night.

John's rental car was in a parking lot across the street behind the buildings. I suggested getting a nightcap at a popular bar that was right on the way to the car. I think John was ready to leave but he said OK just to appease me. We drank our drinks then made for the car.

The parking lot was so well lit it almost seemed like daylight. John thought he turned on the lights because all the dash lights were shining like a new dime. The traffic was still slow because the area was a busy entertainment district, so we moved along with it at a snail's pace. I asked if he would stop so I could grab some cigarettes. That's when the blue lights came on behind us, and John stopped the car.

It was two female officers, and after all the rigmarole we were arrested and taken downtown to the Shelby County jail. It was 2:30 in the morning by the time we got there, and they asked me if I wanted to make a call. I asked them how long I had to stay since I was charged with public drunk. John got the DUI. They said I had to serve five hours, so I declined the call, thinking I would be released at 7:30. We both were fingerprinted, photographed and sent to a cell with a few other guys.

I remember as soon as we thought we had the situation figured out we would be moved to another cell. The third cell we were sent to was about 8 feet wide and 12 feet long with a lonely commode in one corner. I counted 22 of us in this cell, pretty much shoulder to shoulder. Guys were talking randomly to whoever was standing next to them.

John was across from me when I asked if I could have a smoke. It happened just when there was a lull in the conversations, and the ceramic tile walls made every word much louder than I said it. So everyone heard what I said. John looked at me with his all-knowing eyes like I was the dumbest person who ever had drawn a breath. He slowly took the pack out of his shirt pocket and opened the flip-top box. I could see he was down to about eight or nine Marlboros, and he tried to not let anyone see the exact total. When he gave me one, he couldn't really get out of giving one to a few of the other guys who immediately asked for one. So that brought it down to very few left in the pack.

John was the kind of guy who would give you the shirt off his back if he had it to give, but I felt about as low as an alligator's belly about the predicament I put him in.

The jailer came around and moved us again.

This cell seemed like one you would see in a movie. It had room for two people, and the other guy in my cell wasn't John. This guy was nice enough, I guess. He was in for a domestic disturbance or something like that. A few more hours went by when I was moved yet again.

A VERY SHORT TIME

By this time all the residual alcohol in me had gone wherever dead alcohol molecules go. I suppose it's to make room for the hangover army to march into my brain and make me uncomfortable for as long as possible. As a result I was hoping one of the jailers would let me out.

Gone were the offhand jokes and comments that were so cute when I first arrived. This reality was going from stark to bleak in a hurry. A jailer came by, and I got his attention long enough to show him my wristband clearly showing I was merely a public drunk and not a drunk driver. He smiled politely and walked off, never to be seen again.

We were all given a sandwich in a plastic bag.

Mine had something that vaguely resembled something like tuna spread or something from Mars between two slices of white bread. I took it out of the bag, peeled the slices apart, smelled the contents, then quietly placed it back in the bag and into my jacket pocket. I kept it so I could show it to someone on the outside, because I knew no one would believe me without some evidence.

Just when it seemed like this night would never end, I was taken to the checkout part of the facility and my stuff was returned, along with my walking papers. I found a phone booth and called Jerene.

Let's just say she wasn't in the best of moods. I held the phone as far away from my ear as my arm would allow and listened as she explained what had taken place.

John had called her an hour or two before and told her what had happened. It goes something like this: The people at the jail had figured out who John was, and he was taken to get fingerprinted and photographed several times because they all wanted to spend a little time with him. The last time he was taken to get photographed, the jailer left him in the room alone with a phone right there on the desk, so he called Jerene. She didn't pick up on the first ring. Or the second or fifth or 10th. When she finally did pick up, she lit in to him with an uncommonly loud barrage of adjectives and verbs.

"Jerene," he said, as soon as he could get in a word. "It's not Keith, it's John. We haven't been out partying or anything, we're in jail."

He tells her our story, and she called Irvin Salky, an attorney friend of ours, who set the wheels in motion to get us released. I was in there for 15 hours and John for 20.

The trial was held in a courtroom in the same building as the jail. I was there to testify that John was not drunk. My part went kinda like this: I told the judge that I was the one who was drunk that night and John was in full control of his faculties. I said I've known him for years and have never seen him be what I considered drunk, or out of control, and he certainly wasn't that night. The judge asked me if John had been drinking that night. I said yes. The judge said the arresting officers said he was over the limit. I said "I guess it all depends on your yardstick of drunknisity." Everyone in the courtroom laughed. Out loud. Yes, the judge, too.

John had to go to jail for a weekend with 20 hours being dismissed for time served. I still consider it my fault. But John never said one disparaging word to me about it, and we've had many a good laugh about the whole ordeal since then.

67

CO-WRITING

I would co-write every time I went to pitch songs in Nashville. Of course I had some experience co-writing before, but it wasn't until Rodney Crowell and I got together that I saw another side of how it's done.

Rodney was working on a new Rosanne album in New York and had a few days off. He called to see if I might come up and work on a few songs. His publisher, Bo Goldsen, and I had done some deals on songs before, and he asked if I was willing to offer a percent of the publishing on the songs we work on in exchange for my expenses. That sounded fine to me, so away I went to New York.

Compared to me, Rodney has the concentration of a Harvard-educated neuroscientist.

I mostly just wrote off the top of my head, and if it didn't come soon, I just put in a filler or quit working on it altogether until I got back into it. Rodney's workflow helped me see another side of the craft that I had never explored, and I liked it. He could work on a line till the end of time if he thought the song needed it. Some of that rubbed off on me.

So, when I was back in Nashville co-writing, I had gained that experience with Rodney, and I put it to use. The people I usually wrote with were used to co-writing from doing it on a daily basis, and I could adjust to pretty much whatever style made them comfortable. After a while I had a batch of songs, and I wanted to make a record.

68

NAOMI JUDD

In 1991 I was pitching to Brent Maher and getting nowhere in a hurry. He passed on everything I thought might be appealing to the Judds, so I finally just asked what kind of song were they looking for. And believe it or not he said, Chuck Berry.

OK. New data.

I was writing with a guy in Memphis who had given me some ideas I thought I could make into a Chuck Berry kind of song. I asked him if I could run with it. I laid out what I thought was an amicable split, and he agreed. He said he wanted to get his "foot in the door," and this sounded like it a good way to do it.

Using his ideas, I got a verse and chorus of "This Country's Rockin'" together and sent it to Brent, thinking he might like to finish it. To my surprise, Naomi Judd called me a couple of weeks later saying she wanted to write on it. Believe me when I say I said yes with enthusiasm.

In a few days she sent me the last verse, and I thought it was killer. She asked me if I could come to her condo and write on another song or two. Again, I said yes.

Writing with her was very cool. At one point she said something I'll never forget, "I'm so square I can't roll out of bed."

We had an interesting time that day and tossed around some ideas, but nothing seemed to work. Which is fine. That's the way these things happen sometimes.

At Christmas that year she sent me a little prayer book called "God's Promises" with the most wonderful inscription written inside. It's one of my most favorite things.

Alas, before we could write anything else she was diagnosed with hepatitis, which brought her professional career to an end.

She was beautiful inside and out, and I'm a lucky man to have met her and worked with her, even this little bit. RIP, Naomi.

69

IT'S ABOUT TIME

For some reason I still don't understand, Ardent refused to let me book Hampton anymore. I had helped bring at least a million dollars of business to Ardent, and now they were locking me out.

OK. Readjust again. I called Gary Belz and worked out an arrangement to record an album at his studio, Kiva.

Kiva was another state-of-the-art studio in Memphis. It was much newer than Ardent and therefore it didn't have Ardent's cachet, but it more than made up for it with its equipment and the great sounding rooms. It didn't hurt that Joe Walsh was Gary's partner.

I programmed the drum parts at my house so when I got in the studio, I simply dumped them into the multi-track and then added the other instruments. I could have done better by getting an actual drummer to help me create the nuances of real playing.

Dave Cochran was on bass. Jack Holder played the guitar parts I couldn't play as well as him, along with other parts on synths and keyboards. Rick Steff played the squeeze box, and Tommy Burroughs played fiddle. Mickey Raphael played harmonica, and I played everything else. The album became *It's About Time*. I liked the title, because it had been a while since I made an album so it seemed to fit the bill.

"Train to Dixie" was written back in Key West, so it was about 20 years old by the time I used it on a record. It had been cut several times, but this was the first time it made it on one of my records. I still like it, and I believe it's a keeper.

"I Was Right About You" was an idea I'd had for a few years. When Ralph Murphy and I got together it coalesced, and in my opinion we made it into a real song. I've played it many times in my shows.

"Mi Casa Su Casa." Russell Smith was the lead singer and songwriter in the Grammy winning band, The Amazing Rhythm Aces. We went into his cubicle at MCA Music in Nashville, and all I had was the title. Russell was still hurting from a divorce and used those feelings in this song. The line "I know you loved him, and I know he hurt you so badly" sprang from his heart and I wrote it down as soon as he said it. I love co-writing like that. I believe in this song, and I always will.

"Back in the '60s" was a title I had when I went to write with Don Singleton. Don had a studio in his house, and it was a wonderful place to write. He was in the band Shiloh and had quite a few hit country singles on Columbia Records. This is the only song we've written, and I've played it many times. I don't believe Don has ever played it, but I still think it's worth it.

"Letting Go" is one I wrote with Fred Knobloch. Fred was one of the musicians who played on the demos I did for Warner Bros. back in Jackson, Mississippi. When we met in Nashville he remembered me, but I didn't remember him because I was the artist and only thinking about me, me, me.

Fred is a successful Nashville writer with many hits to his credit, and on the day we started this song he was breathing fire. He was singing lyrics off the top of his head, and it made me glad I had a recorder running. If not, a lot of these ideas would be gone. Over a few months I kept working away at it, and this is the result. "Letting go is the hardest part of goodbye."

"I Wanna Go to the Islands." Jerene and I went to Hawaii in '81 for a two-week vacation. During our stay an idea kept rolling through my mind of having words over the top of percussion like they were floating over waves. I worked on the lyrics for the next nine years, and when I recorded it I was satisfied that it was all worth it.

Tony Gottlieb, a manager friend in Nashville, called and said he heard it on the radio and had to pull his car over to listen to it and find out who it was. That's the best compliment you can get. Thank you, Tony!

"Goodbye for Real" is me trying to capture the moments that come at the end of a relationship. I didn't want to be maudlin, or flippant, but I also didn't want it to come off like "just the facts ma'am." The word "real" was my northern star, and I followed it the best I could.

"Buzzin' Fly" is a song by Tim Buckley I've been singing since the late 1960s. Nick Holmes and I would sit and listen to this song, and we'd both get lost in it. Buckley's version is so good it's transcendent, and I loved it so much I wanted it to be a part of my life.

"Your Love" is a song I wrote with Rodney in New York. I think we may have started it in Nashville, but we finished it up there. In any case I love this song. I'm so glad we stayed with it and worked on those lines until they were waterproof.

I did a single version of it with Hampton for Memphis Records, and the big commercial radio station in Memphis was all over it. It is beyond me why a major artist hasn't cut this one.

"I Love Football" is a gas to sing during football season. I wrote it with John Kilzer, and I wish I had done a better job on it. The San Diego Chargers used it a few times after the record came out.

When I finished recording I played the tapes for either John Prine or Al Bunetta. I can't remember which one heard it first, but they wanted it for Oh Boy Records. I was blown away by that and so happy they were releasing it.

They got me booked on *Mountain Stage*, the radio show out of West Virginia, and on *Nashville Now*, the daily country music show hosted by Ralph Emery.

After it was released, I noticed there's a truckload of albums with that title. If I'd known that beforehand, I might have come up with another title. I don't know.

70

TODD SNIDER

A package arrived with a handwritten note inside that had Todd Snider's name and phone number, along with a cassette with three songs on it. All three songs were good, but the one that made me laugh was the one I gravitated to. "I Can Drink Any Girl Pretty" had a classic melody and very clever words, and it was impossible to keep it out of my head. I called the number and Todd answered. "Hey man, this is Keith Sykes, and I like your songs." I knew how he was feeling on the other end because I'd felt the same way myself. We talked for a minute or two. I can't remember what we said, but it seemed like I put the phone down and almost instantly I heard a knock on the door. I opened it and this fellow said, "I'm Todd Snider."

That's similar to the story Todd tells, or one of the versions he tells, and it's correct until it gets to the part where he knocks on the door. It actually took longer for him to get to the door. In any case, his stories are always much better than mine.

Jerene's sister was working at the Hyatt Regency Hotel in east Memphis as a bartender and server. Dan Snider, Todd's dad, was staying there. He was in Memphis working for David Goodwin, a man whose family are some of our closest friends. Everything's a circle, isn't it?

Dan tells my sister-in-law his son is a musician and songwriter who's trying to get things going in Austin. She tells him about me and gives Dan my address. That's how I got the songs.

A VERY SHORT TIME

A few weeks later I got a message saying Todd was playing in Memphis at a place I'd never heard of. This place was way off the beaten path from all the other places I knew that had music on a regular basis. Lyn Jones and I were doing gigs together in those days, so I asked him if he'd like to go with me to hear this guy from Texas. Lyn knew about the place, so off we went.

Todd was on stage when we walked in, and the crowd was singing along with some of his songs. This was the first time Todd had played Memphis, and people were singing along with the songs! What in tarnation is going on around here? (That's the first time I've ever used "tarnation." And it was fun, so I might do it again).

After his set I introduced myself and we talked a while. We stayed in contact from that night on, and we became closer as time went by. After about a year I told him I'd like to work with him, and we signed a songwriter agreement.

We got into a routine where he would come to my house, go to my computer, and type in new lyrics he had written since the last time he was there. We would then record them on my cassette recorder, so I'd have a sketch for reference.

Todd is a writer with a capital "W." The stories he tells are always compelling. His love songs run the gamut from poignant to comic—sometimes in the same song. Like all the writers who can really do it, there was never a bad song. By that I mean average. There was always a depth and maturity to his songs. How do you do that, and be so prolific? Well, I don't know, but I sure wasn't going to give him any reason to slow down!

Along with his songwriting prowess, he was the best solo performer I've ever seen. Period. It's impossible to describe adequately. You just have to go and see him yourself. I can't tell you how he does it, but I can tell you he does it very well.

He'll come out with a song that's really an over-the-top "Hello!" Suddenly you're in the palm of his hand, and that's only the first song.

Around the third or fourth song he'll plant a seed of a story and then let it be. Then it's on to some familiar songs to keep you with him, then off to some new songs just to show you what he's made of. Then he tells you a story that makes you laugh until you cry. This goes on in a random but purposeful direction, so you're never far away. But he will make you wonder where it's going. And when you least expect it that seed he planted returns fully grown and flowering, and he nails you with its petals. It's just fucking great.

I was taking his songs on my trips to Nashville, but I never had any illusions about him being a country singer. He wasn't. I always thought I knew what he was, and when he became successful I believe I was proven correct. He had some fantastic country songs, and I pitched them at every meeting.

I was at Columbia Records and pitched "She Just Left Me Lounge" for Rick Trevino, and it worked. The album was Trevino's first gold record, and Todd was right there.

I can't remember if we did a development deal with Capitol Records before or after the Rick Trevino cut. In any case we did a deal with Capitol for six months, whereby the company would finance agreed upon sessions, and at the end of the period they had an option to keep Todd or not.

The first sessions didn't work. After that they wanted me to stop being involved with the project and most likely hoped I would just go away. Todd and I had a meeting, and he decided to stay with me, which was a breath of fresh air after my experience with Kilzer.

Buffett moved to Nashville around this time and opened Margaritaville Records with MCA. As soon as the six months were over with Capitol, I took Todd with me to meet Buffett in the Margaritaville offices. It had been a while since I'd seen Jimmy, and he seemed as glad to see me as I was to see him.

Todd was set to play a showcase on Beale Street in Memphis a few weeks later, and Bob Mercer, Margaritaville Records' main man, came to see him perform. Todd played with a band and did a great show that night, and Bob went away impressed. A few weeks later Todd and I went to L.A. where he opened some Buffett shows there, Portland, and Seattle. That sealed the deal.

It took me 13 months to get Kilzer's deal. Todd's deal took three years. But Todd was much younger than Kilzer when I started working with him, so maybe it all squares in the grand scheme of things.

The papers were signed, and I was set to produce the album with Tony Brown. Tony is one of my all-time favorite producers, and I was really looking forward to working with him.

But alas, it was not to be. Even though it was written in the contract that I was co-producing the record with Tony, I got a call, or letter, or whatever, saying there was another producer along with us. Hmm. Guess who didn't like that? So I quit the project. My idea of making a record didn't have three producers.

Songs for the Daily Planet came out in '94 and did very well. It set the stage for Todd's career, and Keith Sykes Music published many of those songs.

One cool thing that happened, among many, was that "Talking Seattle Grunge Rock Blues" went to No.1 on Billboard's College Radio Chart, and USA Today put it on the front page. Only Todd could do that!

71

THE BIENSTOCKS

I was talking with Max Kittle, an agent I met when we were working *The Way That I Feel* album. Max had moved to Nashville and knew Cliff Audretch, who was working for Freddy Bienstock in his Nashville office. How's that for another circle?

Cliff was interested in investing in some publishing companies, and Max told him about mine. I went to Nashville and talked with Cliff, which led to a meeting with Caroline Bienstock.

After a couple of months, we had worked out the terms for a deal. When the papers were signed, I had enough money to build a studio in the building behind our house that once was a body shop.

I got to tell you one story about Freddy Bienstock. He pitched every song Elvis Presley recorded from 1956 to 1974. OK, not every song, but most of them. He was also in a group that bought Chappell Music Publishing in 1984. Chappell has a long history going back to Beethoven. Probably further. Freddy went to the main office in London after the sale was completed and found a safe that no one had the combination to. So they hired a locksmith to open it, and inside there were two letters. One was from Charles Dickens and the other was written by Beethoven.

I was in Freddy's office the day we signed our deal, and I saw a large frame with four aged, yellowed pages written in German, I think, surrounding one typed translation in the center. Just above the typed letter was a picture of Beethoven. So I read the translation. It said, and I paraphrase: "Dear Reese,—Reese was an officer at Chappell at the time—As you may know, the city has been difficult this winter and I need to get to the country where I can enjoy my sister's children and let my health return. I've worked on several pieces and I'll be sending them soon. Is it possible to get an advance?" When I read the advance part I couldn't help but laugh.

I looked over to Freddy, who had been quietly watching me read, and with the widest grin and a twinkle in his eyes he said, "Nothing has changed."

72

THE WOODSHED

One day I heard a knock on our door. There stood a woman who told me her name was Anita Hiner. She turned out to be what I call a super fan, and we began a friendship that has continued ever since.

After we'd known each other for a few months she found out I was in the process of building a studio. She told me her husband, Tommy, was a carpenter and could build the studio for a fair price. When I met Tommy he impressed me as being a very skilled craftsman. I explained I could afford him, but I would have to be his helper.

Money was tight, but if I put in the "sweat equity" I'd have enough for him, the building materials, the recording equipment, a tech to wire everything, the heat and air, and an electric company to rewire the building. He agreed to work with me, and by the spring of '94 The Woodshed Studio was born.

The following couple of paragraphs are about the technical parts of the studio. If you don't know anything, or don't care about such things, skip this stuff.

The control room was 23 feet deep, 17 feet wide with 10.5-foot ceilings. The studio was 16-by-30-14 feet with three ISO booths and no parallel surfaces.

It had 32 ADAT tracks, and a Mackie 8 Bus console with automation. 10 Shure 57s, an AKG 414, AKG D 112, four Alesis compressors,

A VERY SHORT TIME

a Lexicon LXP 15 Reverb, and other assorted mics, outboard gear, stands and everything you need for a nice little studio.

I needed a place to record demos for the publishing company. I figured it was less expensive to spend $50,000 on a studio than it was spending $300 to $600 on every song I needed to demo. That said, I could make some money recording indy artists, or ads for radio, or whatever anyone might want to spend on recording.

In the first 18 months after the Woodshed opened I recouped everything I had put in the studio. It wasn't all at once, but it sure helped, and I was able to make demos to take to Nashville and record some songs for my own records.

It was wonderful having a studio at my fingertips. At any time of the day or night I could make as much racket as I wanted, and play the same the song for days on end without bothering another soul. It was a songwriter's paradise. Maybe that's what I should have called it. Songwriter's Paradise. Why didn't I think of that?

73
ROBILIO

Gigging at this time was not my main source of income, but when something nice came along, or something I could have fun doing around town, I would. There was a place near us called Hastings Place where we went to eat occasionally, and over time it became our "Cheers." Everybody knew our name!

By the 1990s I started playing there regularly as a solo act. It was there I met people who weren't musicians, or in the music business, but they became some of our best friends. The cornerstone of these folks was Michael Robilio.

Robo, as we all called him, never met a stranger, never missed a party, and would work from sunup to sundown, and then work until past midnight. In any conversation he would always mention at least one cousin. If you talked about politics, he had a cousin or two who did that. If you talked restaurants, he had some cousins who did that. No matter what the topic he had some cousins who did it. So, one day I finally asked him, "How many cousins do you have?" He thought for a long minute and said "2,000." That was the only time I'd ever heard about one person having that many cousins. Except once when I was talking to Teenie Hodges.

74

TEENIE

Teenie is among my favorite songwriters. He and Al Green wrote "Take Me to the River," "Love and Happiness," and "Here I Am (Call Me)."

Teenie and I were talking about Drake, the phenomenally successfully rapper, and that he was Teenie's nephew or cousin, I can't remember.

Teenie was another who would tell me about his cousins. Again, no matter the subject, he had some cousins who were into it. So I asked him how many cousins he had, and he too thought for a long moment and said—and I swear this is what he said—6,000. Six thousand cousins! That has to be a record.

75

SONGWRITERS ON BEALE

In 1993 Bob Cheevers asked me if I would play a songwriter in-the-round with him at the Bluebird Cafe in Nashville. He said Dan Penn and Spooner Odom were gonna do it with him, and I would be a good fit because of my Memphis connections. Bob is a really cool writer, and Dan and Spooner are heroes to me. I said yes.

I'd played the Bluebird since it opened in 1982, but since I didn't live in Nashville, I didn't see it transformed from a little club in the suburbs to the premier songwriter club in the world. But when I started going to Nashville to pitch and write, I saw some great shows with formidable writers, so I revered the Bluebird very much.

The in-the-round thing it's famous for was largely the idea of Fred Knobloch, the Jackson, Mississippi, guitar player who moved to Nashville to be where the action is. He and his friends Thom Schuyler and Don Schlitz would play the Bluebird in the center of the room rather than the stage, and people enjoyed it. Voila, in-the-round with songwriters was born.

Don Schlitz is among the most successful writers in Nashville. He could have done that with "The Gambler" alone, but his credits include so many great country standards he really does stand out in a city of greats. Schuyler wrote "The Boys on 16th Avenue." Knobloch wrote "A Lover Is Forever" with Steve Goodman.

Amy Kurland, the Bluebird's owner, started booking more writers, and the rest is Nashville music history.

After I did the show with Bob, Dan, and Spooner that night, I couldn't get to sleep. I just stayed up, completely inspired, with an energy running through me I'd never felt. Hearing those writers play their songs reverberated in my head and kept me thinking of how it affected the people listening. There was not a sound to be heard except the songwriter—and the bottom of the soul of the song.

I wanted to bring professional songwriters to Memphis. Beale Street was breathing life into downtown Memphis, and the clubs were buzzing. Joyce Cobb, the Memphis institution who has been singing in Memphis since the '70s, has a well-deserved status as one of the top jazz singers of her era. She was among the first musicians to open a club there since the redevelopment of Beale Street began in the 1980s.

I asked Joyce if she might be interested in having a songwriter night on the last Thursday of the month from February through October. That would be nine times a year Memphis would have the chance to be part of the listening room experience with—in my opinion—world-class writers singing their hits. Joyce agreed, and so it began.

The first night was the same four of us who were at the Bluebird—Bob, Dan, Spooner and me. Joyce's club is quite a bit bigger than the Bluebird, and the Memphis crowd is decidedly not a listening audience when it comes to clubs. Sometimes it seems they think the louder they talk the better the music gets. Or something like that. So when the show started I tried to get everyone's attention and spell out that on this night, Joyce Cobb's is a listening room. And it worked for, I don't know, maybe 20 seconds. I can still see the resentment on the faces of the people I was trying to convince to shut up and listen.

Were we not charging a high enough cover? What was it I said that didn't relate? It did stay mostly quiet that night, but for a few years I had to do the listening room speech before every show. It did get to the point that the fans were doing the shushing when some patrons would talk too loud. And so there you have it. Memphis can listen after all.

For 10 years I hosted songwriter nights on Beale Street. The first two years were at Joyce Cobb's. The next three or four were at Blues City Cafe. After that situation went away, I didn't really know what I would do, but Jon Hornyak, the Executive Director of the Memphis Chapter of NARAS, introduced me to Fran Scott, who owned the Black Diamond. I put a show together that went so well I wanted to stay there till the end of time. It was the closest to the Bluebird in size, and it had the feel of a real old-time Beale Street café—or at least what I think an old-time Beale Street cafe would be like.

Then one February a few years later I was told the Black Diamond was rearranging the layout of the bar. The gift shop was gonna be the cafe, and the cafe was gonna be the gift shop. So our time at the Black Diamond came to a close.

I ended my run on Beale Street without actually being on Beale Street. The Gibson Guitar Company had a fantastic guitar factory, museum, and great restaurant and bar just around the corner, so I did songwriter nights there. By 2003 things had changed, and doing the kind of shows I wanted to do did not compute with the new reality. It would take famous songwriters to do the kind of shows the club wanted. I liked the songs being famous and the writers being mostly anonymous. I know there is an audience for that, and I still love doing songwriter shows.

I have scores of "favorite" writers, and many of them came to Memphis to do my show. Here's a story or two.

One of my favorite writers was Wayne Carson. Wayne did a lot of shows with me in Memphis and later in Dallas and other places. Every time he came to Memphis he would complain about something to do with the food, the room at the Peabody, the drinks, the sound system, just everything. I've got to tell you it would get right inside me.

Once in a while a writer would ask if something could be rearranged. Of course I'd try everything possible to accommodate them, but Wayne was something else. He made me feel like everything was wrong!

But when the show began and he was singing "The Letter" or "You Were Always on My Mind" or any of his hits, he settled down. You can imagine the applause he would get after singing these gems. It was deafening.

After the show he would turn to me and say, "Man that was the best time." And just gush about how he enjoyed himself. Whenever I asked, he said, he would be there — anytime, any place.

When he said that, it was very much like a cloud lifted off my head. But then a year later he would be back, and it was always the same script. He didn't like anything until after the show. After the second time I caught on and got to where I kinda liked it.

He was truly one of the greats of his time, and his songs will live on.

Unlike Wayne, Billy Joe Shaver only came once to Memphis to play my songwriter night. I met Billy Joe when I played Rodney's "Austin City Limits" show. He had become good friends with Todd Snider, and it was Todd who put me in touch with him. I asked him to play, he agreed, and I was very excited.

In those days, Gary Belz would get me rooms at a special rate for my out-of-town guests at the Peabody, and of course I had Billy Joe booked there.

On play day Billy Joe called and said, "Hey Keith. I'm driving up and I'm going through Little Rock, and I've got my wife with me, and she's got her mother with her, and Eddie's got his wife with him, and they got their dog with them, and would you mind giving me the money you'd pay the Peabody so I could get another place that takes dogs? This dog don't like ducks." I'm paraphrasing here, but it's one of my favorite memories.

76

BEN – WILLIE – DARRELL

Alex Harvey had a string of hits a mile long. I guess the biggest one was "Delta Dawn." We had met over the years, but I can't remember where or when. I do know in the years I was doing the shows on Beale, Alex and I became close.

He called me and asked if I would like to go to Austin to play the Ben-Willie-Darrell Charity Golf Tournament. It sounded good to me. I knew Darrell Royal and Willie Nelson, but I didn't know who Ben was. Turns out he's Ben Crenshaw, and he'd just won the 1995 Masters tournament. No, I still don't know him but, damn, sometimes I feel like Forrest Gump meeting people like him simply because I write songs.

On the way from the airport to the event, Mickey Mantle got in the same cab as I was in. And that's the kind of thing that went on all weekend.

Seeing Darrell and Edith Royal again was so good. Edith told me Darrell had shot 70 on his 70th birthday.

The tournament was at Willie's golf course, and so many people were there. It was amazing. We played a song swap that night and the writers—I think there were six of us, I can't remember everyone's name—were Willie, Kris, Alex, me, and two up-and-coming writer/stars who sounded like a million bucks. We each did a song or two. I know I played "Coast of Marseilles," but I don't have a clue as to what, if anything, I played other than it. I mean if you're trading songs with Willie and Kris …

After the songwriter show I met a man named Cliff Harris. He seemed to me to be the world's biggest fan of "Coast of Marseilles."

We were talking and I naturally asked him what he did. He said he worked at an energy company, but he was a Dallas Cowboy for 10 years, played in five Super Bowls, and won two of them. I thought to myself, 'I can shoot 120 on 18 holes.'

The golf match was the next day, and I don't remember who I was paired with, but they had conversations along these lines: One says "Yeah, we made the deal." The other guy says, "How was it?" First guy: "We cleared about $140 million." The other guy: "Yeah. That's pretty good." I'm thinking they're speaking in English, and I understand it, but my sentences usually don't have "millions" in them.

At one of the holes Mickey Mantle was signing baseballs. I shook his hand and thanked him for all the joy I got seeing him on TV and how I was always hoping to get his baseball card with every pack I bought.

Willie and his whole band put on a show that night, and I rode to it with Mark Rothbaum, Willie's manager, and Kris. We arrived, and thousands of people were all around like a regular show in a large hall. I was thinking it would be another small gathering like we did the night before. It was the most amazing thing to see all these legends from so many backgrounds.

After it was all over, I was in a van that was taking us from the hotel to the airport when Bill Curry, who was the center for the Green Bay Packers in the first Super Bowl, was sitting in the right front seat. He was talking to the driver, and others, who seemed to know each other. In the very back—I was in the middle aisle—there was an astronaut, I think it might have been Charlie Precourt with some of his family. I overheard someone asking Bill Curry about the first

Super Bowl. I asked if they gave rings for it back then, and he took the ring off his finger and tossed it to me.

Now we're traveling about 50 miles an hour in traffic, and the van is doing what vans do. Mild shifts and turns as you bounce along. In my mind, this ring is some almost holy thing and no dollar value could be placed on it. It's one of the first Super Bowl rings. One the actual center for the winning team had just taken off his finger.

It didn't matter, because time stood still as that baby was launched through mid-air, heading my way. I got into position to catch it, and at the last possible millisecond it snapped into the cups of my hands. I held it with a death grip that rivaled anything a pit bull could do.

Time seemed to begin again as I looked at the treasure I held. I wanted to look like I was really appreciating everything about it—the way age had softened its edges, and the weight of it. The fact was, I couldn't wait to give it back to Bill. I was so glad I caught it. I reached over and handed it back to him, then thanked him profusely for letting me see it.

It's times like these that make me very happy to be a songwriter.

77
CLIFF HARRIS

Cliff Harris and I stayed in touch. He told me about his charity golf tournament in Dallas and asked if I would be interested in playing it. I was intrigued. I didn't realize there were more of these events all around the country. I said yes. Cliff, and his team who helped to put it together, did a fantastic job with the details. I called Alex Harvey to get him on board. On the appointed day we all met in Dallas.

Cliff's charity benefited the Dallas Casa, which raises funds for kids needing a home. I'm being a bit over simplistic here, because I don't know all the things Dallas Casa does. But I do know it's good stuff.

The event was held at Los Colinas Country Club, and we didn't even have a PA. We went into a room that looked like it may have been an office, but there wasn't any furniture. Alex and I just stood up singing our songs like we would have at home, and Cliff and a few of his friends were in there with us. It was a joy.

From that one on, Cliff and his team made it better with each passing year. Wayne Thompson, Guy Clark, and Richard Leigh all came down. Teenie Hodges was soon to follow. When Roger Cook joined us, we knew we had found the missing link. One year Teenie even got Sir Mack Rice to come.

We did a lot of great shows over the years. Every time we had just as much fun singing in a hotel room as we did on stage.

In 2020 Cliff was elected into the Pro Football Hall of Fame. When he gave his acceptance speech he mentioned me. I told you he's the world's biggest "Coast of Marseilles" fan!

78

KELCY WARREN

Cliff Harris worked for Kelcy Warren in a business called Energy Transfer. Cliff introduced me to Kelcy in '96, and we started KSM Warren Songs and Syren Records in 1997.

Kelcy ran marathons, played golf a lot, and is a highly successful businessman. Through it all his passion is music.

When we talked he was in music mode. He would listen when I would go off about Bob Dylan or Chuck Berry. When I played a record 10 times in a row, he would sit back and watch me go.

When he talked, he always went back to Jackson Brown or some of the Texas artists, especially Jimmy LaFave.—If I may interject right here, if you've never heard "River Road" by LaFave you gotta stop what you're doing and play it right now. You can thank me later.

It was always solid, soulful music that brought Kelcy the most joy. If I brought up a rock song or some pop song he'd look at me with eyes that seemed to say, "I hear this music, but it just doesn't move me."

Kelcy put new gear in the Woodshed Studio, and I went about writing and recording demos and looking for artists who I thought could get a major deal.

79
ADVANCED MEDICATION FOR THE BLUES

I had recorded an album's worth of basic tracks using my original equipment with Greg Morrow playing drums and Rusty McFarland on bass, but I hadn't finished any songs. So I overdubbed all my parts and sang the vocals, got Earl Randle on electric piano, Greg Redding on organ, and Danny Flowers on slide guitar. Robert Hall played drums on "The Whole Nine Yards" and "Hard Enough," and Jimmy Davis and Tommy Burroughs sang background vocals on "Those Were the Days." I mixed it, and it became the *Advanced Medication for the Blues* album.

I wrote the songs after I started doing songwriter shows. As a result, I took my time, and made sure I fell in love with every line. It's strange. When I perform a song—and I mean "perform," not just "play" a song—it's easier to fully realize that song. Then all it needs is a little fine tuning. When I perform a song, I'm really paying attention, and the flaws rear their ugly head. Anything that doesn't work annoys me to no end, which motivates me to work until I finally find the right words in the right place.

Danny Flowers and I used to get together to write quite a bit. We would talk a little to get into the spirit, then once we locked in we just went for it. Once Danny came down with tickets to see Eric Clapton when Clapton was doing his blues-only tour. We were buzzing the rest of the night on the blues.

"Advanced Medication for the Blues." I got this title while I was staying in Nashville with Steven McCord for a few days. The TV was on, and an Anacin commercial caught my ear with its "advanced medication for pain" line and I liked it. Danny and I wrote the song at his house a few days later.

"I Know an Angel" was written for my granddaughter, Kelsey Fletcher, when she was a little girl. "I know an angel, she's got the darkest brown eyes. She doesn't know how to be unfaithful. She doesn't know how to tell lies." She was 3 when I wrote it. The other lines are the way I thought she might be as she got older. I was right.

I wrote "Flyin' Low" with Swain Schaefer. I started on it but couldn't get it finished, so I went to Swain's house and we got it done. I love the motif. A bar. A guy comes in and gets harassed by a local. Fight ensues. The guy leaves on his motorcycle before the law gets involved.

"The Whole Nine Yards" was a title I had when Kenny Evans came to the Woodshed one day, and we finished it in an hour.

Again, the scenes were playing out in my head: A guy and girl are the cool couple in town until he cheats and she doesn't like it. The guy's days are numbered. Hers are, too. His are in the ground, hers are in jail.

"One World." This is one I'm gonna do again someday with a little editing on the music and likewise with the words. Stay tuned.

"Give Me All Your Love." I wrote this about the song in the liner notes for the record. *When the weather is cooperating, I ride my motorcycle to the river, sit down in my chair and write whatever pops in my head. I hope you get to meet the Loch Ness monsters.*

I named the logs that float just under the surface Loch Ness monsters. Good sailors know how to manage them. Bad sailors don't get very far on the river.

"Baby Please (All the Shrimp in New Orleans)" was written with Hank DeVito and Danny Flowers at Hank's house outside Nashville. We had a lot of fun putting it together.

"Hard Enough." Jamie Hartford was just coming up when we got together and wrote this song. We had just finished the melody and got the direction going when we decided to stop and get a bite to eat. I recorded a quick version with what we had before we left, and I'm so glad I did. By the time we got back we had lost the energy, and if it hadn't been for that work tape it would have been gone forever.

"One Up, One Down." I knew I wanted a slinky, laid-back feel with a solid smack on the snare drum. Greg Morrow and Rusty McFarland were just the ticket to make to happen. I played it at Joyce Cobb's when Paul Craft was on the show, and he said over the mic that it reminded him of John Lennon. Well, if he thought so, that's a great compliment.

"Those Were the Days" was written in Nashville in about 30 minutes when my co-writer didn't show up. Sometimes when I play it, I wonder if it would have been the same if I had a co-writer. Jerry Jeff recorded it for his *Cowboy Boots and Bathing Suits* album he recorded in Belize. As always, he made it his own.

"Better Than a Husband" was inspired by old blues records when the artists would sing almost anything that had to do with sex. It's not my proudest songwriting moment, but it is what it is.

"I Want You, I Need You, I Love You" was a hit by Elvis Presley and one I like to sing, especially when I've been drinking wine. That's about the only time I sound exactly like Elvis.

"The Fireplace" is another blues I wrote with Danny Flowers. It's a gas to play with a band.

If you listen long enough after the song ends, you'll hear a song I wrote for Jerene for our second anniversary.

Having a "hidden track" was all the rage in the '90s, so I hid this one real good. I think it takes a full minute before it starts playing.

A VERY SHORT TIME

Looking back, that's about the dumbest thing I've done so far on a record. My advice: don't try this at home or anywhere near a recording studio!

The gear Kelcy Warren put in the Woodshed was a giant step up for me. I should say again, if you're not a gear head please skip this part and go to the next one.

Multi Track; 24-track Otari RADAR with 6.2 gigs of memory for 42 minutes of 24-track recording time, controlled with the R8 remote.

Speakers; KRK 7000B powered by Crest Audio 3301

Mic's; 1-Neumann M149, 2-Neumann KM84i, 2-Coles 4038 (matched pair), 2-AKG C414 EB, 1- AKG C451 E, 2-AKG C3000, 1- AKG The Tube, 1- AKG D 112, 3- Sennheiser 412 II, 1-Shure VP 88 Stereo, 10- Shure SM 57, and a few odd ones

Outboard 1-TUBE-TECH LAC 2B, 1-Drawmer 1960, 1-Amek 9098 stereo compressor, 4- DBX 160, 4-Neve 1073 mic pre/eq, 2-API 550 eq, 2-API 550A, 2-Troisi 517, 2- Troisi 518, 2-Lucas tube eq's

Reverb/FX 1-Lexicon 480L, 1- Lexicon LXP 15, 1-Eventide H3000 D/SE, 1-Alesis Q2, 1- Yamaha EMP 100,

2-Tr.'s 1-Panasonic SV 3800 DAT, 1-Tascam 122 mk 3, 1-Otari CDR 18 CD Recorder

Misc 1-Avalon U5 Direct Box.

80
AMBERGRIS CAYE

Jerry Jeff and Susan Walker built a house on Ambergris Caye in Belize, and Jerene and I were guests many times.

That area of the world is as beautiful as anywhere you can imagine. Sub-Tropical temperature—making it gorgeous all year. Locals who are personable and friendly. The Caribbean Sea, mahogany trees, and the second largest barrier reef in the world. The list goes on and on.

When it was just the four of us are some of my favorite memories from an ocean of favorite memories with Jerry Jeff and Susan.

Wake up and start laughing. At least for me. I mean everyone wakes up differently and I know that. It's just sometimes the world conspires and everything seems to be alright!

As time went by we were there as part of Jerry Jeff's birthday bash and we met a lot of his fans who became friends we treasure.

Being with the Walkers was absolutely a joy every minute we were there. I fell in love with Ambergris Caye. The deck at the end of their 300 foot dock put me in touch with a feeling that everything really can be good, even if it's just for a little while. It was like a piece of heaven that slipped to earth that I was lucky enough to catch.

from top; Christmas gift from Naomi Judd, December, 1990; Inscription from Naomi on the inside page of "God's Promises;" Songwriter Night pics; with Dave Gibson, Paul Craft, Todd Snider; with Danny Flowers, Russell Smith; with Rob Jungklas, Guy Clark. ~Anita Webb.

from top; Songwriter Nights, with Danny Flowers, Tracy Nelson; with Jim Dickinson, Ralph Murphy, Tony Arata, Fred Knobloch; with John Prine, Roger Cook, ~Anita Webb. Todd Snider signs with Margaritaville/MCA Records, 3rd from left Jerene Sykes, Steven McCord, Left, smiling Bob Mercer, center, Todd, ~Anita Webb.

from top; Songwriter Nights; with Rivers Rutherford, Paul Craft, Wayne Carson; with Steve Earle, Tim Krekel; with Tommy Burroughs, Jimmy Davis, Rodney Crowell; Billy Joe Shavers. all photos Anita Webb.

from top; with Richard Leigh, *Adv Med* party; with Kelcy Warren, *Advanced Medication for the Blues* CD release party, Memphis, 1998; with Jon Inmon and Jerry Jeff, Belize, late '90's, Jerry Jeff and Susan Walker, Belize, late '90's ~Jerene Sykes; with Kris Kristofferson, Jerry Lee Lewis, '90's ~Skipper Gerstel.

John and Fiona Prine and Keith and Jerene Sykes
Millennium New Year

from top; Poster for Hot Springs Songwriter Weekend, '05; NARAS Memphis Chapter Premier Player Awards, Premier Songwriter, '99, '00, '02; with Teenie Hodges, KS Songwriter Celebration, '08 ~Ebet Roberts; with Richard Leigh, Red River, NM, ~Finn Fredriksen; Program for KS Songwriter Celebration, '09.

from top; with Memphis Mayor AC Wharton taping video for "City of Good Abode," at the Wearhouse, Memphis, 2011; with John Prine and Jerene, Hot Springs, AR, 2012; with Phillip Rauls, House Concert, Camano Island, WA, 2012; with Guy Clark, last picture together, 2014.

from top; with Jessie Winchester, 2013; Note on Beale St party, 2016 ~Anita Webb; with David Porter, 2019; with Gordon Alexander and Jerene, '00's; with Jamaica group, 2012

from top; with Richard Leigh, Larry Joe Taylor, Doug Montgomery, John David Montgomery, Stephenville Park Show, 2017; with David Hough, sound engineer for Austin City Limits since its inception; with Bonnie Raitt and Prine, NYC, 2019; with Lucinda Williams, Kelsey Waldon, All The Best Fest, Dominican Republic, 2019; with Steve Earle, St Jude's Research Hospital, 2019.

from top; with Jeff Hanna, Jimmy Buffett, Ramblin' Jack Elliot, Rodney Crowell at Jerry Jeff Celebration in Luckenbach, 2021; with Django Walker, Mac MaAnally, JJ Celebration ~Jerene Sykes; Mr Bojangles Award; with Jeff Hanna at You Got Gold, Country Music Hall of Fame, Nashville, 2023; with Roger Cook, Loudon Wainwright at Keith Sykes Songwriter Weekend, 2021 ~Jerene Sykes; Last picture with Jimmy, 2022; Group shot with Tommy Prine center, You Got Gold, 2023.

81

MIDEM

Kelcy Warren, Krista, his girlfriend, and Jerene and I went to the world's largest music conference in Cannes, France, the coastal city on the French Riviera famous for its film festival. When I say largest I ain't just whistling Dixie.

Every morning at 9, one of us had to be at the convention center to man our booth. When I took a break, I'd walk and walk and still not see it all.

In the afternoon when the day at the booth was over, we would go for drinks at one of the hotels that were just a short walk from our room. We met people from all over the world who were there to meet people from all over the world.

After dinner, we would meet at a club where Alex Harvey had arranged for me, along with other writers, to play a few songs each.

It was a revolving door kind of a thing, and a lot of cool songs were played. One night Donovan got up and played a few songs.

You didn't have to do an original if you were a good singer, and Alex was a very good singer. He sang "My Funny Valentine" and blew that room away, as Paul Simon might say.

We would all visit over another drink or two after the singing was over. It wasn't too long before it was way past bedtime, and being back at the booth would come around way too early.

MIDEM

The last night, when we were in a hotel lobby, Daryl Hall was playing piano. Jerene and I were talking to a friend of ours who knew Daryl, so we all walked over to the piano and listened.

Hall seemed like he was into an idea and started playing loud, filling that marble-walled lobby with his music. I could tell when he hit the final chord and slowly opened his eyes with a faint smile on his face that he enjoyed wherever his muse had taken him. All I said was, "You were right down in the bottom of it." He looked up at me and said, "Yeah. I was down in the bottom of it."

The trip was a success because I met an Italian distributor, and they picked up *Advanced Medication*.

82

AMSTERDAM

After MIDEM, Jerene and I went to Amsterdam with our friend Steve Moore. Steve was an attorney at the time, and we had known him since he was a student at Ole Miss. We checked in to the American Hotel. It turned out, the only thing American about it was its name. We loved it.

Steve and I wanted to check out the coffee bars, because we wanted to try some legal weed. Enough of this inferior, illegal weed you get at home. We wanted some of the superior, legal weed they have there.

Jerene and I were arguing about something—I have no idea about what—so I went downstairs for a local beer while Steve went across the square—which was actually a circle—and came back with all this pot.

He had bud and hash and a lot of it. He said he spent $20 or the equivalent, and it filled a paper bag to the top. We were only gonna be there a few days, and it looked like he had a year's supply. More like a few years, to me. Steve ended up so high trying to smoke all that stuff before it was time to leave that I don't think he ever left his room. I'd knock lightly on his door. No answer. Knock again and speak up. "Hey Steve, you in there?" The door would open enough to see Steve's face—his eyes still opening, squinting in the light. I'd say, "We're gonna go have dinner." He'd answer, "Y'all go on without me." After a few times like that we stopped asking. Our thinking was he'd say something to us if he was interested in doing something.

AMSTERDAM

We were enchanted with Amsterdam. I went to the Van Gogh museum and walked to the house where Anne Frank hid from the Nazis. Jerene and I took a canal boat ride.

On the night before we left we went to a bar and watched the Super Bowl. It didn't start until midnight, but the place was packed. Jerene and I were pulling for the Broncos because John Elway was always knocking on the door but never sealed the deal. Until that night. He and the Broncos were finally Super Bowl champs.

The next day we headed back to Memphis.

83

NEW ORLEANS

In 1999 I went to Kelcy Warren's house in New Orleans to write during May and November. I hadn't put myself in that situation in years. Instead, I would write when the notion hit me or I when I had set up a co-write with another writer.

When I lived in New York, I wrote every day. I wouldn't always come up with a song, but my headspace was in songwriting mode all the time. It was my universe and my university. I think of the time I lived, worked, and wrote in New York as my classroom.

I didn't have the instruction nor the experience to find shortcuts to writing songs, so it was live and learn on my own.

The skills I have now were all developed over many years. When I met writers that I admired, I listened to them play live. Then I tried to squeeze out every ounce of what I heard so I could figure out what had such a large impact on me. To hear John Prine's "Sam Stone" for the first time is what I'm talking about.

After the two months I spent in New Orleans, I looked over the songs I had written and I believed my time was well spent. I don't think I would have written "Broken Homes" or even "Lavender Blue" by happenstance. My earliest songs like "A Very Short Time" were written in a flash of inspiration. And I love those songs that come to me like that. I just didn't have the experience to know how or why it happened. That's why I believe songwriting is something that is given to you at birth and you work on it over a lifetime. And giving myself the opportunity to do it well, if for only a month or two at a time, is way better than trying to write in the busy swirl of my everyday life. At least that's the way it works for me.

84

THE MILLENNIUM NEW YEAR

The millennium New Year was the most anticipated event of its time. Everyone was talking about computers and how they were going to stop the world and eat our children, among other things.

John and Fiona Prine invited Jerene and me to come to Ireland and spend the New Year with them and some of their family and friends. "Oh yes," I said to myself, "that sounds like the way to commemorate something that only comes once every thousand years."

Considering the long journey we were taking, we decided to arrive a few days early and leave a few days after so we could see and do as much as possible while we were there.

Roger and Kitty Cook, and their daughter, Sophie were there, as well as Linda and Keith Chapman from Virginia. A couple from Dublin—I'm sorry I can't remember their names—were also there. We all stayed just outside Donegal town in a four-bedroom vacation house.

Jerene and I were the first to arrive, and neither one of us had any experience lighting a coal-burning stove. It was cold, and at that time of year the days only lasted about six hours. We found as many blankets as we could and snuggled close, trying not to freeze.

THE MILLENNIUM NEW YEAR

The first morning I remember waking up, and Fiona was looking down on us wondering if we were alive. All I could say was something like, "Is it going to be this cold all the time?" She assured me things were going to be much better very soon. And after Roger and Kitty arrived they did.

Roger grew up in Bristol, England, and his family home was heated by coal. He built a fire in the coal stove in short order. As soon as it caught the house was as warm as the smile on the Mona Lisa. And no one was as happy about it as me.

Jerene and I would go exploring in our rental car. We were traveling down a county road, and everywhere we looked we saw something amazing. Sheep just walked out into the roads and sometimes just stood there looking at us about the same way as we were looking at them. At one point there was a sign that said, "Scenic Road." We looked at each other thinking, 'If this ain't the scenic road we better go take a look.' After all, these regular roads were pretty damn fine. We were never disappointed.

In the afternoons we'd stop in a pub and drink Guinness. It tasted like coffee to me and had the most wonderful "high" attached to it. The bartenders always told us stories about the area and people who came from there.

On the afternoon of the big night, we went to Donegal to a pub called "The Stable," and listened to the locals sing and play. I was in heaven.

When I had to use the john, a fellow came in and took the urinal next to mine and casually asked if I'd like to go out back and fight. I answered no. He seemed so nice about the whole thing I never felt threatened. I thought to myself, 'maybe that's how people get to know each other over here.'

We stayed until the revelers started to arrive, and it was getting crowded. We all went back to the vacation house and began our night in earnest. Jim Rooney, John's friend and producer from Nashville, and his wife, Carol, came. Philip Donnelly, John's Irish guitarist, was there, too.

John, Roger, Philip, Jim, and I started singing songs at around 6:30, and we sang until the only ones left were John and me. No one ever sang a song they wrote!

When it was close to midnight we stopped playing and got a glass to make our toast. As anyone who was celebrating that night will remember, when it struck midnight in a new time zone the TV would broadcast a variety show from the major city in that time zone. When it was midnight in Dublin, one of the biggest country stars in Ireland sang "I Just Want to Dance With You," a song John and Roger wrote that was a number 1 hit for George Strait. Roger was excited and called out from across the room, "Hey Johnny, we're dancing." John was standing not too far from me, and I saw him as he nodded slightly and that's about all. I thought to myself, 'I wonder if he is doing what I might do when I get a particularly good phone call—just acknowledging the accomplishment on the outside but on the inside he's rejoicing like Roger.' I'll never really know. That's not something you ask someone.

We were back trading songs after we drank our toasts and sang "Auld Lang Syne." I played every Sam Cooke song I could remember. John played Johnny Cash, and all manner of country songs. Roger played old pop and rock 'n' roll songs, and Philip sang some Irish folk songs and played a lot of great guitar. Rooney played folk and bluegrass songs, and we went on and on. It was more fun with each passing song.

At about 5:30 in the morning John and I were the only ones left singing. For the last hour or so we finished every song we played with "Get a little drunk and land in jail," going as low as we could on "jail."

Fiona's niece and her boyfriend were the last ones listening. As shyly as she could say it, Fiona's niece asked if her boyfriend could sing one. "Of course," we said. He sang, a cappella, an old folk song

THE MILLENNIUM NEW YEAR

in a voice that was old and young at the same time, and it was most beautiful to hear. When he finished, John and I looked at each other and without a word we sang "and you get a little drunk and land in jail. ..."

And the Millennial New Year came to a close.

We meandered from Donegal Town to Galway beginning on the second of January and saw some crazy good sites. Hugging the west coastline as much as we could, we came to a part of Ireland that looked like the surface of the moon. That was the second time I saw a place that looked that way. The first was the volcano on Montserrat.

We'd get out and walk around to soak up as much of the vibe as we could. After we had taken some pics and inhaled the scenery we would drive until we came to the next place that compelled us to stop once more.

We passed a castle on the ocean side and what we thought might be a pub on the other. Or was it vise versa.

We stopped to watch the angry waves that pounded the craggy rocks on the shore.

When we got to Galway we met up with John and Fiona for a bite to eat. Jerene handed her camera to someone who snapped us together. That pic is one of my favorite things. When I pass it I feel us together at that place and time.

We left from Shannon airport heading home, both of us marveling over the time we had.

85

KEITH SYKES, ARTIST

When we got home Todd Snider asked me to do some shows with him. I hadn't done anything like that in a while, and the idea sat really well with me.

We covered a lot of ground on those tours. I remember Chicago, Madison, and places in that area. Dallas, Oklahoma City, Austin and Gruene, Texas, along with all the others. After it was over I felt like I had just touched something I didn't know I missed. Playing live. Opening for Todd, or someone else, or on my own. With other songwriters or in a band. I just wanted to be out there again. So that's what I did.

In my mind I wanted to be an artist full time again. I figured I couldn't ever be just an artist again, but I could center it around the other things I do. I could still pitch songs in Nashville and do the secretarial work that goes on behind the scenes in music publishing, too. If someone wanted me to produce, I could do that.

Writing is the first thing I did, and it'll be the last one, too. Truth be told, it's the one thing I do best. And like everything in music, it's all subjective. One man's trash is another man's treasure. Which makes me think—have you ever heard Gary Nicholson's song by that name? It's killer.

86
DON'T COUNT US OUT

In 2001 I recorded *Don't Count Us Out*. It was the first record I made for Syren Records from start to finish. Unlike *Advanced Medication*, this record was made when Kelcy and I owned the company together, so I wanted it to be extra good. I hoped it would make a statement that our company was for real, and our aim was to be an Americana music record company.

"Country Morning Music." Thanks to Guy Clark "Country Morning Music" was finding an audience with Americana fans by way of *Heartworn Highways*, a movie made in the mid-'70s about some of the best of the new "Outlaw Country" writers making a name for themselves in Nashville. At the end of the movie Guy and Rodney are playing it, and Guy says, "Keith don't even play it anymore."

I hadn't recorded it since I did it on *1,2,3*, my second Vanguard album, about 30 years before. I never played it unless Guy was around. He made it seem like if I didn't play it, or at least make an attempt to play it, he was going to have my head.

Dave Cochran played upright bass, and Paul Buchignani played percussion on the top of my D-28 case. I played the D-28, Fred Knobloch played his acoustic, and William Lee Ellis played dobro. We sat in a circle in the Woodshed control room with a mic on each of the instruments and one on my vocal. Jeff Powell engineered, and we had it in a few takes. It set the tone perfectly for the rest of the record, and I owe that to Nancy Apple for sequencing it first.

A VERY SHORT TIME

"Everybody Wants To Feel Like You." I was still doing songwriter shows when John Prine had hip replacement surgery. His first outing to play after the surgery was with me on Beale Street at the Black Diamond.

John and Roger Cook came to Memphis together, and the club was packed to the brim. John did the show without a hitch. He had to sit on a four-inch-thick telephone book, but he sounded great. Roger was his usual "coolest man in the room," and I did the best I could. I mean, how do you follow "Sam Stone" or "Long Cool Woman in a Black Dress"? Like I say, I did the best I could.

John stayed over the next day, and we had breakfast at the Arcade. After we ate, we went to the Woodshed and recorded his vocal.

We had written the song years before at my friend Rick Moore's house in Germantown. We worked on it most of the night, and when we finished, we took the cassette to John's Corvette, put it in and turned it up. We drove around and played it for a while thinking this was a good one and would be fun to play with a band.

When John cut it for "The Missing Years" album in 1992, he had it stripped down to finger picking it solo. So, this little song has a storied past, having been a rocker and folkie. The cut we did in the Woodshed sounded much more like we wrote it. I could never thank him enough for singing it with me.

I wrote "Sally Got Jack" with the mighty Roger Cook. Roger had his first hit in 1965 with "You've Got Your Troubles, I've Got Mine," and it was a worldwide hit. He told me once that a hit like that is remarkable in a lot of ways. To have so many stars aligned in so many places with vast amounts of miles between them is a minor miracle. He said having a hit like that pays really well, too.

I was staying at the Spence Manor, and had this title. Roger came over and I said how about "Sally Got Jack," and he caught fire, and the lines and ideas were coming fast as lightning. Then as quickly as it started, we hit a snag.

I couldn't remember the names of the highways we were writing about, so I wanted to go to the store and get a map. We walked to the store, which was only a couple of minutes away, and bought one.

Back at the Spence, Roger started talking about his glasses being worn out and how he could hardly see through them. When I looked at them, they looked like the lenses were covered with Vaseline. I said why not give them a wash in the sink. He did, and when he sat back down he was marveling about how well he could see. We found the real highway numbers on the map and put it all in this song.

I used to play it as a singalong and would ask the crowd to answer me when I say, "Some (some) Time (time) living in the country is a pain on earth. But Sally got Jack and Jack got Sally and y'all know what that's worth."

"Lavender Blue" was written in New Orleans when I went to Kelcy's house on Burgundy. I went down in May and November of 1999 and got some of the best songs I'd written in a long time. This one came during the November trip. The day was very pretty. I had the French doors open overlooking the street, and everything conspired to give me this simple, beautiful little song.

I became tired of writing what I thought might sound good on the radio—always thinking about the bells and whistles that really don't matter to real songs. To me, a real song is one that sounds right on a a single guitar, or huge ensemble with every trick in the book to tickle the ears. To me, it must have that quality before anything else. It must be able to stand alone. So, when I wrote "Lavender Blue", I felt liberated.

The best I could do when recording it was ask Iris DeMent to sing it with me. When she said yes it was such a joy. She sounds exactly like she is. Both honest and true. I would never have met her if it wasn't for John introducing us. John = Cool Dude.

Sunny Sweeney recorded it on her first album as a duet with Jim Lauderdale.

A VERY SHORT TIME

"Broken Homes" is one of those songs that came to me and patiently waited for me to scribe it on the paper. The music in me just poured forth. I was on fire that day, and it felt so good. My family that I loved so much when I was a kid was with me that day, just like they were at my grandma's house when she would cook so much the table couldn't hold another dish.

We recorded it the same day we did the session for "Country Morning Music," and it went down like soft butter on a hot biscuit. Thank you, Lord, for Your many blessings.

"Talking to a Stranger." Rodney Crowell and I wrote it in 1988 at his home on the outskirts of Nashville in a room that looked just like a writing room should. I didn't even have a guitar with me, and Rodney didn't know what to think about that. I was in my "I'm a publisher" phase, and sometimes I forgot I was a songwriter first. I used one of his guitars and came up with the guitar counterpart to Rodney's Buddy Holly kind of melody. He recorded it for his *Greatest Hits* album as a duet with Mary Chapin Carpenter in '89. He came down from Nashville to record it with me at the Woodshed for this version. It's one of my favorite songs we've written.

"Chain." I met Rickey Ray Rector through Alex Harvey. When we got together, I had this title. I guess everyone's had this title at one time or another. It's a good thing titles aren't copyrightable, or we all would be in copyright jail. I think we got a good song, and I love to sing it. Teenie Hodges and Howard Grimes came out to record it with me. Howard was one of my favorite drummers, and of course Teenie was a sublime guitarist.

One quick Teenie story. The Woodshed had a nice-sized control room, and Teenie liked the couch, so we set him up right there. He handed me his guitar cord to plug in the amp and said, "Absolutely no distortion whatsoever." How's that for cutting to the chase? He was happy with the sound of his guitar, so I guess I did OK.

"Broken Down Engine." When I first moved to New York in '68 I went to visit David Bromberg. I knew very few people, and Bromberg was someone I really admired, so hanging out with him was a treat for me. One of the first records he played for me was Blind Willie McTell, and I fell in love with his voice as soon as I heard it. This song played in my mind years before I made this record. If you haven't heard of McTell, listen to his album *The Early Years 1927-1933*. It's the real deal.

"It's Just You" is another New Orleans song. I was going for a simple '50s-style country song, and here you go. Is it cheating if you get Iris DeMent to sing it with you? I knew no one would ever say it sounded bad if I did.

Tony Kamel and Emily Gimble have a great version on You Tube you can check out.

"She Loves to Ride Horses." Guy Clark opened the door when I got to his house. I walked in and said hi to Susanna and we talked for a few minutes. Then Guy headed down to his workshop and I followed right behind.

I had this title and ran it by him. He liked the idea of it, and away we went. The lines came, and we both threw some in the pot. The last few always seem a little harder to come up with because they have to be as good as the ones you already love. When we felt we had it right, Guy stepped out to pee.

I was running through the chords and singing the first verse when it hit me to use a 5 chord rather than stay on the 4 for the third line of the verse. Guy called out from the next room, "Hell yeah, man. Keep that." So we did. He recorded it in 2002 for his album, *The Dark*.

Acoustic Guitar Magazine did a great interview with him about that record. Every time they do an article like that, they pick a song from the record and print the sheet music to it in the magazine. They picked "Horses" for this one. I have a copy, and I will get it framed sometime before I leave this earth. I promise.

A VERY SHORT TIME

"She Will" came from a story that Camille Harrison, my co-writer, told me that day. It came together in my mind as she was talking, and I still love the girl in this song. "When the time comes in for her to leave her windowsill, she will." Thanks Camille, we got a good one.

"Why Do You Treat Him Like That" was my question to the talk radio DJs who trash their political foes. Larry Crane is playing some badass electric guitar parts with me.

"Sweet Emily." Kelcy Warren wrote the lyrics and was a little shy about giving them to me. But when he did I was fascinated by the story and the way he had written it. It's like a movie. I've never heard a song about someone who was sad to be in heaven because the love of his life isn't there.

Sometimes I revisit songs trying to make them better. This is one of them. Don't get me wrong, this record was just the way I liked it when we recorded it back then. It's just that I think it's better now. Plus, I haven't recorded it with a band yet, so look for that one day.

"Don't Count Us Out." Bill Lloyd and I got together when he was going through a divorce. I had this feel on the guitar, and we wanted to express the "outer feelings" you can have along with the inner ones. I had always wanted to do a "number" verse so we did, "One time in a million two people love the way we do. Three words I swear I heard said forever I'll be loving you."

Jerene and I were staying up late with the songwriters after a songwriter show on Beale listening to the mixes of this record playing in the background. Kelcy Warren and Cliff Harris were with us, too. Everyone had a good feeling about the show that night, and it was a good after party. When "Don't Count" came on and played for a bit, Jerene and I looked at each other and said at the same time, "This sounds like the title of the CD." And so it was.

Don't Count Us Out, the album, was well received and sold consistently at shows. I don't know how many people have told me it's the best record I've done. That kind of thing makes it all worth it for me.

87

I'VE NEVER SEEN ANYTHING LIKE IT

WEVL is Memphis' listener supported radio station and it's been voted Memphis' best station in polls in the *Memphis Flyer*, Memphis' alternative newspaper. In late August of each year they have a benefit show at the National Ornamental Metal Museum on the Mississippi River, and fans of the station, called members, come out and support it. The station invites some of the best artists in the area to perform, and it's one of the most treasured events in Memphis. I played it in late August and did several songs from *Don't Count* that night.

My next gig was near Redding, Pennsylvania, for my friends Pete and Jan Prydybasz, on September 8th. We got home on the 9th and were going about our lives as usual. We were getting ready to spend the next few days in Hot Springs beginning Tuesday, the 11th.

That morning, I was about to take my daily forty minute walk, and as I was leaving I opened Jerene's door. She was watching the news and said a plane had crashed into the World Trade Center. It sounded unfathomable to me. I looked at the TV, and it showed the video of the plane turning into a fireball.

On my walk, the postman had one of those cars with the steering wheel on the right side and was stopped by a mailbox as I was walking by. We looked at each other and I said, "I've never seen anything like it." He said the exact same thing to me.

When I returned, Jerene told me another plane had crashed into the second tower. I looked at the TV in disbelief. I said we better call Rusty—Rusty Mathis is our friend in Hot Springs we've known for years and have done shows for since the mid '80s—and see if the event is still on.

He explained that the people attending the show had all arrived the day before, and since there was nothing going on in the outside world, he still wanted us to come play. There was nothing we could do to help or hurt at that point, so we agreed and kept our plans.

Even though everyone was in a kind of zombie mode to one degree or another, I would like to think we offered a bit of relief from this tragedy. Every time we thought it couldn't get any worse, it did.

I played outdoors that night, and when I looked at the sky it was as beautiful as I've ever seen it. The moon and Venus were a glory to behold, and the temperature was sublime. Just before the sun went down, that reddish gold color that washes over the edge of the sky where the sun once occupied, tinted my soul with a question. How could something so beautiful happen on a day so frustratingly horrible?

A lot of us gathered in the hotel lobby that night. The hotel was small and on the edge of downtown Hot Springs and the lobby bar had a cozy atmosphere that invited a good time. And we'd have a nice time for a minute or two, then the TV that hung on one side of the bar would show the video of the planes. Then the video of the towers crumbling. It was all so surreal. And I bet if you were living that night, you had a similar experience where you were.

Most Americans went about our lives like it was a show of how we were supposed to be. Like, look at us you fucking terrorist. You did not defeat us. It probably wasn't any solace for the families of 3,000 people who will never be the same. Solace was hard to come by for them.

I'VE NEVER SEEN ANYTHING LIKE IT

Doing shows—and everything else—was so weird. Soldiers in full battle gear at the airports and things like nail clippers being confiscated by the baggage checkers seemed like we were in another world. My new CD seemed so inconsequential in the grand scheme of things I felt strange promoting it.

Then I started hearing "Only Time" by Enya on the radio. It was so soothing it took my mind off the terrible catastrophe, and I again thought that getting on with life would be the best way to cope in the new reality. It confirms that music is among the best healers we have. I can't think of anything that does it so well.

88

LJT

In 2002, John Inmon called and told me the guy he was playing for has a festival in Texas and wanted to know if I might be interested in playing it. I said yes. Jerene combined it with a gig she booked in Austin, and we made the trip.

The festival gig was on Thursday, and Austin was on Friday. When we got to the fest gig it really piqued my curiosity. Here we were in a very small Texas town, and there had to be 10,000 people at the festival. They camped all weekend and had campfires going all night after the stage shows were over. People were swapping songs and having a high old time.

After the Austin gig—which was set up by our friend Margie Lemons—I wanted to go back to the festival and check it out without having to play. I walked the grounds both day and night, marveling at how this thing was running. There were no "radio stars" on the bill, just popular Texas and Oklahoma bands, and they packed the place. The staff consisted of a few employees and a bunch of volunteers who made us feel completely welcome. We felt like we were part of the scene right off the bat. Keith Cabaniss was assigned to Jerene and me. He was so personable that we became good friends.

They asked me to come back the next year, and I drove down alone. I managed to listen to every artist that was on the bill that year. It was magical.

It was also a good trip because I met Larry Joe Taylor and got to know him a bit. The festival is called "Larry Joe Taylor's Texas Music Festival and Chili Cook-Off." And that year, 2003, it was held in Stephenville for the first time. I stayed at Larry Joe's house and met his wife Sherry and son Zack. I met more folks who were incredibly good to me and made me feel like one of the family. Maybe second cousin, but I was one of them. Over the ensuing years we've bonded over our love of music, both recorded and played live, guitars, seashores, islands, and other good life-affirming stuff.

Later that year Larry Joe asked me to play a show with him in Port Aransas, TX, at the Third Coast Theater. I didn't know what to expect, but it was cool. Inmon was there so I had someone to hang with, and it was there he told me; "After a long tour I always know when I'm getting back to Texas. The server always says, 'Be careful, the plates are very hot.'"

I didn't know then that a big a piece of my life would one day be centered around Port Aransas.

89

"ALL I KNOW"

After 9/11, a song started forming in my soul. This was 2003, and the song was still just vapors. Every few days, or even weeks, I'd find myself thinking about how I felt when the terrorist attacked.

I have to be honest here. When it first happened I wanted the president to go on TV and say, 'We are not going to retaliate with acts of war. We will fix ourselves and the damages that have been heaped upon us and come together as a nation that still believes in our Declaration of Independence and our Constitution. But if you so much as harm one hair on a citizen's head we will destroy one of your most treasured sites. If you continue to harm us we will continue to harm you a thousand fold. You, our enemies, must find the people who did this to us and kill them. You must police these cowards. Every time America is attacked, we will know who is responsible, so do not fail.'

As time went on, I became less naive and understood that nuking temples of worship would not cure our ills.

So that was my dilemma.

I took a walk down our drive on a beautiful spring afternoon with my guitar strapped over my shoulder when I turned around and looked back and there stood Daunder, Jerene's gorgeous thoroughbred stallion, standing 10 yards away, looking at me with his handsome face shining in the sun.

"ALL I KNOW"

From deep in my heart I sang "All I know, we're all in this together. All I know, we're not so far apart. We're good enough to do the things that make the whole world better. Don't you think it's time we start?" I said to myself, "If that ain't good enough for you, you should find a different profession," and walked back to the house as fast as I could and started writing.

To me the best 9/11 song will always be Alan Jackson's masterpiece, "Where Were You (When the World Stopped Turning)." It came out at the perfect time with the perfect person doing it, and may I say, with the perfect frame of mind behind it. Still, I never stopped wanting to speak my piece about 9/11 and "All I Know" says what I wanted to say. I'm very proud of how turned out.

Now get this. In the back of my mind, I've always wanted Paul McCartney to do it. Of all my songs, that one is the one I'd love to hear him sing. I know. Hell will look like a beach on St Martin before that happens, but a guy can dream, can't he?

90

KELCY

Kelcy Warren wanted to pursue other opportunities in music, and I didn't blame him for that. We still have our publishing company and the records we did on Syren Records. You never know how it will all pan out.

91

CRUISIN'

Larry Joe Taylor asked if I'd like to play on a songwriter cruise that he hosts. The cruise ship sails from Galveston in January. He explained that Jerene could come, and a high old time would be had by all. Jerene and I talked it over and decided to do it.

Neither one of us had ever been on a cruise, so we asked a few friends if they thought we'd have a good time. Susan and Jerry Jeff Walker had tried it once, and they did not enjoy it. Susan told of having her privacy invaded pretty much every day and all the time. They didn't like the food or accommodations, and by the time the ship sailed back to port they were out of their stateroom and sitting on their luggage on the baggage deck waiting for the doors to be opened. I still wanted to experience it for myself.

A week or so after Jerene and I signed on, Larry Joe asked if I thought Richard Leigh might be up for it. I said "I'll ask. If he says yes I'll give him your number."

Next thing you know it's January and Richard, and his wife at the time, Shannon, Jerene, and I, are all on a ship sailing for Mexico.

I remember standing in our cabin looking out the porthole at the giant terminal with people moving in every direction when I noticed the ship was about a foot from the dock. I called my friend Ronny Russell and said, "Man, you need to do this next year. It's great!"

The ship on that trip was small compared to ones we sailed on later. On the morning Richard and I did our show we were sailing through a storm, and the boat was rocking. We played seated and set our Bloody Marys on the floor beside us, and they slid away. But when the ship tilted the other way they slid back to us. It was like having some built-in effects. Forget Kiss. We had sliding drinks!

92

ALL I KNOW, THE ALBUM

By 2004 I had enough songs to record again. Ronny Russell is one of my best friends and he happens to own MadJack Records with Mark McKinney. They've released records on so many songwriters they should have a damn fine catalog by now.

Jerene and Ronny worked out a way for me to record what became *All I Know*, and I set about calling musicians and singers.

Zack Taylor started playing drums with his dad when he was really young. By the time he was 12 he was doing gigs with him. I'd sat in with Larry Joe's band enough to know Zack had a great groove, and he lived in the pocket. He played on most of the album. Sam Shoup, David Cochran, and Dave Smith played bass on various songs. John Inmon played most of the electric lead guitar with Eric Lewis adding some lap steel and electric leads. Kurt Ruleman played drums on "Monkey River Town Girl" and sang with us on the chorus. Ross Rice played piano and organ, and Kelley Mickwee and Jed Zimmerman sang harmonies.

I look back at these credits, and I'm amazed I've been able to collaborate with musicians and singers of this caliber all through my recording career. Thank you to all of them.

"Sailor's Prayer." By the time I finally finished this song it had taken me almost 20 years. When we cut it, it was the one song I really wanted to put in the extra effort to get it just right. And I'm glad we did. By a wide margin it got the most radio play of all the songs. SiriusXM's Outlaw Country and Buffett's Radio Margaritaville both gave it a lot of spins, and I could tell at gigs there were people who knew that song because of it. Kelley Mickwee's harmony fit me like a glove.

"Baby Took a Limo to Memphis" is a song Guy Clark wrote about the time his wife, Susanna, hired a limo to come to Memphis to write with me. According to Susanna, Guy and Townes spent a lot of time and money tossing coins after gigging. And this wasn't exactly sitting well with her. Since she and Richard Leigh just had "Come From the Heart" go to No. 1 with Kathy Mattea, she decided it would be a good idea to hire a limo to take her to Memphis. When Guy found out how much she paid for her trip he wrote this song. As usual, he nailed it. My version is mighty loose, but Guy told me liked it that way.

"Shut Up and Talk to Me," is the song Susanna and I worked on when she took the limo to Memphis. Guy wrote on it later and recorded it for his *Dublin Blues* album.

"It Don't Matter." I thought this was gonna be my first co-write with Jerry Jeff.

He and Susan had bought what I considered to be the coolest house in the French Quarter. It was on Burgundy and had a pool in the back, a great kitchen overlooking the street, and a guest room that was almost soundproof. Jerene and I went there every time they asked us. When I told Kelcy Warren about it, he bought an elegant house just across the street, and we stayed there after that.

Jerry Jeff was enchanted with New Orleans and relished talking about it. When he and guitarist John Inmon were talking, Inmon said he enjoyed being there because the people "seemed like they just ate or they're fixing to." This rang Jerry Jeff's musical bell, and he called me to see if I'd like to write it with him.

I was overjoyed by the prospect. I'd already been talking with Kelcy about the possibility of writing at his house, so it all fell into place.

I went down in May and November of '99 and wrote some of the best songs I had written in years. This was one of the May songs.

I found out that writing with Jerry Jeff, at least for me, was like herding cats. He would come up with these incredible lines, and before I could get them on paper he was off to new lines that were as good as the ones he had just came up with. And then he'd go off on an entirely new subject. It made me wish I knew shorthand.

We got the basics down the first time we worked on it, and I think we traded ideas over the next few weeks until it was set.

Not long after I thought it was finished, Jerry Jeff called to tell me he didn't think it was right that we didn't include Inmon and we should make him co-writer. We should have, and we did.

I love his recording of it. It came out in 2001, and it has a heavy load of creativity going on. On mine I just played pretty straight-ahead bluesy rock, and it works fine.

Jerry Jeff's version went to number one on the Americana Music Chart and mine … didn't.

"Monkey River Town Girl." When Jerene and I vacationed with Jerry Jeff and Susan at their home in Belize I became fascinated with the maps of Belize that were ubiquitous. I first noticed one at the tiny airport when we arrived. Then at Jerry Jeff and Susan's house. Then at the Victoria House bar. And every place I went I saw this map. I could take my time and study it at Jerry Jeff's and read the names of the towns and counties—the counties may be called districts, I can't remember—and one name stuck with me. Monkey River Town.

I imagined a place with monkeys in the trees that lined the banks of a river that flowed into the sea.

Fast forward a few years, and I'm on a radio tour promoting Larry Joe's festival. It was a two-week run that finished in Johnson City, and we celebrated a bit too much to avoid a good-sized hangover the next morning, which was a Monday. I mention Monday because we were planning to have lunch at a Mexican restaurant on the way to Larry Joe's house in Stephenville.

Going north on US 281 looking for a Mexican restaurant doesn't seem like much of a stretch seeing how we were in Texas, but as it happens, I think it must be illegal for Mexican restaurants to be open on Mondays on US 281. It's only about three hours from Johnson City to Stephenville, but when you're hungover, and thinking the next time you roll through a town there will be a Mexican restaurant that's open for lunch and offers a nice meal accompanied by an ice-cold Dos Equis on tap, and it doesn't, well I kept getting more and more hungry.

I can't remember if we ate anything on the trip up to Stephenville, but I know without a doubt it was not Mexican.

I do know I was feeling a bit better because of the passage of time, but not by much. When we sat down in his office and began writing "Monkey River Town" I'd had this antique melody since I was in Belize soaking up the vibe. I also had the first line or two to get started.

I'd never written with Larry Joe, but I'd been listening to his songs almost every night, and I had every confidence we would come up with some good stuff.

We needed something to really hit home after a good three-line set-up, and he came through like a skyrocket. When he had the line "more fun than a barrel of you know what's" I had all but forgotten my indefatigable hangover and couldn't stop smiling for hours. When I do an all-trop rock record, this one will surely be on the list.

"All I Know" is my 9/11 song. I wrote about it a few pages back, but I have it here because I want it in this context.

I didn't finish it until 2003 because the event was so huge it knocked my spirit into a tailspin. I had some of the lines rolling through my mind, but nothing could get me over, around or through, the quagmire that was heaped in my head.

It finally came together when I was out in the east pasture, and Jerene's beautiful horse, Daunder, came up and looked at me from a few yards away. He stood in the perfect light of the afternoon sky, and through some mental telekinesis I knew what I needed to say to finish the song. I know. There's probably some of you thinking I've lost my mind, and you may be right. But the chorus came to me when I was looking at Daunder and the rest came when I went back to the house.

"A Night Out in Paris" is a song inspired by the patrons of my mother-in-law's bar, "The Freeloader." They must have broken the mold when Jerene's mother was born. She had already raised five children by the time she bought this little bar in a working-class neighborhood in Memphis. We would go over there on weekend nights when we were in town, and I would see the couples slow dancing to fast songs. Or slow dancing to slow songs. Or mid-tempo. Sometimes they would dance to no song at all. I never really stopped thinking about that. The way you do when a memory gets etched into your mind. So it was perfectly natural for me to make a song out of it at some point.

On the original release there is a video of this song embedded in the CD. You can see it if you have the right player in your computer. Sad to say, I don't remember what player that is. I'd like to see that video myself.

"A Long Monday" took John Prine and me a while to finish. Compared to "You Got Gold," it took forever. The last time I talked with John before I recorded this album I was sure we had decided to change the "stuck like a tick of a clock" line to come first and the "sitting all alone on a mountain" line to be last. So I recorded it like that.

My record came out before his, and I was surprised to hear his with our original version. Oh well. Things happen. This song seems to gather more fans every year, all because of John's version. Guess how I sing it now? You got it!

This song has been recorded many times, including by Drew Holcomb. Underhill Rose has a magic version, too.

"Hard Luck and Old Dogs" is a Nancy Apple song I fell in love with. It tugs on my heart strings every time.

"That Ol' Songwriter" is the first song I wrote when I went to New Orleans to write at Kelcy Warren's house in May of 1999. It was the first time I went away from home to write, and Jerene was not looking at it the way I was. I wanted her to know that she's the only girl for me, and I wrote it to try and let her know that.

After writing for a dance band for years, and doing publishing full time for years, I needed some time to figure me out. I think the songs I came home with are well worth it. This song very much included.

"The Devil Is in the Courtyard" is the second song I wrote at Kelcy's New Orleans house. That house is old, and I believe spirits inhabit it. I tried to put some of that in the soul of this song. Sal Valentino, who sang as the lead singer for The Beau Brummels, did a really great version of it.

"Take Me, Take Me" was written in Key West when I first spent time there. I think I worked on it in New York when I got back home as well.

Rosanne Cash did the definitive version as far as I'm concerned, but when all the stars align, I can do a pretty good job on it. It's a soulful country song any way you look at it.

"Keith Sykes Is Sorry" sums up my experience after missing an important appearance at a major commercial radio station. It's the first, and only, time I've missed any work-related event in my over 50 years of doing this stuff. I embarrassed myself and Jerene and killed the best shot I had at reaching a morning drive-time audience with thousands of listeners. It still irks me that it happened since I consider myself a pro who can rise to the occasion no matter the circumstance. This song never fails to get a laugh, but in reality, it should never have had to be written. Sorry. I guess I should lighten back up.

"Once Around Stephensport" is the only instrumental I've ever released. You'd think I would have spelled the title correctly in the liner notes, but I didn't. It's correct here.

This is the town my artist friend, Edward Perry, moved to and lived until his death in 2007. He died on Jerene's birthday, and Gordon Alexander, Jerene, and I miss him every day. This music doesn't at all sound like Ed's personality. He liked Dylan, and that's about all. But as I took my morning walks in Stephensport this music played itself to me, and I think it fit the environs well.

I played behind *All I Know* for the next year and a half doing shows anywhere anyone wanted me to play. One of the best tours I did was with Jerry Jeff on the West Coast. When we got to San Francisco he was in his element. The people loved him, and he loved the people, and the shows were full of energy. When he was on—and that was pretty much every time he hit the stage—he took them on a ride that was so satisfying I could feel his energy return from the seats back to the stage.

When Larry Joe and I did shows we had "Monkey River" to run with. Looking back at those days is good for me, because I see where I was in my life much more clearly now than I could then.

Touring through Red River and Taos, Austin and Port Aransas. San Diego and Petaluma. All the towns and all the songs have their own set of memories.

Richard Leigh and I did more shows together in those days than we did with any other artists. Every day was a joy because we let every day be new to us.

93
RETROSPECTIVE VOL 1

Sometime in 2004 I gathered up some songs and released *Retrospective Vol. 1*. It has songs from my first album up through *It's About Time*. I picked songs that marked turning points for me and used 20 of them for the record. You can go to Apple Music, and the other streaming services, to check out the playlist. To me the interesting thing is the way I changed over the years. I'm due for Vol. 2, and my mind's a-thinking.

94

HOT SPRINGS

Rusty Mathis was in his mid 20s in 1984 and managing The Sawmill Depot, a restaurant and bar in downtown Hot Springs, Arkansas. He was a Buffett fan and was aware of my connection with him, so he reached out to Jerene and booked me to play for a weekend. Rusty grew up in northeast Arkansas and also remembered me from my years playing on the Memphis music scene. The Sawmill shows evolved into many gigs and a deep friendship that's lasted for decades.

Years later he left the Sawmill Depot and after a couple of other stops he ended up as general manager for Ben E. Keith Foods Mid-South Division. He eventually became a sponsor for Keith Sykes Hot Springs Weekend, a songwriter event we held annually in the historic hotels there.

In the early aughts, before the Songwriter Weekend materialized, we had an event we called Jerene's Birthday Weekend. About 60 of us stayed at the Park Hotel. I would play there on Friday night, we would all go to the races at Oaklawn Park on Saturday. I'd do another show that night. It was always great fun, and we kept it going for several years.

I kept wanting to do a songwriter fest, and we decided to try it at the Majestic Hotel in 2008. We called it Keith Sykes Hot Springs Weekend, and Ben E. Keith was our sponsor. By 2010 we had moved to the Arlington Hotel, and we had Richard Leigh, Larry Joe Taylor,

A VERY SHORT TIME

Susan Gibson, Jimmy Davis, Susan Marshall, Buzz Cason, Jed Zimmerman, Nancy Apple, David Cousar, Grace Askew, and Delta Joe Sanders. It was a great start. There was always a lot of camaraderie between the fans and the writers, and many folks came year after year.

Over the years I added Roger Cook and Shawn Camp and more to the mix, and it became a truly wonderful event. John Prine even played it for us once.

One year Jerene and I stayed over on Sunday at the Arlington which had a fire that forced us to walk to the Majestic to spend the rest of the night.

Here's what happened: Jerene had decided to rent "Brokeback Mountain," and we were in bed watching it. There was a scene when the camera panned out over a wide shot of a valley surrounded by mountains when we heard a sound that seemed like a distant horn going on and off. I just thought it was part of the soundtrack.

When that scene was over and it cut to the next one, that sound keep on going. After a while, we began to wonder what the hell was going on. I paused the movie, and the sound still kept going. Hmm. What is happening? That's when a person from the front desk called and told us about the fire, and said we have to come to the lobby with only what we're wearing.

Since we weren't dressed, I draped a bedspread over me, and Jerene put a blanket over her. We put our shoes on, and of course I grabbed my guitar. When we opened the door you could smell smoke, but it wasn't thick, so we walked down the stairs to find the lobby filling with guests.

Rusty, being the natural leader he is, got behind the bar and started serving everyone drinks. Then management at the Arlington told us we had to walk down the street to the Majestic to spend the rest of the night.

That was a new one for us!

95

LET IT ROLL

I'd been writing with a lot of Nashville writers and writers I crossed paths with on the road. Michael Hearne and Django Walker, Jerry Jeff's son, come to mind right off the bat. Django had a hit with Pat Green's "Texas on My Mind" when he was seventeen years old. He's among the best writers I've written with because he's fast and comes up with great lines. By 2005, after writing with them and the Nashville guys, I had enough songs to record *Let It Roll*.

Pete Prydybasz was talking to Jerene about me recording for his Fat Pete Records, and they worked out a deal for me.

I touched base with my "first call' musicians and booked Eric Lewis on guitars, Al Gamble on keys, Dave Cochran on bass, Kurt Ruleman on drums along with Jimmy Davis, Susan Marshall, and Jackie Johnson on backing vocals.

"Midnight In Tupelo" was written with Roger Cook. I'm hoping by now that you know Roger from reading this book. If I haven't said it before, he's a trip to write with. Sometimes he makes me think he doesn't like a single thing I come up with, and then he'll go right through the roof from the next line I come up with. At the end of the process, I'm always happy with the songs we put a fork in.

The images we found—and Roger has a heap of them—hug this title so well it puts me in some bar in Tupelo doing all the things we conjured up. "Hey bartender turn that AC down." "8 ball in the pocket." "Elvis on the radio." It's fun to listen to.

"Let It Roll." I produced an album for Syren Records on a band called The Moonshine Cherrys. They had some very cool songs. Ted Thompson was the lead singer and writer for the band, and he came to Nashville to write with me a time or two. He was a fine collaborator.

I got the idea in Destin on a little week-long family vacation one night when I was the only one still up. In Nashville, Ted came up with a lot of lines that were playing hard to get with me.

Steve Huntington at Radio Margaritaville put this record in the mix, and it rode the waves quite well.

"Old Rock N Roller" was a title that came to me when Jerene and I went to the Mid-South Fair after we had not been in decades. The sounds of the rides, the loud music that played when they were in motion, along with the smell of the cotton candy and Pronto Pups, all came together to create this song. Or, at least give me the bones of it. When Django Walker and I got together, he had just the right finishing touches on the places where I was drawing a blank, and bang! This song presented itself in full regalia.

"Make Up Sleepy Head" is another Django Walker co-write, and he was on fire during our session. "The buzzer is buzzing and ain't gonna stop," "can't lay there forever pretending you're dead" and more sprang from his pen.

"Peggy Sue" is the rock 'n' roll chestnut from Buddy Holly. No one can do like he did, but it was fun to try it like this.

"That's the Way You Do It." Danny Flowers wrote "Tulsa Time" and has been one of my favorite writers ever since. We've had such good times working on songs and this one in particular.

Marcia Berry, a producer at WMC-TV in Memphis, wanted to do a piece on how a song was pitched to record companies and artists.

I suggested it might be fun if she videoed the writing of the song, recording the demo, and pitching it in Nashville. She talked it over with the station and got the go-ahead for the project.

I called Danny to see if he'd like to do it with me, and he came onboard. He came up with the title driving down to Memphis. When he arrived the TV camera crew were setting up in the Woodshed and became the fly on the wall during the writing process.

Somehow it was easy for us to start working on this song and forget they were there. We wrote most of it in that one session. Over the next few days we finished it and I set up a demo session with Kathy Jerry, a/k/a Miss Kitty, singing.

All this took place in the mid '90s when I was doing some gigging at Harrah's Casino, and I met Kathy there. She was a cocktail waitress who was very pretty and told me she was a singer, so I wanted to hear her voice. I asked her to come to the Woodshed and sing any song she'd like. We recorded a couple songs to prerecorded tracks and I was intrigued by what I heard. When this opportunity came along I thought it might work out for us both.

The camera crew returned and videoed us making the demo. The next step was to pitch it in Nashville.

I called Tony Brown, who was the president of MCA Nashville at the time, and asked if he would book a meeting with me and let me video the proceedings. He said yes. So on the appointed day at the appointed time, we did just that.

Marcia took the footage from the writing session, the demo session, and the meeting with Tony, and made a mini-documentary that won a regional Emmy. How's that for things coming together? It doesn't happen too often. And having Tony Brown in the mix was remarkable, because he was one busy fellow.

Here's the rest of the story on that song. Tony Brown didn't have an artist who wanted to do it, but I still believed in it very much, so I cut it on this record. I've enjoyed playing it every time I perform with a band.

"Tearing the House Down." Todd Snider and I used to get together occasionally to write, and this is one of the fruits of our labor. A lot of the images came straight from him. And the machine gun melody line I believe is what we both wanted. It's a lot of fun to sing because of the surprise line at the ending of the verses.

"What Are We Waiting For" is a Richard Leigh and Layng Martine song I fell in love with when we were at Larry Joe's festival one year. I just couldn't get it out of my head, and the best solution for that is to go ahead and record it. So I did.

"Pictures" is a song I worked on off and on over a few years. I love the image of the brokenhearted man pining his life away over a love that faded, but his love stays as clear as her pictures.

"It Just Don't Get No Better Than This" is another Larry Joe Taylor and Keith Sykes song I believe in. My secret desire was that George Strait would record it. Hey, there's still a chance!

"You Can't Lie About Love." I was in one of my "listen to Jimmy Reed all the time" modes.

Roger Cook had a publishing company called Picalic on Music Row, and sometimes we would write in his office. He had a picture of Queen Elizabeth posing topless that sat on an upright piano, and it always coaxed a chuckle out of me. I think that's where the idea for this song originated. I guess you could say this song is a mashup of blues royalty and English royalty.

"You Better Be Ready to Dance" is the first song I wrote with Michael Hearne. I was driving to Red River and Taos to play some shows, and had plans to meet Michael in Cleveland, New Mexico. I'd never been to that part of New Mexico, and the terrain I experienced along the way was blowing my mind. I recorded some ideas with my handheld cassette recorder, and we used those ideas in this song. When he sings it—he does a killer job—my mind never fails to go right back to the Cleveland Roller Mill where Michael was playing that night.

The title says at all, because the people in New Mexico dance like nowhere else I've ever been. It must be something in the water or the air or both. But whatever it is it's a wonder to behold. As a matter of fact, it may be the only thing more beautiful than the scenery.

I love the songs on this record. When it came out, I toured behind it quite a bit, but records were becoming harder and harder to promote.

96

THE NEW REALITY

The entire music business was going through some of its most dramatic changes ever due to what became known as "file sharing." Writers who spent the lion's share of their working life in small cubicles from Tin Pan Alley to Music Row suddenly found their royalties falling like temperatures in December. It took time to deal with all the shape shifting.

To me, I had a feeling of how sheet music publishers must have felt when Edison's talking machines took off.

And then radio came along, and like the tide it lifted all boats for a while. Then movies could sing and dance. Every time a new technology exploded, the music business was rearranged. After adjustments were made, all the related businesses came out in better financial shape.

Each year the overall business grew and grew. Big bands. Rock 'n' roll. Teenagers with money. Recording technology breaking new ground. 78s, 45s, 33s, CDs. Huge national tours. And like the ending of "A Day in The Life," everything went up and up and up and until there was a loud bang that left a long sustain that faded into silence. In the midst of the silence was a thing called Napster.

When I was touring on "Let It Roll," I didn't think too much about Napster. After all, I thought it was affecting the major stars and their huge revenues but not working-class artists like me. In 2006 on into '07, and '08, I played gigs coast to coast—everything from

THE NEW REALITY

people's living rooms to beautiful small halls like the Manship Theater in Baton Rouge, Louisiana. Opening for John Prine or song swaps at festivals, I kept busy.

Gradually, I started seeing my royalties fall, but I just chalked it up to not having a serious cover lately. My catalog of songs that I wrote and/or published was paying on sales of around 500,000 records a year. That's nowhere near the top, but still enough to keep me working in music.

It would take the genius of Steve Jobs to really turn the page on recorded music. When the iPod, iPhone, and iTunes came to be it opened the door to the digital age of music.

97

JED AND KELLEY

I produced the Jed and Kelley albums during this time.
Jed Zimmerman and Kelley Mickwee were playing gigs in Memphis, and I was out one night when I happened to catch them in a small club on Madison Avenue. "Loose" is the word that came to mind as I listened to them play. Their brilliant harmonies were delivered in a laid back, liberated way. It pinned my attention to them in a way that hadn't happened for a while. I loved the off-the-wall sense of humor and the catch-as-catch-can approach they seemed to have. I think subliminally I must have needed a dose of how music could be loose and not so professional all the time.

Sometimes—and I think I'm as guilty as anyone—we try to make music so perfect it sounds good, but there is no lasting soul to keep you coming back to it time after time. Jed and Kelley had found a way around all that, and I became a fan.

After getting to know them I made them an offer whereby they could do an album for pay-as-you-can. And they took me up on it.

It was so cool watching them mature in the studio. When the second record was released, Mark Jordon gave them four stars out of four in his review in the Memphis' *Commercial Appeal*.

When I think back on them as a duo, I'm sad they broke apart. But such is life and music. The wheel keeps turning—sometimes with us and sometimes against us. No matter. I believe they could have been a great success, but they made the decision they needed to make.

98

THE DELTA FAIR

Jerene got a call from Darrin Hillis of the Delta Fair to see if we might put a songwriter show together. We met him and Mark Lovell, the owner of the Delta Fair, talked it over, and we decided to do it.

Our first show had Guy Clark, Roger Cook, Rodney Crowell, Teenie Hodges, Fred Knobloch, Todd Snider, Larry Joe Taylor, and me. Anyone in the songwriting world would have to agree that's a great lineup. Here's what happened.

The stage was right smack dab in the middle of the midway. Seems cool, doesn't it? When the songwriter show started, the rides did too. As a result, the "Coast of Marseilles" included me and my acoustic guitar, accompanied by the cacophony of the screams of the riders as the machines made them pull g's, while the engines of the rides revved up, straining to pull the contraption along. And it seemed to be the loudest during the softest parts of the songs.

This went on all weekend. I can't tell you how proud I was to have Guy Clark trying to do a set with all this clatter going on. Oh, and imagine Rodney singing "After All This Time" covered up by all this mess.

On top of everything the PA sounded dreadful on stage. It was somewhat better out front, but all in all it was just F'n bad.

The Delta Fair folks couldn't have been better trying to help us get through all this, and the next year we moved the stage away from the midway. One of the highlights that year was Rodney Crowell brought his friend Vince Gill, and they did a superlative show.

Things went better, but it just couldn't power us into a better situation because our event is essentially an acoustic affair. Most of the fair goers aren't in the mood for being that quiet. After all, it is a place for an exchange of energies. And all things cerebral are better fitted to a place where the energy is focused in one direction.

In 2010 we tried one last time. I really didn't have my heart in it, but Jerene did so we gave the old college try. But we finally decided we had a great idea but the wrong place. It wasn't our fault or the fair's fault. I just realized you can't mix oil and water.

99

COUNTRY MORNING MUSIC, THE ALBUM

2008 came around and Todd Snider and Peter Cooper came to our house in Fayette County, Tennessee, to record me playing a batch of songs solo. They were in and out in two days, and before I knew it Aimless Records released an album that included solo versions of songs that I had become known for. The record was called *Country Morning Music* and has 13 songs covering 38 years of songwriting.

After the first pressing was sold it was never made again. I mention that because there will be some collector out there who will look for it. It was CD-only with liner notes by Peter Cooper. Good luck trying to find it.

100

START AND FINISH

Todd Snider asked me to do a couple of tours with him in 2009. We would do one in the winter lasting though the spring and another in the fall lasting into winter. I was excited and I think Todd was, too.

It was the dead of winter when we began, and from the start, I could feel a strange vibe. I don't think I'll ever be able to put my finger on what it was, but it was real.

A few weeks before the tour I got an email from Todd with a list of "rules" for the tour. I thought it was just another joke and didn't pay it any mind. Especially coming from Todd, a rule breaker if there ever was one.

The first show was at Blueberry Hill in St. Louis, and from there, we made the long haul to Colorado. We made another long haul from Colorado to Phoenix. I was fired from the tour after Phoenix. It wasn't the first time I was scratched from a Todd Snider show, but this time I wanted to make sure it would be the last.

I still don't have an answer as to why, but I will say I was hurt by it, and Todd and I never said a word to each other for 14 years. Maybe an exchange of greetings if we met by chance but that was it.

I never stopped singing his praises because his songwriting is beyond compare, but it was not worth it to me to have a relationship with him. I never knew when I might be hurt by him like that again.

101

PORT A AND *20 MOST*

Two things stand out for me in 2010. The first was I started going to Port Aransas to write. I learned in New Orleans that I really do thrive in a dissimilar place where I only know a few people, and have no distractions except for the ones I can't get by without—like grocery shopping, laundry, and the occasional trip to the post office. But generally I have nothing to intrude on my muse when I'm alone.

By the end of the first week, I'm so zoned in to my music, everything I do, and say, and feel, all hinge on songs—what they say and how they say it. They become extensions of my psyche, and I don't separate them from my reality for the entire time I'm working.

I stayed for three weeks the first few times, but now I go for four.

I have a friend in Port A I met the first time I was there, but that was such a whirlwind trip we hardly said more than hello. His name is Jim Urban, and he owned the Seashell Village Resort. After I had been to Port A a few times we became friends, then good friends, and now we are real friends.

He used to say, "Keith, if you ever want to come down, I can usually find you somewhere to stay. It might be in the laundry room, but I'll put you somewhere."

When someone says something like that to me when I'm on the road I take it more as a compliment than I do as an invitation. But after five or six years I was still getting the invite. That's something else. So in '09 I called Jim and said, "Are you for real about me coming down?" He answered yes. I told him I've been thinking I could do it in January after I do Larry Joe's cruise, and if that worked for him it would work for me. He assured me he was ready, and so began my writing sojourns in Port A.

I have written over 100 songs and a screenplay in Port A since 2010, and I have only missed two years. One for an illness and one for the COVID pandamn. (Jerene always calls it the pandamn so I do too).

The second notable thing for me in 2010: I made a record I called *20 Most Requested* that's like the *Country Morning Music* album I did for Aimless. This one, and all the ones I have done since, are on KSME Records. It's my plan to keep it that way. *20 Most* does have a lot of songs that are requested when I do my shows. And I freely admit I requested a few myself.

It sells well. I take that back—it sold well back when people bought physical records—and I have been through several pressings of it. All the usual song suspects are on it, and you can find the track listing at the places where folks listen to music. Pete Mathews recorded it at my house, then did the editing and mixing at his studio.

102

BUCKSNORT BLUES

I've had a love for the blues since I didn't even know what it was. That is to say, when I was very young I didn't put the songs I liked in a genre. But by the time I finished school and was playing guitar I began to hear things differently.

My mother worked for the Veterans Hospital, and when I was a junior or senior in high school she went to Washington, DC, on a trip involving her work. On her return she brought me two Library of Congress albums. One was called *Afro-American Blues and Game Songs*. The other was called *Folk Music of the United States, Play and Dance Songs and Tunes*. They were both made with red vinyl and had blue labels in the center. Guess which one I gravitated to? Blues by a mile. This is how I first heard McKinley Morganfield, a/k/a Muddy Waters.

Every song on that album became my favorite song. I would get so completely mesmerized by the songs, in my mind's eye I could see the people singing in the places where they were.

Not long after, I bought a Mississippi John Hurt album called *Today!* and it became my favorite record. Not long after that I learned these blues are called country blues, which was just fine with me. They were recorded out in the country by artists singing blues.

Then I learned about urban, or more precisely, Chicago blues. After a little more digging I found that one of my heroes, Sam Phillips, recorded a lot of the records from Chicago in Memphis. How do you do that, you ask?

In those days Chess Records was always looking for new artists, and if they were from Memphis, or elsewhere, they didn't much care. As long as they had a chance of becoming popular, Chess would take that chance. Howlin' Wolf is a prime example.

For the time being I stayed caught up in country blues. I'm thinking it was mainly because I was learning to play on an acoustic guitar, and Chicago blues were electrified. In a few years I opened the door to all kinds of blues, and I still get just as caught up in a good blues song as I ever did.

Which led to recording *Bucksnort Blues*, the only all-blues record I've made so far. *Advanced Medication* most definitely includes some blues songs, but it also has some singer songwriter things on it, too.

"Bucksnort Blues" was written by Jed Zimmerman, and when I heard him play it in Red River at the Lost Love Saloon one night it hit me just right.

I love that I made it the title track. It's got just enough rock—the way I did it anyway—to become a country song and blues song all at once.

I was lucky enough to have Greg Lundy play drums and Leo Goff play bass. Eric Lewis played guitars, and Al Gamble played keys. Reba Russell, a true Memphis treasure, sang the harmony vocals. Paul Cantieri was the executive producer.

"Capt. Pete's Blues Cruise" is a song I wrote during my first writing trip to Port A. Cap'n Pete was the moniker of Dee Henderson, a DJ at Memphis' WEVL listener-supported radio station. Cap'n Pete's show was a favorite of mine long before I found out he was the same guy I would see at this auto parts shop when I needed parts for my '50 Studebaker. He was a cool guy when I would see him there, and even cooler when I met him as one of my favorite DJs.

I listened to his Friday night *Cap'n Pete's Blues Cruise* show for years. One afternoon while I was watching the news on TV, I saw a story about him being killed at his home by his grandson. It just completely blind-sided me.

I wrote the title in my notebook, and it stayed there on the top of an empty page until I wrote the song two years later.

Anyone who loves the blues in Memphis revered Cap'n Pete.

About the title of my song and Cap'n Pete being spelled differently. My bad! I didn't think to check before the record came out. Just another in a loooong line of stuff I didn't do right.

"Texas Blues" is mash up of incidents that happened to me over the years in Texas. Just so you know, I'm overwhelmingly in love with Texas. But the blues are blues — no matter where you are. Maybe I wrote too many words for this song. It may have been perfectly fine with only one verse. Keep that in mind if you ever feel like cutting this song. Feel free to pick a verse or two and jam!

"Hot Fed Ex Man" is a song that was inspired by a TV commercial. And check this. It may not have even been a Fed Ex commercial, but for this story it is. It shows an office with several secretaries jockeying for position to catch a glimpse of a Fed Ex man delivering packages.

"Bucksnort Blues" was written by Jed Zimmerman. Bucksnort is a very small town -- I've never seen the town, but there must be one around there somewhere. What the song is really about is the human experience of a tangled relationship.

"Unkind Blues" was written when I was 18. My songwriter/bluesman friend, Delta Joe Sanders, has played it from time to time, and that keeps me into in it. It's about as basic as blues gets, and maybe that's part of its charm.

"City of Good Abode" was written in the mid-1970s when I was converting myself from a folkie to a rocker. I really can't think of why I didn't do this song for the "I'm Not Strange" record. Oh well.

I name-checked Furry Lewis and the Amazing Rhythm Aces because Furry's a Memphis legend, and I was running with the Aces a lot in those days.

A VERY SHORT TIME

I was walking through Memphis International Airport one morning and heard it on the ceiling speakers. I was so happy I got my phone and recorded about 30 seconds of it to play for Jerene.

"I Got That Going for Me." I wanted a blues that pictured some of the dumb things I do — the ones I keep doing, like forgetting where I parked my car at the grocery store. I also just wanted to pick on some pet peeves like political ads on TV. I recommend it to any of you who want to vent a little while you play and sing.

"Trouble Woman." I'm a true believer that everyone has had a "trouble" person in their life.

"California Coastline" sums up my state of mind when I was in California for Todd Snider's 40th birthday party. Jerene and I left John Prine's 60th birthday party in Florida the day before to be there. It was our first time to be in Santa Cruz. If I had to describe it in one word ... magical.

"Tonight It's Just Me and the Blues" is the song Grace Askew liked the best on this record. I always put weight on what good songwriters tell me.

The *Bucksnort Blues* album made it on some of the satellite stations and generated my first royalties from Sound Exchange, the company that pays artists and rights owners — which is record companies and other rights owners — when their music is played on non-terrestrial radio stations. Pretty cool.

Jack Holder was working for a company that did a video for "City of Good Abode" and I got the mayor of Memphis, AC Wharton, to appear in it along with my granddaughter Kelsey Fletcher, Teenie Hodges, Leo Goff, and a bunch more.

All the albums I've made mean a lot to me for any number of reasons, but connecting with the players and studios is the best.

103

JAMAICA

In 2012 and 2013 Pete and Jan Prydybasz held a retreat at the Coral Cove Resort in Jamaica. They had found it a year or two before when they were at a concert in nearby Negril and were looking for something a little more off the beaten path. Coral Cove had it in spades.

They organized everything around me playing at night, and about 30 of us had the most wonderful time. There were side trips and excursions you could go on or you could stay there blissfully doing as close to nothing as humanly possible, which is what Jerene and I did. I keep thinking we should continue to do this more often.

104

PHILLIP STAFFORD

In 2013 I played a house concert at A2H, an engineering company owned by Grace Askew's father. After the show a man named Phillip Stafford introduced himself and said he wanted to gift me with a ukulele he made.

Well, that took me by surprise. I gladly accepted, and we walked out to his car. He opened the trunk and several ukuleles were in there. He said, "Take your pick." I was a kid in a candy store. They were made really well and looked great, so I played what little I knew on each of them and decided on the one that felt the best to me.

From that time on we'd talk on the phone about instruments and how they're made and what I liked about various brands. We became good friends in the process.

He built several guitars using the measurements I favor, and all of them had things about them I liked very much.

My favorite looks like a miniature dreadnought style guitar. It's made of cocobolo rosewood and has the big, rich tone of a much larger guitar. It plays exactly like I like. I named her Rosie, and she is the only guitar I played on the *Songs From a Little Beach Town* EP.

Phillip has become a dear friend, and I learn something from him all the time.

105

SONGS FROM A LITTLE BEACH TOWN

After Larry Joe's songwriter cruise around the first of January, I head to Port A, where I work on songs five days a week. I use the weekends to recharge and come up with titles or fixes on songs I'm working on. None of it would have happened if not for Jim Urban. By extension I could say it was due to knowing Larry Joe Taylor. But that goes back to knowing John Inmon. And that of course goes back to knowing Jerry Jeff Walker. And that goes back to knowing Delmark Goldfarb. And that goes back to the Holiday Inn circuit. I don't know where that came from. I suppose it was me. But I digress, literally.

Jim Urban told me he'd always find a place for me in Port A, and he has. Acquaintances don't do things like that for you. Only friends do those kinds of things. True, when I'm there we hardly ever see each other on weekdays. Sometimes not on weekends either. But there are times we're able to spend some hours talking about everything under the sun. And we don't always agree on everything. Only friends can talk over differences of opinions and enjoy it — proof that if you listen you will hear. Crazy how that works.

I was in Port A talking on the phone with Jerene about how it was going, rattling on and on about some song, when she just blurted out, "Why don't you write some beach songs?"

I told her I'm concentrating on the ideas I already have, and I'm working on getting them on paper and into the recorder. After we hung up and I was about to watch something on TV, or go the store, or get ready for bed, whatever it was, I started thinking about what she said.

Beach songs. Hmm. Well, I am in a beach town. And the ocean is two blocks away. I walk on the beach every morning. Maybe Jerene might have a good idea. I'm not saying for sure. After all, I didn't think of it myself. But she may be on to something. Note: I'm saying all that with tongue conspicuously in my cheek.

The next day when it was time to get to work, I decided to give it a try. I made a list of potential beach song titles and went out for a beer at this place that's overlooking the beach.

Bear in mind, when I'm in Port A I'm not there in the "season." It's not the time of year to go for a dip in the Gulf. I wear long sleeves most all the time, and more likely than not I'll have a light jacket on when I go out. I usually don't go for a beer at midday like I did this time. But this was work related. I had some gears to shift, and I needed some outside influence to get it done.

When I got back I was still wrapping my head around what in the hell a beach song is. I decided it's a pretty broad category. I love good songs. I don't care if they take place on a beach or in a bar in Kansas. A beach town has everything a non-beach town has, it's just that the ocean is involved. And that really does make a difference.

I thought about classic beach songs—at least what I think are classic beach songs—like Steve Goodman's "Banana Republics" that Buffett made his own. I know, Steve has some co-writers on that song, but it's so Steve Goodman I just think of it like that. Buffett's "Cuban Crime of Passion" that he and Tom Corcoran wrote comes to mind, and practically any Buffett song, for that matter. Harry Belafonte's "Jamaican Farewell" is a beach song, and so is Zac Brown Band's "Toes." There's a host of them.

SONGS FROM A LITTLE BEACH TOWN

I know Jerene, and I know she wasn't talking about the cheesy country-sounding songs about drinking on the beach with your drinking buddies. I knew she was talking about "Boats to Build" by Guy Clark. Or Steven Stills' "Southern Cross." She meant for me to write some real songs with the beach as the atmosphere.

I have written a few over the ensuing years, and I think a few have hit the nail on the head.

Crowd funding became a thing around this time. Being naturally shy it took me a couple of years to get in the headspace to pursue it, but when I did I went full tilt. I set up my account on Kickstarter, wrote my pitch making my case about why I was doing it, and made videos of me singing the songs I wanted to record.

The EP would be called *Songs From a Little Beach Town*. I went on my Kickstarter page, pressed the go button, and it was on.

When I reached my goal, I was staying with my friends Dave and Lora Hanson just outside of Stephenville. Dave was working in his home office, and Lora and I had gone to a grocery store when she texted me from two or three aisles over to tell me she was just notified that my goal was reached.

Back home, I got busy getting the packages together to send all the things I promised the backers. I had various levels of pledges. Level one was a copy of the record. Level two was a giant taking dog—I just made that up.

It was a ton of work, but what it meant was I was going to get to record with Brent Maher producing with some amazing musicians. Brent has made some of my favorite records as an engineer, producer, or both, and now I could work with him. Hot dog! We recorded four songs, and they turned out just as I had hoped. And they were all beach songs.

One other thing. When I took this record to my distributor, Johnny Phillips at Select O Hits in Memphis, he told me EPs were at least six songs long.

A VERY SHORT TIME

When I was a kid, back before electricity, EPs were four songs, and that's why I only recorded four. So, I took two cuts from the *20 Most* album, "Coast Of Marseilles" and "Drive Myself to Drinkin,'" and filled out the EP with them. Those cuts are played solo, but they seemed to fit the record well enough.

Nir Z played drums and percussion, Willie Weeks played bass, Body Ogden played keys, and Brent Mason played electric guitar. These guys are top pros in Nashville, and I was excited to be in the same room with them. Tom Flora sang the harmonies, and Charles Yingling engineered. Terrific work, all around.

I called Joe Hardy to see if he would master it. When he sent me the results, I asked him if he would do a mix of "Come as You Are Beach Bar," and he did. It's the mix that's on the EP.

"Come as You Are Beach Bar." I felt like I was on to something when I finished the first draft. I worked on it some more, and just when I liked it enough to think it was finished, I would think of something else I wanted to include. This went on for a year or so. By the time I went to Nashville, I thought it was ready. When I heard the playback, I knew for sure.

I was in Key West for the Meeting of the Minds, a/k/a MOTM, the annual Parrothead convention, and played it for JD Spradlin at the Radio Margaritaville booth. It was on a jump drive, and JD plugged it into his computer and played about 15 seconds of it and stopped. Of course I was thinking he didn't like it but would be polite and say something like, "I'll take this home and give it listen and maybe I'll get back to you" when he said, "Stay here. I'll play it next."

Well, a lot of things were running through my mind right then. Mainly that the record wouldn't be out until next March, and this was in November. I was wondering if I should ask him to hold off until it's released but I said to myself, "screw that. Play it now, anywhere, anytime there is an opportunity. This is most defiantly an opportunity.

Take it!" So I sat there looking around like the proverbial Cheshire cat. Smiling away. Then JD played it.

That was the first of its many spins around Radio Margaritaville. It must have hit home with someone, because I would get texts from around the country with screen shots showing that song playing on Radio Margaritaville.

I asked Elizabeth Cawine, who was doing promotion for the record, if it was too soon to be playing the record. She said, and I'm paraphrasing here, "Are you out of your mind? I've talked with Kirsten Winquist and Radio Margaritaville is in to it. Let it happen."

I finally got the message that this wasn't the 1960s or '70s anymore. Back in those days if you created a demand and didn't have the product you would lose sales because the audience would be gone by the time your record could be sold. Today, it's the wild west. People are making up the rules as they go. Digital records are something your service provider has and you just listen to them—no physical record necessary. Which is cool. I'm just trying to get along in a brave new world that doesn't like timid attitudes. It's best to jump in and figure it out as you go. Everyone else does.

"Beach Bar" was No. 1 for seven non-consecutive weeks on the Trop Rock Music Chart and voted Favorite Song by TropRockin' Magazine's People Choice Award.

"The Best Day" is an amalgamation of two events I really treasure. One is my first day in Key West when I met Buffett, Ashley Simmons and all my future Key West pals—Benjamin "Dink" Bruce, Pat and Phil Tenney, Tom and Judy Corcoran, Chris and Sonia Robinson, and more. I'm sorry to say there are some with names I can't remember but the trip out to Woman Key for an all-day party still lives vividly in my memory. And it really did all happen in 24 hours.

Two is a Labor Day Weekend show I did with Larry Joe Taylor in 2005. After the weekend show was over a lot of us stayed around for a much-appreciated day off that Sunday.

Jim Urban took about 20 of us out on his boat, the "Cajun Queen," to one of those little islands off Port A. I don't know if it's an island or an isthmus, but we went there with a boatload of beer, wine, and spirits. By late afternoon I was bobbing in the water, watching dolphins swim, and looking up into the spotless sky thinking to myself, 'If nothing swims over here and bites my leg off, this is gonna be the best day ever.'

I mentioned this to Finn Fredricksen, my Norwegian friend who was bobbing with me — is that even a thing? Bobbing together? — and he seemed to take it in the spirit I intended and laughed out loud. I also noticed a seabird on the water just a few feet from us and remarked, "That bird must have really, really long legs." Finn liked that one too, but I couldn't work it into the song.

This is one of those songs I get into as soon as I write it and I play it all the time — so much so I tend to wear it out early. And then comes a period when I never play it. And finally I'll hear it unexpectedly somewhere and get back into it again. I don't know why I do this. I wonder if other songwriters do it, too?

Jim Urban bought a house in the Bahama's. After he renovated it he named it "The Best Day." That's put a permanent smile in my mind.

"I Pick You" is a love song through and through. Sometimes I think I should never sing songs like this even though I wrote it. If I could just get my inner Dean Martin working in real life, I'd have it made.

"Little Beach Town" is an ode to the towns that embody that description. Even big beach towns have some of the charms of the small ones. But when you can drive around the entire town in less than a quarter of an hour, those are the ones I love. I guess Key West spoiled me. Port A was such a fishing village when I first went there that I fell for it right off. Now that it's going through some gentrification, it still is a little beach town through and through. Every beach town has some similar things, and my fav is the storefront shark jaws. Once I see those things, I think to myself, 'Oh good, I'm here.'

I've recorded "Coast of Marseilles" several times, and thanks to Jimmy Buffett I still get a lot of requests for it.

This is the second time I've used this recording of "Drive Myself to Drinkin'." I predict I will record it with a band of some kind and get a performance that makes it sound like it is in my head. I produced it on Konner James and it came out well. He did a killer video of it, too.

Songs From a Little Beach Town has been my most successful record in terms of actually making more money than it cost in the least amount of time. The artwork came directly from the T-shirt art. That was a first for me as well. Normally it's the other way around.

The EP has been a blessing for me. I know, Kenny Chesney would be moaning the blues if he had a record with sales like this, but it's all relative.

I was on the road all over the country playing festivals and house concerts and events. I could have stayed around doing it year after year, then another opportunity presented itself.

106

NOTE ON BEALE

Around the end of 2015 I was told I was receiving a Brass Note on Beale Street. I thought to myself, 'OK, I must be somebody.'

It came up just after I'd finished recording *Songs From a Little Beach Town*, and Jerene and I were trying to figure out how we could do the promo. She said, "Let's lace them together and make it work."

We called Kris Kourdouvelis and Sharon Gray. They are friends who live in one of the coolest places in downtown Memphis. It has a performance space called the Warehouse, and it's got everything you need to have any kind of function you want—a stage, dance floor, cafe type seating, a bar area, and it was perfect for what we were doing.

We chose March 16th, and I asked Elizabeth Cawein to help organize it, and we were off and running.

I gave a speech. I'd never given one, but I wanted to thank everyone I ever met. Just kidding. But I wanted to make sure I mentioned as many of the key people who helped me through the years as I could.

Even though it shared the night with my new record, the Brass Note is very important to me for a lot of reasons.

If you're ever on Beale you can check it out. I'm in front of King's Cafe. Be careful. You might step on me and my blue suede shoes.

107

PRESIDENT AND CHIEF MANAGER, ARDENT STUDIOS

In 2017 Jerene went to work for Betty Fry. They had been friends for a very long time.

Jerene has been riding horses since she was a young girl when she would visit her aunt and uncle in Mississippi. By the time she was 15 she had a horse of her own and kept him not far from her house in Memphis.

At the time we got together in 1974, she didn't have a horse, so I never knew that side of her until she started riding again in the early '80s. That's when she met Betty Ellis, and a whole host of other women, who became friends through horses. Jerene is still close to a lot of them.

I'm a little fuzzy on some of this history, but I think Betty met John Fry sometime in the late '70s or early '80s. Sometime in the '80s Jerene invited Betty to lunch with her and John.

John and Betty started seeing each other and eventually married.

We all were friends and kept in touch. Betty is an animal lover, and at one point she named one of her many cats Keith Sykes.

After John Fry died in late 2014, Betty became sole owner of Ardent Studios and all its holdings. In 2017 Betty called Jerene to see if she could help her with Ardent, and not long after that Jerene became Betty's personal assistant.

After Jerene started working for Betty, she asked me if I would come to work for Ardent and run the studio. I asked Jerene if it was her or Betty who was really asking. She assured me it was Betty.

I thought about it for maybe 30 seconds and declined the offer. For one thing, things were going pretty smoothly out there on the road, and for another, I didn't want to be in the middle of managing a recording studio—even one as renowned as Ardent.

I was still flying high from *Songs From a Little Beach Town*, so why would I walk out on that? I had long thought that walking away from performing in 1986 was most likely a bad idea, especially after I went back to performing in 2001. I chalked it up to Monday morning quarterbacking, and left it where it lay. I just wasn't looking for a 9-to-5 job.

From a distance I would hear Jerene and Betty talking into the wee hours about this or that concerning the studio and how it was being run since John Fry died. Sometimes I could even tell what they were talking about and think to myself, 'I know the answer to that problem.' This went on for months.

I was in Port A when I finally agreed to come on board. I guess I felt like I knew the answers to a lot of the problems they were talking about. Or maybe being the manager of Ardent Studios would be an appropriate place to retire from the road. It doesn't matter now. I did it.

When I began at Ardent in mid-March, 2018, my first order of business was to get it cleaned up. When I was recording there it was always as clean as could be with a place for everything and everything in its place. Now I found the shop so cluttered it was impossible to find anything, much less get work done in it.

The atrium, which was once a beautiful and peaceful place for some solitude if you needed a break from the tensions of recording, now had no vegetation save for the overgrown trees.

The fountain was in pieces with the bottom third standing at a 45-degree angle in the empty fountain pool. The other parts of it were lying in a corner of the atrium.

When it rained it flooded the entire atrium up to the bottom of the floor-to-ceiling windows that lined its perimeter.

Every fluorescent light bulb in the building was a different color than the one next to it.

The roof leaked every time it rained, and as a result many of the ceiling tiles were badly stained.

It seemed like there was a mess everywhere I looked. In a word, it was sad. And that broke my heart. This majestic place, once the home to hitmakers from all over the world, was now reduced to an unwell geriatric on a downhill spiral. It was time to get busy.

Over time through many trials and tribulations, Ardent made it back to its original luster.

The next thing was figuring out what needed to be done to restore the studios. I was told when I arrived the gear was in good shape. I found out in short order that was not the case. Studio C was in very good condition because it had a less-than-10-year-old console that I could buy parts for from the factory. But Studio A and Studio B had consoles that were over 30 years old and needed a lot of attention. Consoles that old require constant work to keep them in the shape rental studios have to be in. The daily wear and tear compounded by the fact the equipment was in smoke-filled rooms practically 24 hours a day since their installation, stacked the deck against them. Studio gear gets cancer just like people do. When that smoke mixes with the inner working parts of anything as sophisticated as a Neve or SSL console, bad things happen.

I hired Murphy Odom and Rick Caughron to begin work. Studio A had a 60 input Neve VR and Studio B had a 56 input SSL 6000. If you know about these boards you know that it takes a lot of work for them to be in viable condition. Many of the original parts for these units are no longer available because of environmental laws. And there are parts that just aren't made because it's not profitable for companies to make them, so the studio has to have them made and that gets expensive.

Even if you invest the money that's necessary to keep them up there's generally not enough business to justify those costs. It's another way that computers have changed the world we live in.

Today you can make a record in your home studio that is of high enough quality to be played on the radio. When I was coming up that was impossible. In a lot of ways Ardent, and all the large studios like Ardent, are dinosaurs. It's become necessary for those studios to invest in young talent to survive. John Fry did just that when Ardent was in its infancy by taking on artists like Big Star. Even then Fry knew the rental business alone isn't enough to keep the doors open.

I tried to interest Betty Fry in a new record company or reopening Ardent Records, but she wasn't interested.

I did make a single on myself, and one on Roger Cook, and produced an album of my songs for a country singer from Louisiana named Konner James. The pandemic wiped out a lot of the plans I had for it, but I believe it's a solid, original record.

108

TREE OF FORGIVENESS

John Prine and I started working on "No Ordinary Blue" on April 11, 2011, and we got three verses and a chorus. We worked on it again on July 7th. We ended up working on it off and on for the next eight years. I suppose you could say we weren't in a terrific hurry to "get 'er dun."

In all that time parts would be written, changed, discarded, and rewritten again, but the chorus was one constant we always went back to. I finally reconciled it to cooking pork ribs. They'll be done when they're done.

We put a fork in it in Mountain View, Arkansas, during our fishing trip in 2018. And that's the only time we ever tried to write up there. I always thought of it as John's down time. I think we all did. But that night he played it like he was 25 again, with a fire I could feel in my soul. It was spiritual.

He recorded it a few weeks later for the *Tree of Forgiveness* album. When it entered the Billboard 200 Album Chart at No. 5, I thought to myself, 'How's that for a folk singer!'

John invited everyone who co-wrote with him on the *Tree* album to the City Winery in Nashville during Americana Fest—Roger Cook, Pat McLaughlin, Dan Auerbach, and me. Pretty good company and a wonderful night.

The next year John was inducted into the Songwriters Hall of Fame in New York City, and Fiona texted me about coming up for the ceremony. I thanked her profusely, made plans and booked my flight.

Bonnie Raitt was there to sing "Angel From Montgomery" with him, and even though I have seen them do it many times, this may have been the most emotional. I was so proud to be his musical brother. To see him be so respected by his peers filled me to overflowing.

That November the *All the Best Fest* was held in the Dominican Republic. Some of the artists had known John a long time and others were just beginning to know him—Emmylou Harris, Lucinda Williams, Tyler Childers, Nitty Gritty Dirt Band, Nathaniel Rateliff, Steve Earle, were there along with many others.

The Dominican Republic was beautiful, and the hotel was fantastic.

Jerene and I stayed on an extra day and had dinner with John and Fiona. I didn't know it then, but it would be the last time I would see him.

109
THE PANDAM

Jerene was ill (not covid related) when we got back from *All the Best* and needed me to be home to help her get through it. I didn't even think of going to Port A or anywhere else.

I went to Ardent in the morning and stopped at the hospital to check on her after work. She was able to come home after six days, but she had a long road ahead of her to recuperate. She was getting better day by day, and then the outside world closed its doors.

Ardent, along with the entire United States, shut down in March 2020. What a deal. No one had any idea of how to go about doing anything.

Just before the lockdown started, I hired Mic Wilson, a longtime engineer at the studio, to help me get the studio computers updated. Together we checked out all the high-end mics, and sent the ones needing repair to specialists to be refurbished.

When the studios were ready, they were sitting there all dressed up with nowhere to go, so to speak.

The Konner James album, like everything else, came to a screeching halt.

During this time, we resumed Ardent's beautification program. Being closed was kind of a good thing because we didn't have to worry about interrupting anyone who might be recording.

Fiona called and said John had Covid. From the moment I heard, I was hoping for the best and focused on him pulling through. But alas, it was not to be. On April 7th Fiona called again to tell me he had passed.

To say I was bummed would be putting it mildly.

Most of the year I was trying things that wouldn't have occurred to me otherwise. Playing live sets on Facebook is the most obvious one. I didn't even think to keep the first one I did. I didn't even know how archaic I had become. And it had only been a few weeks since the pandemic started.

The year was revolving around quarantining, waiting on the vaccine, putting Q-Tips in your nose, and being paranoid to go to the grocery store.

In my opinion it sucked.

110

JERRY JEFF

Fiona called and said she was sad to hear about my buddy. I thought she meant John. I don't know why. I must have heard it right and thought it wrong, if that makes any sense. She was talking about Jerry Jeff.

She thought I'd already heard and felt bad I'd heard it from her. I told her the same thing had happened to me with Roger. I told him about John when he didn't know. We both knew we should not worry about such things because there is no right or wrong when it comes to a death in the family. We all just get by the best we can.

I called Susan straight away. We talked, and she told me she thought Jerry Jeff was tired, and lost patience putting up with the hospitals, shitty days, and one thing after the other, and just died.

It made sense to me. Life is all about quality of life. When you lose it after you've put up the good fight, then it's time. I guess Jerry Jeff just let go.

It didn't stop me from going off the deep end for a while. Him being the sun, and us being the planets. That's the way I've felt about him for decades.

Having his approval was the most important thing. If he liked a song, then brother it was a song. He never picked a bad one, and he sure didn't sing a bad one. As matter of fact, saying he didn't sing a bad one is a cut. He actually never sang anything less than a great one. Don't believe me? Check it out for yourself.

No matter. They broke the mold on him, and there will never be another.

Guy Clark, Townes Van Zandt, Todd Snider, Steve Earle, Rodney Crowell, Jimmy Buffett, and all manner of singer songwriters, especially the ones from Texas, are Jerry Jeff planets.

I can't wait to see the first few movies they do about him.

111

KEITH SYKES' SONGWRITER WEEKEND

Larry Joe Taylor, his wife Sherry, and his son Zack are some of the best people I know. When Larry Joe called around the first of 2021 and asked if I'd like to do my songwriter show at Melody Mountain Ranch, I couldn't say yes fast enough. Melody Mountain is 380 acres with all the infrastructure you need to have whatever size event you can think of.

Every April "Larry Joe Taylor's Texas Music Festival" attracts about 80,000 Texas music fans.

They have other, more modest events, through the year, and now they wanted *Keith Sykes' Songwriter Weekend* to be one of them. Oh hell yes.

We set the festival for October, and I was excited to put it together. It had been a long time since I had done one, so I wanted it to be as good as I could make it. I asked Loudon Wainwright, Bruce Robison, Richard Leigh, Dickey Lee, Susan Gibson, Larry Joe, Jimmy Davis, Michael Hearne, Roger Cook, Shawn Camp, Django Walker, and Jed Zimmerman to perform. Whoosh! That's a lot of songwriters. And yes, I asked too many but I wanted the first one to be unforgettable.

A VERY SHORT TIME

And this was also an opportunity to create an award I had wanted to do for years. As far back as my shows on Beale, I've wanted to honor Jerry Jeff Walker and his classic song "Mr. Bojangles." And now I could do it. I named it the Mr. Bojangles Story Song Award. My hope was to inspire writers of story songs to one day be the recipient. How do you get it? Write the best story song you can, and get it out there!

112

LEO GOFF AND THE DOLBY ATMOS ROOM

Leo Goff lll was an engineer who had worked at Ardent at one time, but since then he had been working for the rap artist, Yo Gotti. Leo III is the son of Leo Goff, the bass player, who I've been lucky enough to have play with me many times over the years.

Leo lll was investing in the equipment to build a Dolby Atmos system and wanted to know if I was interested in putting it in Ardent. I said yes before he could finish his sentence.

I'd been reading about Dolby Atmos for months, and the thought of having the first one in the region seemed to be very Ardent to me. Ardent always tried to have the best equipment, and this was the next logical wave.

I called Betty, and she was hesitant at first, but she almost always was when it came to anything new. We talked, and I reminded her she that liked Leo when Gotti had rented all the studios at Ardent for a week a few years back.

After she talked to Leo, she said she was good to go on the Atmos rig going in Studio B, leaving the control room open for other projects.

It took him a while to do it, but after months of calling Dolby Labs in England, and getting all the scaffolding, speakers, the Atmos system, and all the associated wires, stands, amps, and all, integrated into one working system, he asked me to come and hear it.

Guess what he played me? A hi hat. All this equipment and he played me a hi hat. He was so excited, and I tried to give him the impression I was really hearing it. But it sounded like a not-so-good recording of a hi hat to me. I asked him to have me back when I could hear a string quartet. Or anything that had a few different instruments, so I could hear what all the fuss was about.

It didn't take him long until he was mixing Atmos projects for people all over the country. Mostly rap, but hey, it's the most popular music of this era. It was revenue, and I thought to myself, 'Yeah!'

113

JERRY JEFF'S SEND-OFF

With covid always lurking around every corner, it was crazy trying to have a celebration of life for Jerry Jeff. Same thing with John. It seemed like as soon as a date was on the calendar it had to be moved. I can only imagine what Fiona and Susan were dealing with.

Finally Susan set June 4th for Jerry Jeff's graveside service and the 5th for the concert in Luckenbach.

She asked me to deliver a eulogy, and on one hand I was flattered and on the other I was doubtful I could do it justice. I mean, should you be flattered to do a eulogy? And if I was gonna do it I wanted it to be something that would say how much he meant to Jerene and me, and everyone else, all at the same time.

When the time came, everyone she had asked to speak delivered their eloquent remembrances in a just a few minutes. Mine was gonna be closer to 10.

I spoke about how we met, how generous he was to me, and how deeply he loved Susan and his kids, and what a great artist he was.

As I left the dais I stopped in front of Susan, who in a short second or two made me feel like she appreciated what I said even though I had taken so long.

I sat back in my chair, and Buffett asked me if I would give him the papers I had written. I politely refused. I don't know exactly why, but I said I'd like to keep them. In hindsight I wish I'd given them to him. After all I had them in my computer. Oh well. As I have said many times, there is no right or wrong in these circumstances. You just do the best you can and leave it at that.

I think Jerry Jeff would be mighty proud of the show Susan put together in Luckenbach. So many artists and writers that Jerry Jeff loved gave everything they had on that stage. It was a joy to behold. Django, Ramblin' Jack, Jimmy Buffett, Emmylou Harris, Rodney Crowell, the list was long, and the tributes were heartfelt. I was so proud to be a part of it, and at the same time wishing we didn't have to be there. My run with Jerry Jeff came to a close within the echos of the past.

114

LET THE SHOW BEGIN

When the time came for the *Keith Sykes' Songwriter Weekend*, I had a big dilemma. I had an accident at the end of August. I was on an eight-foot ladder with a ten-foot pole saw trying to cut a limb out of a tree in our front yard. I was almost done when the limb fell on the ladder. I broke my fall with my left hand.

When I went to see a doctor, the x-ray showed I had moved the luna bones in my hand to somewhere they did not belong. It took surgery to fix it. I didn't know if I would ever play again.

My surgeon, Dr. Benjamin Mauck of Campbell Clinic, told me I should get back to within 90 percent of my playing ability. I still wasn't sure. When I tried to move my swollen fingers, I could get them to move about an eighth of an inch. Day by day they got a little better. The show was October 21-23, and there was no way I was going to be able to play. I was still wearing a cast.

Since I was unable to play, I had been trying to improve my voice. It was liberating to just sing, and I actually liked it. I still hated the thought of losing my ability to play guitar. It had brought me so much joy over the years. But you have to go on. Not going on would have really put the hurt on me.

I called Shawn Camp and Michael Hearne to see if they would work up enough songs for me to do a show. They both said yes, and I sent them MP3s of the songs I wanted to do.

A VERY SHORT TIME

On Saturday morning, the day of my show, we got together in Shawn's trailer and ran through everything. It worked for me. That night I went out there like I had been doing it all my life—or at least giving it all I had—and we did a show I'll always be proud of. As matter of fact, I'd like to do more like that. Maybe I was supposed to be singer after all. You sure can't tell it by my first record.

115
LEO GOFF III

In the summer of 2022 Leo told me he was going to the Bahamas for a week or two to work on a Gotti project. He was so excited because it was his first time to leave the country. He was even excited about getting his passport.

He was away for maybe a week when I got a call from his dad—who we all call Big Leo when we're talking with or about the two of them—telling me Little Leo had an accident in Mexico. I didn't even know he was in Mexico. I thought he was going to the Bahamas. I asked what happened, and Big Leo said he had taken a fall. He was still alive but not responding.

It was crushing for everyone who knew him. I kept thinking about him. The last time we talked he was telling me his plans to move the Atmos room into the Studio B control room, which I thought would be killer. That, and him working with me on some songs I wanted to work on. Those were the last conversations I had with him.

I knew Leo was good in the studio, but I didn't know just how good until we did a few things together in Studio A. Studio A wasn't in great shape, and Jody Stephens wasn't comfortable renting it until it was. So I tried to do things in it to find out what we needed to do next.

I was recording a song solo using a click track so I could add other instruments later on. Leo knew what I was going to ask for before I could say it. I'd record a take then ask to do another right away. And then again, for a total of three tracks. I was still deciding which takes I liked best when he had already picked the ones he knew I'd like, taken the best parts of each, and edited them together. That, my dear readers, was amazing. And it made me all the sadder knowing he was in Mexico and not knowing if he'd return.

 I don't remember where I was when I got the news he was gone. That day cast a great pall over me, and I was left in a state of disbelief.

116
WINDS OF CHANGE

Things at Ardent were changing. Leo had introduced me to a tech I hired to work on the studio equipment. The thing was, he didn't work on the studio equipment. What he did do was things a janitor would do.

When I told Betty what was happening, she said she had talked to this tech and they had worked it out so he would be doing janitorial work. Hey, it was all fine with me as long as that's what she wanted, but I still didn't have a tech.

I finally found out about another former Ardent engineer who was also a tech. He also had the same model Neve as Ardent did. It seemed like a win-win to me. Betty agreed and he was hired.

This tech said he found some much needed Neve parts on the internet from a guy who would deliver them. Great!

117

A NIGHT AT THE HALLORAN

In September I did a show at the Halloran Center with the band. It's such a beautiful venue with astonishing acoustics, and I was more pumped about it than any gig I'd done in a long time.

Ron Jewell, the VP of Operations at the Halloran, and Jerene worked out the details over several weeks.

I hired some of my very favorite players—Pee Wee Jackson on drums, Dave Smith on bass, Al Gamble on keys, and Andrew Saino on guitar. Angela Burton and Mandi Thomas-Moore sang background vocals. As a bonus, Angela sang "Natural Buzzes" and Mandi sang "Hey World." Konner James came all the way up from Louisiana and sang "Mr. Phillips" and Canale Tagg sang "Do It All Again."

The show sold out, and as a performer, no matter if it's 30 people or thousands of people, if the room is full you're stoked to do the very best you can. And we did.

My sister and brother-in-law came from east Tennessee, and Dane was there with a lot of our family to make it a night to remember.

118

YOU GOT GOLD, THE EVENT

The days around the 10th of October were marked by the first *You Got Gold Celebration of John Prine's Life and Music.*

Fiona had been trying for over a year to make it happen, and every time another bout with Covid would cause it to be postponed. But this time it finally came to fruition. I remember her calling me more than a year before to tell me she had decided on the name. I was so honored I was practically speechless.

When we hung up, the thought of it went through my mind in wide circles. It was a perfect name because if anybody in this world had gold in their heart it was John Prine. On the other hand, the name could have easily been taken from another one of his songs. So, this was big for me.

I asked if I could go to every event they were having this first time. After that I'll be satisfied with whatever they would like me to do in future years. Fiona said yes, so when the time came, I went to all the shows that were held at night.

I called Dickey Lee to see about staying with him for the week, and he said he was happy to have me. At least that's what he told me! So, I was all set.

I played at the City Winery twice, the Country Music Hall of Fame, and The Basement East.

I didn't play the Ryman, but I was there both nights and the concerts were unbelievable.

The tributes to John were so touching, so appreciative, so inspired, I was transformed. At one point I felt like a beam of light streaming through the night. It was John's light somehow inside me. I can't think of anyone whose music connects with the soul of man so completely. I was lifted many times over the course of the celebration, and I'll never come all the way back down.

The caliber of the artists who played over the course of the week was astonishing. And not a single one of them wasn't humbled by John's work. Among them were Brandi Carlile, Margo Price, Kacey Musgraves, Allison Russell and JT Nero, Kurt Vile, The War and Treaty, Tyler Childers, Jason Isbell, Amanda Shires, Tre Burt, Hiss Golden Messenger, Nathaniel Rateliff, and Shawn Camp.

It was the most beautiful music event I've ever witnessed, and I couldn't believe I was there. Thank you, Lord, for Your many blessings.

119

KSSW 2022

Jerene and I were en route to the October 2022 songwriter show in Stephenville when I got a call from the guy who was selling Ardent the Neve parts.

It seems Betty had hired him to rebuild the Neve from the ground up. He decided he was going to fire the tech who bought the parts from him for Ardent's Neve.

I stopped the car as soon as we got to a rest area and called Betty. I asked her if I was still the Chief Manager of the studio. She emphatically said I was. With that understood, I called the guy who was rebuilding the Neve to tell him he can't fire Ardent's tech. I told him he couldn't fire him because he didn't hire him. I also said it was fine if he didn't want him to work on this project, but he stays at Ardent. We seemed to have an understanding, so Jerene and I went ahead with our plans.

The songwriter show was wonderful again due to the songwriters. We had Steve Earle, Jed Zimmerman, Walt Wilkins, Susan Gibson, Chuck Cannon, Dickey Lee, Richard Leigh, Larry Joe Taylor, Shawn Camp, Deborah Allen, and Roger Cook. If you ever see the poster, you will see Django Walker's name on it, but Django got one of those gigs you can't refuse because the money is so good, and he couldn't do our show. I've always said when that happens you have to take that gig.

A VERY SHORT TIME

Roger Cook got Covid just a couple of days before the show. Bummer. And since he couldn't be with us, I made a playlist of 10 of his biggest hits and played the original versions over the PA. We all took turns saying something about each song, so he was with us in spirit.

120
LAST PHONE CALL WITH BETTY FRY

My time at Ardent was some of the least musical years of my life, but I did enjoy a lot of it because I like solving problems. I was told when I came on board my job was to make the studio beautiful again. When I believed we reached that point Betty Fry didn't agree.

I got a phone call from her in November. She informed me the guy doing the work on the Neve console in Studio A was going to "pick up his tools and leave the project" if I was physically at the studio. She said she would continue to pay my salary, all I had to do was stay away.

As we talked, I told her she wouldn't have anyone there for checks and balances. She said she didn't care. I said I may occasionally need to stop in for a reason I couldn't define at the moment, but when I do I'll make sure all I do is go to my office and be gone as fast as possible. She agreed to that. After all, I have a lot of personal stuff there and may need something from time to time.

Since I began working at Ardent, Betty had told me when she sold the studio Jerene and I would never have to work again, which was one of the big reasons I took the job. We looked at it as part of our retirement plan. She reaffirmed this again during this conversation. I agreed to stay away even though I didn't believe anyone would walk away from a project like the one this guy was working on. It didn't make sense to me, and I found it strange, but hey, that was just my opinion.

A VERY SHORT TIME

121
THE NEW YEAR AND PORT A

Jerene and I rang in 2023 like we usually do—being together at home. We've long thought New Year's Eve brings all the amateur drinkers to the streets, and we are better off toasting at home. And since Jerene doesn't drink anymore, I got her a bottle of alcohol free Champagne and I had some white wine.

I traveled to Port A in the middle of January and I set my things up in what Jim Urban calls the Boat House. It was my first time to stay there, and it turned out to be my favorite. I'm usually in one of the condos or at Jim's house, and it's wonderful. But the Boat House is situated in a commercial area, and I could play my electric guitar on 11 at 4 in the morning, and no one could hear.

And although I started this book there, I soon realized I'd be much better served to take advantage of being able to sing and/or play at stage volume at will, at any time. I figured I could finish the book at home. So I set the book aside, and the songs turned out really well. I can't wait for you to hear some of them.

122

BYE, ARDENT

In the morning, before I begin to write, I go through my emails. It doesn't take more than an hour on most days and sometimes even less. And I was still reading my Ardent emails because I thought I should. When I'd get one I thought Betty should see I would forward it to her.

One day I received an email from Betty asking me to send her the password to my Ardent email account. That was fine except I didn't have it with me. I figured since the studio was closed for business I'd send it along when I got home. Ninety percent of my Ardent email was junk mail anyway. Everyone's email was being delivered, and I couldn't see what difference a couple of weeks would make so I just continued writing songs.

I got a terse email from Betty a few days later asking again for the password. I felt a tinge of apprehension about telling Betty I didn't know the password. I didn't respond, thinking I would tend to it over the weekend. That way I could tell her my dilemma, thinking she would understand, and I wouldn't be in the middle of a song. Let me say that turned out to be WRONG!

The next email I got from Betty said I was terminated. And that was all it said. Not Dear Keith. Not anything but I'm terminated.

123

THE BEAT GOES ON

In June I did a song swap in Mountain View with Roger Cook and Shawn Camp, two of my favorites.

The Ozark Folk Center in Mountain View is a marvel to behold. It's situated on many beautiful acres of hills and valleys and has rooms for rent, restaurants, and an area for RVs. Its central theme is the music of the Ozarks, but it also honors its arts and crafts.

We played the 1,000-seat concert venue. The sound was delicious, and the audience was so into the music it made it easy for us to do a really great show.

The night was also a tribute to John Prine. Roger, Shawn, and I have all written with John, and we played songs we co-wrote with him. I'm hoping one day there will be a John Prine Folk Festival there, because John really loved the area and the area loves John.

That night I introduced "Shirley," my song about the famous elephant. It's six minutes long, but if I get it right it holds the audience really well. The single came out the day before, and this was a great place to introduce it.

124

STAR AT THE HALLORAN

In July I was presented with a star on the new Sidewalk of Stars at the Halloran Center. It caught me completely off-guard, but I appreciated being among the first to be awarded. It had only been a few months since I played there, and I was still reeling. Now I have a reminder of it on the sidewalk right in front of the building.

Some days are better than others, and this one was way cool.

Many thanks to Ron Jewel and the entire Halloran staff.

125
TODD 2023

Just a few weeks after the Mountain View show Jerene asked me if I'd like see Todd Snider play a benefit for WEVL Radio at Minglewood Hall in Memphis. Now that's something I hadn't thought about in a long time.

Even though I'd been out of touch with Todd for years it didn't mean Jerene was. She would tell me from time to time they were emailing back and forth, and he was doing this or that. I didn't get involved. I still loved his songs and the powerful way he performs them, but I was reconciled to keeping my distance.

She didn't push me or cajole me or anything like that. It was just a matter of fact thing. She was going, and I could go if I wanted.

For years I'd hear about Todd singing my praises at one gig or another. And I'm always flattered by it. It's just been a lot for me to deal with since I was fired from that tour.

After I thought about it, I decided to go. After all, I didn't think I could be fired for being a fan!

When we met backstage, I rediscovered the Todd I loved to be with. He told me about a record he had made and how the song "The Resignation vs. the Comeback Special" had background singers that were all him via overdubs. As matter of fact, he played everything on the entire record. He sang me the the background singers' part, and it cracked me up.

When it was just about time for him to do his show, he told me he was playing another show for WEVL the next day at the Railgarten in Midtown. Both Joes—Joe Mariencheck on bass, and Joe McLeary on drums—were playing, and he asked me if I'd like to do it, too. I couldn't resist.

I grabbed a seat out front and saw the way he'd matured over the years. I was more blown away by the show that night than any other show I'd seen him do. And believe me, I've seen a lot of Todd Snider shows. It was astonishing.

The next day I joined him and the Joes for the afternoon show, and we played in that loose way you do when everything comes right off the top of your head. It's like being a part of a Van Gogh—more impressionist than perfectionist. Lyn Jones was there, and Todd asked him up for the next two sets. I must say it felt great, and I enjoyed every minute.

A week or so later Todd invited me to his house near Nashville, and I spent a couple of days writing, visiting, and hanging out. He took me to see his studio in East Nashville, and we had lunch at a nearby restaurant. It made some memories I'll keep close, and I owe it all to Jerene. It took 14 years to get back together, but like all my music friends, when we did it was like no time ever came between us.

126

THANK YOU, JIMMY BUFFETT, ONE MORE TIME

I finished all the Jimmy Buffett parts of this book around April of 2023. And even though by June I'd heard he wasn't going to make it much longer, the reality of it all still didn't register with me. Then September 1st came down the line.

I began to get text messages from all over the country from people offering their condolences. I did, and still do, so appreciate those messages.

Here are a few of my thoughts about Jimmy;

I haven't been in his inner circle for a long time, but like all my music friends, when we would see each other it was as if no time had come between us.

The last time we were together was at Jerry Jeff's celebration of life. He seemed as healthy as a horse, and I believe everyone there would agree with me on that. But as I'd heard since then, he was in fact undergoing treatment for the rare form of skin cancer that took his life just a little over a year after I saw him.

I was so hoping he would be here to read what I've written about him in these pages just so he'd know how much he's meant to me all these years. But alas, just as John Prine and Jerry Jeff will never read how I've been captivated and awed by their immense talents and friendships, neither will Jimmy. Even though I know all three had a pretty good idea as to how I've felt about them, there's something about committing your feelings to paper that seems to take it to another level.

I didn't want to write this chapter. I wanted Jimmy keep on like he always did. Being my hero. Being my friend. Keep being an inspiration to always be better, to always look for new ways to do what I do, and to never settle for anything less than my very best. I suppose, in a way, he still is being all those things and I should be grateful for that.

For years, before playing "Coast of Marseilles," I've said something about him recording it and as a result it brought me into the world of recognized songwriters. And after I've said my piece about that, I continue by saying, "Where ever you are tonight Jimmy Buffett, thank you one more time." It has deeper meaning for me now, and I've decided to keep saying it.

Here's to you Jimmy Buffett. As long as my heart's beating, you'll be in it.

127

YOU GOT GOLD, THE EVENT 2

I was invited to play You Got Gold again! It absolutely made my year. I didn't stay for all of it this time, but nevertheless, it had a profound effect on me. Being that close to John's spirit lifts mine. Meeting so many great music people who essentially feel like I do about him really connects people. It's just another example of the mysterious movements music makes.

I played the Country Music Hall of Fame again and Jason Wilber, John's guitarist, asked me if I would kick off the night's proceedings. Oh my yes! We sang "You Got Gold," and the night began. How cool is that?

I also got to sing "Long Monday" with Mindy Smith. All the artists who came are legends. Connie Smith, Lucas Nelson, Zac Brown, the impressive list goes on. One thing we all have in common is our respect and admiration for John Prine. And I'm quenched knowing his music will live as long as people listen to his music.

128

KSSW 2023

They say the third one is the charm, and so it was for *Keith Sykes' Songwriter Weekend*. With the help of our sponsors, Doug Montgomery of Texstar Kubota, and Bumpus Harley Davidson in Tennessee, we had the most successful year yet.

It still comes down to the writers. I've been lucky to have a lot of them hang with me while KSSW builds. Dickey Lee, Susan Gibson, Larry Joe, and Shawn Camp have played all three. Roger Cook missed 2022, but he had a doctor's excuse. Chuck Cannon and Jed Zimmerman have played twice. Tony Arata and Max Gomez were there this time, and I hope they'll come back every time they can.

The fans are truly why we do it. These are the folks who sit and listen to every word and melody line and give us their appreciation, admiration, and financial support.

It all coalesces to make a celebration worth celebrating. I'm looking forward to the KSSW being around long after I'm gone, and if you ever have the chance to come, I surely believe you will never miss another.

129

WHY I'M HERE, THANK YOU, AND GOODBYE

When asked about the blues John Lennon said it's like a three-legged chair. It strips away all the embellishments, right down to the fundamentals. Or something close to that.

My three-legged chair is Hank Williams, Chuck Berry, and Bob Dylan. They each in turn came into my life at just the right time and place, which made an indelible mark on me that I wear like a tattoo on my spirit.

Anytime I need inspiration, or a reminder of why I'm here, or a taste of the excitement that fueled me to be me, I listen to them, and I'm quenched. Their records are present and forever young. They take me to the time I was free from corrections, advice, criticism, or directions. They keep telling me who I am and why I should feel for my fellow man. They give me reasons to be joyous and have sympathy for me when I'm feeling sorry for myself. They give me freedom to explore and be wild about a new song when I hear one that moves me. They give me all that and more than I can explain. I can't explain because I don't have their power of words to do it. I only have my own words and melodies to express my take on the world inside and outside of myself.

WHY I'M HERE, THANK YOU, AND GOODBYE

I'm like everyone else in that everything I've ever done has led me to where I am now. I've had highs, lows, and in betweens. I'm way lower than some and higher up than others. As Todd Snider says in his song; "I'm Happy to Be Here at All." I hope you are, too.

Here's a street joke you might like: A woman is standing in a courtroom. The judge is shuffling his papers, then looks up over his glasses and says, "Ma'am, it says here you were given a citation at 2:45 a.m. on the morning of June 10th on Interstate 40 West for riding facing backwards on the tank of a motorcycle, performing oral sex on the driver, during a rainstorm, clocked at 94 miles per hour." The woman said to the Judge, "What night did you say that was?"

Good luck can happen to anyone at any time. Bad luck can too. My luck has happened whether I wanted it or not. Most of the time I don't think about luck, I just do my thing and hope for the best. To those who do their life differently, very well. Oscar Wilde said "Be yourself; everyone else is taken." I'm with Oscar on that.

I wish the best for everyone. I always have. When I was walking to my baseball game one Saturday morning in Murray, I saw another kid I knew dressed in his baseball uniform and yelled out to him "I hope you win!" He yelled back, "Why?" He was wearing another team's uniform, but it didn't seem like I should wish him ill.

Jerene says I'm a perfectionist. If I am, I have failed miserably. Truth is, perfection isn't a reality. Well, it is if you think something or someone is perfect. Then you know what perfect is. More precisely you know what perfect is to you—which, by law, has to be classified as subjective. So much for perfection.

The people I've met along the way are the most important parts of my journey. I wish I could write every one of their names in this book right now. I've found during the writing of this book that books are very limited in the amount of information you can cram into one unless you go about it like Shelby Foote and write big-ass volumes of books on one subject. Thinking about that is pretty wild. Imagine me saying "This is a five-volume set, three books in each volume, containing every conceivable facet of my life. Every breath from birth to death." Oops. I can't write about my death.

That's the kind of crap that goes through my mind. If I had space, and you had the will to read it, I'd stick everything I ever did in here. Since that doesn't make any sense, I decided to write about my music life. I don't care that you might want to hear about me being drunk somewhere or when I'd take a 2,000-mile motorcycle trip. So I've tried to stay with my musical self. After all, that's the only reason anyone would wanna read about me.

Here's another street joke: Shakespeare and Longfellow are at the pearly gates. St. Peter decided to have a poet's contest. The one caveat is they have to use the word "Timbuktu."

So Longfellow thinks for a bit then recites, "While walking along the ocean shore, I heard a mighty cannon roar. A clipper ship came into view, its destination, Timbuktu."

Then Shakespeare comes up with, "Tim and I, away we went. We met three maidens in a tent. As they were three and we were two, I bucked one and Timbuktu.

You're probably thinking, "For the love of God, is this man ever gonna stop writing?" The answer is yes. But wait! I've got a few more syllables to heap upon you.

I was a singer-songwriter of contemporary folk songs when I was young, drifted into rock 'n' roll when I was in my mid-20s, went behind the scenes to be a publisher and producer when I was in my 30s and 40s, then back to being an artist again in my 50s and 60s, manager of a studio in my early 70s, and writing a book in my 75th year.

It's been nice looking back with you. I'm gonna go look forward some more. Hope you do too.

Have a good one ~ks

THE END

ACKNOWLEDGMENTS

Before I began writing this book I reached out to Robert Gordon, the Memphis based writer and film producer, to ask for help and to get some guidelines on how to go about doing this. His help and encouragement is the foundation of my work.

Kelly Bass, longtime newspaper writer and music aficionado from Little Rock, sent me a text saying he heard I was writing a book, and if I wanted a proofreader to look no further. I certainly did need that, and true to his word his steady hand has been invaluable.

John Cunningham, who has written and published over 10 books, has lent his considerable skills to help guide me though the final stages of book creation and publishing.

Beth Goodwin McDonald read this book and came out with both guns blazing! I'm so glad she did. She gave me much needed perspective just when I needed it most. I'm forever in her debt.

Jon Scott, record man par excellence and true friend, saved me many hours with his insights into the world of book writing and publishing.

My heartfelt thanks to each to each of you for sharing your experience and knowledge to help me reach my goal. You are busy, creative people, who took time away from your projects to help me with mine.

It don't get no better than that.

THANK YOU

This list contains some, but surely not all, of the people who have helped me in my musical journey. I apologize for leaving any deserving people off this list.

Russ White
Marjorie and Berry Miller
Sandy Foster
Bruce and Kate Friedman
James and Adela White
Eddie and Paula Albenetti
Alex Green
Amy LaVere and Will Sexton
Amy and Ronnie Wright
Andy Black
Art and Nancy Bowman
Claud and Michele Appel
Ed and Ann Dirmeyer
Joe and Judy Ables
Mark and Debbie Hallacher
Brandon Severs
Bruce and Casey Zimmerman
Cassandra and Dave McKinney
Dave Ladage
Drew and Joann Balton
Emily Randle
Grady and Beth McDonald
Henry Nelson
Jeff and Susan Powell
Jer Lile
Al Capone
Billy Prine
Mike and Lisa James
Brian and Jeremy Holmes
Brian Craig
Bruce and Barbara Newman
Buddy Cannon
Billy Tagg
Claudia Kleefeild
Clay Bradley
Cody Dickinson
Craig Yarbrough
Dan and Kathleen Garber
Darryl Rhoades
Dave and Cid Tartaglia
David and Jaye Fleischman
David Porter
Dawn Hopkins
Don McNatt

A VERY SHORT TIME

Doyle and Debbie Grisham
Eugene and Pat Smith
Garth Fundis
Greg and Melinda Smith
Greg Hamilton
Michael and Paulette Sykes
James Ramsden
Janice and Jason Gibert
Jared Callen
Jason and Jamie Blair
Jeff Gordon
Jeff Hana
Jeff Phillips
Jerry Phillips
Jim Sykes
Joe Elmore
Jor Forlini
Joe Glaser
John Bifuss
John Earl
John and Margo Frinzi
Josh and Lindsey Holley
Kathy and Doyle Scoggins
Kelsey Sykes
Kelsey and Cody Fletcher
Kent and Patches DeShazo
Kevin and Bethany Page
Kevin Carroll
Kevin Cubbins
Kliff and Molly Black
Kyle and Julie Kiker
Larry and Tammy Francis
Leon Griffin
Linn Sitler

Lloyd Maines
Lulu Buffett
Mac McAnally
Mark Parsell
Mark Edgar Stuart
Matt Blake
Matt Lindsey
Matt Qualls
Matt Ross-Spang
Max and Heather Stalling
Mile Addington
Mike McClure
Mike Stoker
Miles Mueller
Missy Querey
Mitchell Drosin
Muck Sticky
Myra Withers
Nadirah Shakoor
Larry Nager
Niko Lyras
Otis Gibbs
Pat Kerr Tigrett
Pat Mitchell-Worley
Paul Ebersold
Paul Speer
Perry Welsh
Phoebe Lewis
Randy and Maggie Kimbley
Randy Poe
Randy and Sandy Eads
Randy Timberlake
Ray Summy
Rhnea Rich

THANK YOU

Remy Miller
Rice Drewry
Rick Clark
Rick Lovett
Rob Junkless
Rob and Kelley Shurly
Robert Hall
Ronnie Narmour
Scott Bomar
Scott Kirby
Mike Shine
Steve and Priscilla Heglund
Steve Roberts
Susan and Gentry Powell
Susan Schauf
Susanne Taylor
Tamara Saviano
Davin and Tammy James
Taylor Craven
Terri Hendrix

Terry Allen
Terry Saunders
Thom and Coley Shepherd
Jimmy and Sally Thackery
Tim Carroll
Tim and Mary Bumpus
Tom and Rita Benike
Tommy George
Tracy Gershon
Trent Johnson
Van Duran
Vicky Loveland
Steve Cohen
Vince Fast
Walker Mimms
Ward Archer
Will Kimbrough
Doug and Sherri Montgomery
Rob Grayson
Gene Holmes and Family

ABOUT THE AUTHOR

Once upon a time in the summer of 1967, Keith Sykes hitchhiked to the Newport Folk Festival and saw Arlo Guthrie perform "Alice's Restaurant." In the fall of that year he got a copy of the album, learned the whole song and sang it at a Holiday Inn audition that led to him playing in Buffalo, NY.

It's pretty perfect that such a rambling tale should be at the start of Keith's own rambling tale—in the more than 50 years that followed, he would become a troubadour and storyteller, a massively successful songwriter with more than 100 songs recorded by artists as diverse as Rosanne Cash and George Thorogood. He would tour every corner of America and play in just about every conceivable kind of venue, appear on *Saturday Night Live* and *Austin City Limits,* and host songwriter nights on Memphis' legendary Beale Street with many of music's most talented songwriters. He would join Jimmy Buffett's Coral Reefer Band, tour the country and record the *Volcano* album—the title track for which he co-wrote with Jimmy.

To date, recordings of Keith's songs have sold more than 25 million copies worldwide. With 13 full-length albums released—and great success with his own publishing company, credited with signing John Kilzer to Geffen Records and the discovery of Todd Snider—Keith Sykes has proven to be nothing short of prolific.

A VERY SHORT TIME

And of course, he's not done just yet. Along with the release of his autobiography, *A Very Short Time,* he continues to tour relentlessly, and is host of the Keith Sykes' Songwriter Weekend at Melody Mountain Ranch in Stephenville, TX. Writing and recording songs remain his first and second musical loves.

Printed in the USA
CPSIA information can be obtained
at www.ICGtesting.com
LVHW010716300924
792358LV00006B/11/J